FOREVER JULIET

To
Elizabeth, Mary and Nova

ABOUT THE AUTHOR

Martial Rose was born in 1922 and educated at Christ's Hospital School, Horsham and at King's College, Cambridge. After obtaining his M.A.he embarked on a distinguished career in teaching and drama. He became Head of English and Drama at Bretton Hall College, Yorkshire, in 1952 and subsequently Principal of King Alfred's College, Winchester, from which post he retired in 1984.
His enthusiasm for medieval drama and for the symbolism of medieval carvings in wood and stone has resulted in a significant body of published work including *The Wakefield Mystery Plays, Misericords of Norwich Cathedral, Stories in Stone, The Norwich Apocalypse,* and many other books and pamphlets.

PICTURE CREDITS

The picture of Rutland Boughton on p.29 is reproduced by kind permission of Ian Boughton and that of Dodie Smith on p.146 by kind permission of Christopher Reynolds-Jones. The other pictures are contained in the archive of Gwen Ffrangcon-Davies, now deposited at the Martial Rose Library at King Alfred College, Winchester. Photographers include Henry Berry, p.6, Window & Grove p.7, 'Sasha' p.32, Alex. Corbett p.53, J.W. Debenham p.77, Angus McBean p.100 (top) & p.158, John Vickers p.100 (bottom), Jane Plotz p.108 (top), 'Anthony' p.113, Houston Toger p.132 (right), Fred Fehl p.156 (bottom), The pictures on pages 4, 183, 186, 187, & 192 were taken by Clive Robbins.

Forever Juliet

The Life and Letters of
Gwen Ffrangcon-Davies
1891-1992

MARTIAL ROSE

Larks Press

Published by the Larks Press
Ordnance Farmhouse, Guist Bottom, Dereham NR20 5PF

E-mail: Larks.Press@btinternet.com
Website:www.booksatlarkspress.co.uk
01328 829207

Printed at the Lanceni Press,
Garrood Drive, Fakenham

First printed May 2003

British Library Cataloguing-in-Publication Data
A catalogue record for this book is available
from the British Library

ISBN 1 904006 12 4

CONTENTS

⧫⫴⫼⫴⧫

List of Illustrations

Introduction

Treasure comes in various forms. It might be in a crock of gold dug up in the garden, a lottery win, or an unexpected and munificent legacy. My treasure-trove was set down in the hall of our chalet bungalow on the 1st January 2001. It was brought by our niece and her husband, Susan and Keith Best. And it came from Yorkshire.

Thirty years ago when Susan was student at a college in Yorkshire her best friend was Maggie. She and her family spent the run-up to Christmas 2000 with Maggie at a house near Ripon. Maggie's aunt had recently died, and this property had been left to Maggie and her sister, Ann. Maggie was in the process of a great clearing-up operation. In the bedroom in which Susan and Keith slept were many boxes containing bundles of old letters. Maggie, apologising for the muddle, explained that the boxes contained the papers of her great-aunt. Susan was told that she could, if she wished, read any of the letters.

On Boxing Day 2000 my wife and I were invited to share lunch with Susan and Keith and about eight other members of the family. In the course of lunch Susan mentioned her trip to Yorkshire and that she had indeed opened one or two of the letters. Most of them, she said, contained phrases such as 'Darling, I thought you were marvellous...'. The great-aunt had been an actress. When I asked Susan her name she replied 'Gwen Ffrangcon-Davies'. I had first seen this actress perform over sixty years earlier and I too, thought she was 'marvellous'. I said how very interesting it might be to catch a glimpse of those letters. I thought the matter would rest there.

On the evening of New Year's Day there was a ring at the front door. Susan and Keith stood there clutching large boxes. They brought them in, and many more were to come from the capacious boot of their car. I was told that, as I had expressed an interest in Gwen Ffrangcon-Davies, Maggie wanted me to see the contents of the archive which she and Ann had inherited and, if I felt inclined, I might consider writing a biography of her great-aunt.

The days that followed were spent picking my way through this mass of material, which comprised countless bundles of letters, diaries, journals, scrapbooks, programmes, and thousands of photographs. There were in addition very many audio-cassettes and videos. Initially my curiosity was drawn more to the letters. These were grouped in bundles, each letter still in its envelope, bearing date-mark and stamp. Among the first that I opened were letters from John Gielgud, Edith Evans, Laurence Olivier, Vivien Leigh, and Sybil Thorndike. My sense of excitement is indescribable. I was finding myself within a sanctuary where I had no right to be. And these letters were not saying 'Darling, I thought you were marvellous'. They were commenting on plays and players familiar to me in my youth, and also referring to many theatrical events that predated my own theatre-going experience. But there were also personal letters between close friends, giving support and encouragement to each other not just professionally but within their private lives as well. I felt an intruder, but I was deeply bitten, and the intrusion went on.

There were over two thousand letters in the archive. The period covered was from the 1880s to 1992. Gwen's father, David, was a world-famous baritone. His letters, photographs, and scrapbooks form a significant part of the treasure trove. Gwen's sister, Marjorie, was also a concert vocalist. Her letters to Gwen reveal a great deal of the family history. The most prolific correspondent was Marda Vanne, Gwen's lifelong friend. Marda's journals, poems, diaries, and scrapbooks form part of the archive, perhaps, in personal terms, the most revealing part. However, as a historical record of the period 1900-1936, in personal, social, historical, and artistic terms, it is the correspondence between Gwen and her mother, Annie, which I found most attractive and illuminating. Both were gifted and engaging letter-writers, and between them were no secrets.

An unusual feature of this archive is the mass of letters from Gwen herself. The family had collected and retained her letters to her father, mother, sister, and brother, and friends – a formidable pile that covered more than ninety years. Gwen's earliest letters to her parents, when she was only nine years old, and the correspondence with her sister Marjorie, who died in 1964, spanned the major part of that period. Gwen herself inherited Marda Vanne's papers when her friend died in 1970, and in this collection is a correspondence that at some stages was conducted on a daily basis. It comprises, of course, both Marda's letters to Gwen, and Gwen's letters to Marda.

The total span of the letters is over a hundred years, and among the correspondents, apart from those already mentioned, are Ellen Terry, Thomas and Florence Hardy, George Bernard Shaw, J. M. Barrie, James Bridie, Somerset Maugham, Rebecca West, and among her friends during the last few years of her life, Nigel Hawthorne, Irene Worth, Wendy Hiller, Anna Massey, Alec McCowen, and Robert Hardy. There was also a wider network of family and friends, not so directly tied to the theatre, who wrote to Gwen regularly, visited her at Tagley Cottage, and offered her hospitality in their various homes.

These letters, together with a massive amount of other material, presented me with a daunting task. I began reading the letters, attaching the envelopes to the back, giving each a code, and placing groups of letters into manila files. There are, at the moment, over seventy files. At the same time I numbered and categorised the scrapbooks, diaries, account books, journals, programmes, photographs, cassettes and videos. These chores were being undertaken at a time when I was receiving hospital treatment for a variety of health problems. In these rather dire circumstances, support was given me by three friends. They agreed to take some of the letter files, read the contents, follow the coding and numbering, make notes, and return the packages to me at regular intervals. These three dedicated assistants were Elizabeth Armstrong, Mary Gibson, and Nova Millar, my sister-in-law. Elizabeth acted as distributor/collector. For the preceding two years Elizabeth and I had worked very closely on a major project concerned with medieval iconography, and that working partnership was to prove a sound platform for the co-ordinating task which was required in imposing a degree of order on this formidable archive. The value of these three assistants is incalculable.

This biography does not pretend in any way to be the definitive account of the life of Gwen Ffrangcon-Davies, but it represents the actress's life mainly through the letters and memorabilia left at the time of her death. During her unusually long life her correspondents comprised members of her family, royalty and nobility, and many of the country's most famous figures in literature, art, and the theatre of her time. Her achievements as an actress have in part already been recorded, but what has not hitherto been recorded is her extraordinary gift for friendship, for men and women, that weathered the trials of age and decrepitude, that matched loyalty with love. Her friendships flourished without any hint of jealousy, envy, or self-centredness. Her generosity of spirit elicits a like response from so many of her correspondents. I have felt it not only a great privilege to have been handed Gwen's papers with a view to writing her biography, but also I have been keenly aware of the daunting task of trying to capture in this work even a part of that rare spirit.

Acknowledgements

Permission to quote from letters has been sought from Gwen's correspondents or their literary executors. The response has been most generous, enabling extracts to be included from the following: Enid Bagnold, Rutland Boughton, James Bridie, Noel Coward, Edith Craig, Gordon Daviot, Robert Donat, Tom English, Edith Evans, John and Susan Gau, John Gielgud, Valerie Grove, Alec Guinness, Nigel Hawthorne, Glenda Jackson, Rayne Kruger, Vivien Leigh, Anna Massey, Alec McCowen, Marjorie Moos, Sybil Thorndike. It has not been possible to trace all of the correspondents quoted, but every reasonable effort has been made to do so.

I am grateful for the help that has been forthcoming from the British Academy, the British Broadcasting Corporation, the British Film Institute National Library, the British Library, the Historical Manuscripts Commission, The National Trust and the Theatre Museum. Advice and helpful suggestions have also been gladly accepted from the following: Brigid Allen, Janet Birkett, Sue Bradbury, David Farley, Bryan Forbes, Helen Grime, Ron Hawkins, Ray Ingram, Susan Knowles, Rayne Kruger, Hugh Melinsky, Sheridan Morley, Christopher Reynolds-Jones, Roger Richardson, Heather Rose, Jenny Rose, Colonel Sir John Ruggles-Brise, Kate Stephens, and Alix Stone.

Victor Pemberton and David Spenser entertained me at their home in Stambourne and were full of lively reminiscences of their long association with Gwen. Particularly vivid was their account of their making the BBC 'Omnibus' programme about Gwen in 1988, 'Juliet Remembered'. I am greatly indebted to them for their kindness and help.

The two great-nieces, Margaret Westwood and Ann Baldaro, entrusted me with Gwen's memorabilia, an extraordinary act of faith in someone they had not met. I must thank my niece, Susan Best, for persuading them that her uncle might not only look after their treasure but also make a reasonable job of writing Gwen's story. I hope that they are not disappointed; nor the surviving executor of Gwen's will, Clive Robbins. Clive has been of immeasurable support in the final stages of completing this book. He has read the text with great care and suggested most valuable amendments, most of which have been incorporated. I have found it a very invigorating experience to have been in constant touch with someone who knew Gwen so well during the last twenty years of her life, someone in whom she put her trust, and someone so enthusiastic that her story should be told.

Finally I must thank the Three Graces who helped with the reading and interpretation of the archive shortly after it landed on my doorstep when, physically, I was under the weather. Their devotion to the task, their insight into what they were reading, and their untangling of names and relationships, made lucid in their notes, were true labours of love. Most helpful was their zest for what they were doing. This was infectious. This book owes much to Elizabeth Armstrong, Mary Gibson, and Nova Millar. I hope that as they read it they will not only enjoy it, but also recall the fun we had in those early days of parcelling out the letters, writing up the notes, discussing them, and wondering what the next pile might bring. Now there are no more piles of letters to read. But here is the book; and in this they will find their signatures.

Martial Rose

Gwen Ffrangcon-Davies with Nigel Hawthorne and Clive Robbins in 1986

Chapter One: Dawn (1891-1918)

Ffrangcon

A service in loving memory of Gwen Ffrangcon-Davies was held in the parish church of Stambourne, Essex, on 30th January 1992. Gwen had died peacefully at her home, Tagley Cottage, three days earlier. The service began with the words of Psalm 139: 'O Lord, thou hast searched me out, and known me!' It was a Psalm close to Gwen's heart. She quotes passages from it in her letters. She read it herself at some of her friends' memorial services. Indeed, at her own memorial service on 18th June 1992, held in St Martin's-in-the-Field, a recording of her reading this Psalm was heard.

'If I take the wings of the morning: and remain in the uttermost parts of the sea; Even there also shall thy hand lead me: and thy right hand shall hold me' (verses 8, 9).

The sense of the omnipresence of God, of the immanence of his goodness, was unwavering in her own life. Her stability, equanimity, unstinting generosity of spirit, infinite care for and thoughtfulness for others, provided for so many of her friends - and there were so very many during that century-long life - a star by which those friends set their lives' course. Countless letters to her testify to her deep and lasting influence on those with whom she came in contact. Quite beyond the consummate mastery of her art, for which she was deluged with fan mail, there was a warm response to her as a person, indeed as a guru, a name frequently given her, that is deeply impressive and very unusual. Audiences felt deeply enriched by her stage performances; but it was in her more intimate friends' response to the way she managed her life and personal relationships that we learn how their own lives had been immeasurably enhanced through the privilege of knowing her. She lived a long and remarkable life; and this is her story.

David Davies, Gwen's father, was born on December 11th 1855 in Bethesda, Caernarvonshire, North Wales. His father, David, was a supervisor at the Bethesda Foundry, and known locally as David Davies, the Foundry. Her mother, Annie Frances Rayner, often called Nan, was the daughter of a Manchester doctor, who had built for himself and his family a holiday cottage nestling in the Welsh valleys at Conway. It was in this area of north Wales that Gwen's mother and father first met.

Gwen's father received his first schooling in Bethesda village school, at a cost of twopence a week. He then moved on to Friars School, Bangor, where the curriculum included Latin and Greek. His father, in his spare time, gave piano lessons to help pay for his son's schooling. The next significant stage in this young man's education was his acceptance with an Exhibition at an institution renowned for its nurture of Welsh scholars, Jesus College, Oxford. He graduated in 1881, and was ordained priest in 1884, serving his first curacy near Pwllheli in Caernarvon.

David Ffrangcon-Davies

The young David Davies was bright, personable, well-liked. He was also very well-known in that Bethesda-Bangor area long before his going to Oxford. He was endowed with remarkable vocal qualities, and he sang first as a chapel choirboy then in a church choir, and later as an outstanding baritone. Before he set off for Oxford he had changed his name to David Ffrangcon-Davies. Without such a change he might have been known locally as David Davies the Voice, but it was as David Ffrangcon-Davies that he was to be known in Britain, America and Europe, as a baritone of international fame. He took the name, Ffrangcon, from the Nant Ffrangcon Pass south of Bethesda. This hyphenated surname was his children's legacy, but he was called Ffrangcon by his wife and friends.

It was partly to find greater scope for his singing, and for the expert training and development of his voice, that Ffrangcon accepted a curacy in Hoxton in the East End of London. But he was shortly to resign his priestly role and set himself the task of earning his living as a professional vocalist. Indeed, it is as a 'Vocalist' that he is described on Gwen's birth certificate and on his own death certificate. His marriage to Annie Rayner took place in 1890. Part of the honeymoon was spent in Cardiff at the home of a friend, Madame Clara Novello Davies, a famous singer and choral conductor. Clara was to be the mother of the greatly gifted Ivor. After the honeymoon Ffrangcon and Annie made their family home in London, and it was there at 195 Finchley Road on 25th January 1891 that their first child, Gwen Lucy Ffrangcon-Davies, was born. Two further children were born: Marjorie in 1893, and Geoffrey in 1895.

In London, to prepare himself for a career as a vocalist, Ffrangcon had enrolled as a student at the Guildhall School of Music. His outstanding qualities were soon realised, and his concert performances at the School were warmly acclaimed by the London music critics. As a professional concert performer fame, if not fortune, came swiftly to Ffrangcon. His range was wide: oratorio, Lieder, folk song, opera. At the height of his career he sang in more than ten languages. He frequently sang extracts from opera, but rarely took part in staged performances. In 1890 he

Annie Ffrangcon-Davies

appeared as the Herald, at short notice, at the Drury Lane Theatre in the Carl Rosa production of Wagner's *Lohengrin*. Eighteen months later he was asked to sing the part, again at very short notice, for a performance at Covent Garden. The reviewer of the Drury Lane performance wrote in *The Figaro*, 3rd May 1890:

> 'Mr. McGuckin was once more an admirable Lohengrin, but by far the greatest success of the evening was achieved by the Herald, a part undertaken by Mr. Ffrangcon Davies in place of Mr. Abramoff, who had been announced in the prospectus. The career of Mr. Davies, who is a Welsh baritone, has been watched with interest by those accustomed to attend the students' concerts given at the Guildhall School of Music, and it is only the truth to say that his success on Saturday was as decisive as it was thoroughly deserved.'

Although he had relinquished his priestly calling, the choice of his work was deeply informed by his religious beliefs, and it is in the field of oratorio that he is best remembered. However, towards the turn of the century, when Wagner was at the height of his popularity, Germany, where music was more highly cultivated and valued than in any other European country, was chosen as the preferred field for Ffrangcon to pursue his talent. It was therefore to Berlin that Ffrangcon took his family in 1898, and there they stayed for three years; that is, the mother and three children stayed. Ffrangcon was away giving concerts in other parts of Germany, in England, elsewhere in Europe, and at least once a year in America, undertaking extensive and exhausting tours. His first invitation for a concert tour of America had come in 1896, and he proved such an overwhelming success that he returned at regular intervals. However acclaimed he was as a vocalist, the financial rewards were not such as to enable his family to live in any marked degree of affluence. Nevertheless, they lived comfortably in Berlin, with domestic and nursery help, even a governess, and the use of a Mercedes car, but for long periods without their father being at home. And when he was at home he was mostly resting and 'not to be disturbed', or preparing for his next concert. It was, however, in Berlin that Annie and the two girls learned to speak and write in German with a fluency that was never to leave them, especially as Gwen and Marjorie were to return on many future occasions to Germany and Austria.

Gwen, Marjorie and Geoffrey Ffrangcon-Davies in 1896

Handel's *Messiah* and Mendlessohn's *Elijah* were the first oratorios that captured Ffrangcon's imagination. In particular he sang the part of Elijah with such fervour and devotion, that he seemed to be truly identifying himself and his life with the Old Testament prophet. The same absorption of the singer with the song became evident when Elgar presented him in 1900 with *The Dream of Gerontius* to sing. Two years later Elgar wrote the part of Christ in *The Apostles* with Ffrangcon-Davies in mind. Apart from the musical collaboration, the two men had built up a friendship which resulted in visiting each other's homes and a continuing correspondence. With this new and flourishing oratorio work being composed by Elgar in England, the Ffrangcon-Davies family moved back to London in October 1901, and were in a position to take up residence at 8 Acacia Road, a large house near Regents Park, in a quite fashionable part of the city. Ffrangcon's engagements took him to many of the main music festivals held throughout the country such as at Malvern, Gloucester, Liverpool, Leeds, and York. He also taught singing to a great number of pupils. He had a studio for this purpose at 8 Acacia Road, where, as a young man, Rutland Boughton, who became a close family friend, would act as accompanist. Reginald Dansie, who played a significant role later in this story, was one of Ffrangcon's pupils. From this teaching experience and from his subsequent appointment as Professor of Singing at The Royal Academy of Music, the seeds were sown for his book *The Singing of the Future*, which was published in 1905. But Ffrangcon's fame was based on his great concert performances at the nation's premier musical venues, such as the Albert Hall and Covent Garden. In a letter to Edward Elgar written in March 1905 Ffrangcon referred to the recent presentation of *The Apostles* at the Covent Garden Festival, conducted by Hans Richter:

'All through these performances at Covent Garden, whenever I was not singing and just before I got up to sing – I whispered to myself "God, The Christ, and his servant Elgar's ideal of Him, are my sole concern." ...I have opened my soul to you because it is a relief, and because I want you to see what you are doing for a man who can scarcely claim that he sees through a glass darkly. It is half past one in the morning and I am going to Leeds to-day – for *The Apostles*. I shall sleep more peacefully after writing to you.' [1]

Gwen caught that intensity, with which her father identified himself with the parts he was singing, in her broadcast talks about him (1949):

'Those early performances of Gerontius with father and Gervase Elwes were more than just performances – they were almost religious observances – something one will never forget. It was this quality of dedication that made father's singing so memorable. His work was his life, and everything else, even human relationships, had to take second place.' [2]

And here she referred to Ffrangcon's remoteness from family life:

'It is in a way difficult for me to talk about my father, because in a sense we always remained strangers. As little children...we saw little of him. We were in the nursery and he was often away. Later, when we might have been able to be companions for him, he became even more preoccupied with his career, and I personally was too diffident and timid ever to feel at ease with him...Though I was barely fifteen when his illness took him away from us, I could sense his greatness as an artist without being able to get near him as a man.'[3]

Ffrangcon's illness came as a major calamity to the whole family. The move to London had been welcomed by the mother and children, and their financial circumstances were certainly comfortable. The girls were attending the South Hampstead High School and Geoffrey was sent as a boarder to St George's, Harpenden. But at home there were frequent stormy scenes. Ffrangcon's time and energy were taken up with an increased commitment of concerts, and furthermore he had set himself the task of writing a book about singing, which included many innovative ideas. *The Singing of the Future,* published in 1905, received an unenthusiastic response. By 1907 his behaviour had become unpredictable, erratic, even violent. His wife was disturbed by his irrational outbursts. In the autumn of 1907 he gave a concert in the Albert Hall. As part of his programme he sang Wotan's Abschied (the king of the gods' farewell) from Wagner's *Ring,* ending with Gounod's setting of 'There is a Green Hill far away'. The applause was rapturous; after taking his bow, he collapsed. He was in a state of mental instability and was taken to the Bethlem Royal Hospital, Beckenham, Kent on 28th November 1907, and remained there, apart from periods of leave, until his death on 1st July 1918.

Annie's Problems

Annie had been terrorised by her husband. She reported that the night before he had been admitted to the Bethlem Royal Hospital he had told her that 'he saw a devil standing behind her chair and that it would strangle her and leave her for dead' and he had talked of cutting her throat. Soon after his admission to hospital Ffrangcon wrote a letter to the Bishop of London, which the hospital authorities kept:

> 'I was tricked into coming here. My wife came to my bedroom one morning and said that someone wanted my help. I got up at once, and stepped, after I had dressed, into a taximeter, with a cigar in my mouth, happy in the thought that I was coming to help a fellow mortal. I wondered at the look of the place when I saw it. But I suspected nothing, until a doctor and two wardens came into the room where I was waiting for the man I thought I was to help. The first question startled me: the doctor said: "How are we this morning?" Finally I saw through the game and asked: "Are you going to detain me by force?" He answered: "Yes".'[4]

During the ten and half years that Ffrangcon was kept at the hospital the records show that he was 'suffering from an intense melancholic, absolute hopelessness, with a conviction that he was for ever damned'. There were times when he had to be restrained in a padded cell. Many of the letters that he wrote were kept by the hospital. One reads as follows:

'...Need I add that I am tired to death of this place into which I was betrayed by that woman and the Doctors who have whored with her at my expense? Fancy my keeping a prostitute for my fellow man!'[5]

There were times when his condition improved and he was allowed to live for short spells outside the hospital. In 1916 he even started to sing again in public, at the Pump Room in Bath; but this phase was short-lived. When he made visits and short stays outside the hospital, it was usually to be with his friend and former pupil, Reginald Dansie, in his home at Streatham, and it was here and occasionally at the hospital that his wife and children would come to see him. During his time in the hospital many letters passed between Ffrangcon and his wife and children, but the family of five had become irremediably fragmented. The approaching war was to break up the family still further.

Annie Ffrangcon-Davies was faced with severe difficulties. Her husband, who at first had been registered at the hospital as 'curable', was soon transferred to the 'incurable' category. There were hospital expenses to pay, letters to write, visits to be made, but even more worrying was the personal contumely poured upon her by her husband, who considered her the primary cause of his unjust restraint. There were the children to look after: Geoffrey was away during term-time at St George's, but the school fees had to be paid, and they were considerable. Serious consideration had to be given to withdrawing him from that school. The two girls at South Hampstead High School showed little academic flair, but both were gifted artistically: Marjorie, following her father, was becoming an accomplished singer; Gwen could both sing and dance, and excelled in the school drama. There is a touching testimony to her acting ability at school in a letter Gwen received, dated 15th February 1988. She was then within three years of her hundredth birthday:

'Dear Miss Ffrangcon-Davies
        When I saw your name in the *Radio Times* my mind went back to my first term at School – South Hampstead – The Seniors were acting "The Pied Piper" and you I believe and I have always thought – were the little girl crying outside the hill that the rest of the children had gone through. I cried bitterly for you (my first encounter with tragedy) and it has always been a vivid picture in my mind! I wonder if you remember it? I hope you do not mind my writing.
        With every good wish
        Marjorie Moos, aged 93!'[6]

Such talents in her children Annie felt duty-bound to cherish. There were some family investments, but now no regular income. Her only recourse was to take in lodgers. She therefore reorganised her house and discovered that she could just make ends meet through working hard and offering board and lodging in this attractive area of London. Her sister Florrie encouraged her in what she was doing and offered her support. The following are extracts from a letter she wrote to Annie dated 12th July 1909:

'We were very pleased to hear from you, and much interested in your scheme for enlarging your premises. It seems to us as if it ought to be very successful.

10

You have really done so very well, so far, and I am sure all the people you have had will recommend you again, so that you will soon have quite a reliable connection. It does seem a pity to work with only at the best a chance of paying expenses – when with a few more boarders, and not much more work in the way of meals, you could feel you were working at a profit...It seems impossible to take Ffrangcon into consideration. As things are at the present, you must do the best you can, leaving him out of it. If he is allowed to leave where he is then other plans would have to be made.

...You do very well to keep your butcher's bill down to 24/-, but you have fish and poultry (sometimes!) bill(s), besides I suppose. It is the hardest part of the work to be keeping down expenses all the time, and yet if that is not done, there soon ceases to be much profit...We have had such very nice letters from Gwen this morning. She seems to be enjoying her holiday, though it is a very quiet one, quite free from any frivoling with the male element! Has she any idea what she is going to do when she comes home? Is she still keen on going to Tree's school? I hope not, but if it must be, I suppose there is no help for it. Would they give her a salary where she is, if she cared to stay?...Your loving sister

Florrie'[7]

A number of letters from Florrie to Annie or Gwen and Marjorie have been preserved. Each of them, like this one, sheds light on the family's history. Annie's plans, however, to extend 8 Acacia Road had to be shelved. Instead she looked for more modest premises, and found them in 18 Canfield Gardens, South Hampstead. The move took place with little enthusiasm. Florrie's allusion to Gwen's 'holiday' refers to Gwen's ten-month stay in Germany. 'Holiday' is not how Gwen would have described her time at the Bryman's Institute, Watzum, Brunswick.

Gwen Prepares Herself

In 1909 Gwen spent her 18th birthday in Germany. She had left school in 1908 and spent some time at a finishing school for young ladies called Sesame House. Here she discovered that she was treated as an adult and, to her delight, that much attention was given to the arts; it was here that she developed her talents for sketching, fashion-designing, sewing, millinery and dressmaking. Her aim in life, ever since she could remember, was to be an actress. She decided that she would spend the time between her leaving Sesame House and the beginning of what she hoped would be a great acting career, by attaching herself to an educational establishment in the hope of improving her German and French. She was also acutely aware of the financial difficulties under which her mother was labouring. Her application, therefore was to the Bryman's Institute, which would provide her with board and lodging in return for her undertaking some teaching of English. No salary, however, was offered. Her application was successful, but her first impressions were extremely adverse. She found herself treated not as one of the staff, but more as a senior pupil, and that with very few privileges. She worked all hours, from early morning until bedtime. Every moment of the day was meticulously planned, even the crocodile walks in which she was obliged to participate. As she became accustomed to the routine she relaxed, and found a few fellow-spirits. It was at this time, away from home, that Gwen's letter-writing gifts took wing. She also looked forward to receiving letters, especially from her mother.

'You are really the *only* person that writes me letters that I care to have, the others are such drivel. I suppose I ought not to say that, but I can't help thinking that the art of writing interesting letters is one that can be very easily cultivated if it doesn't come naturally; it is really so dull to hear that "we went to the concert on Thursday. It was very nice. On Friday I went out to tea. In the evening I went to church," etc, etc. One does so long to hear something of the inner life of the people, what they have been feeling and thinking, their impressions and so on.'[8]

Gwen's letters to her friends and theirs to her, over the best part of a century, graphically meet her criterion here expressed, of revealing the 'inner life'.

At the Institute Gwen's musical abilities were especially praised, and she sang in a number of concerts, agreeably surprising her auditors with her broad knowledge of German Lieder, especially the songs of Hugo Wolf and Franz Schubert, and her general musicianship. Before leaving Germany Gwen was given at least one opportunity to display her acting ability. This is how she described her performance, which was given in German:

'I was dressed up as one of the girls in a sailor blouse and a short skirt; in this attire I acted the sleep-walking scene from *Macbeth*, only I wound the tablecloth round me to make it more impressive. Then we did *Julius Caesar*...Then Weera and I did *Lohengrin, Lorelei, Tannhäuser*, and finished up with the death scene from *Romeo and Juliet*...I was Juliet and lay on the table, for want of a bier, but as it was too short my legs hung over the end and were supported by a chair. Weera was Romeo and killed herself most touchingly, but slightly disconcerted me by falling right on my tummy and making me howl when I ought to have been dead.'[9]

It remained Gwen's firm intention, on her return to England, to enter a Drama School, which Aunt Florrie had regretted in her letter of 12th July 1909, and so equip herself for her chosen profession. No other profession than acting had ever been contemplated. The brightest star in the acting firmament, which young ladies might aspire to follow, was Ellen Terry, a friend of the Ffrangcon-Davies family. In 1890 Gwen's father had sought Ellen Terry's advice on management and presentation issues connected with his own profession, and he had received a copious and most practical response, with details about the manner in which to achieve the very best terms for his contracts. She urged him to take every opportunity to see as much acting as he could, and she even enclosed tickets for a box in the theatre in which she was currently performing. The Ffrangcon-Davies family was accustomed to attending concerts and seeing plays. Gwen recalled the many visits to the theatre with her mother, and on many occasions they were to see Ellen Terry performing a wide variety of parts, which included Queen Katherine in *Henry VIII*, Beatrice in *Much Ado About Nothing*, and the Nurse in *Romeo and Juliet*.

Ellen Terry and her mother photographed in 1865 by Lewis Carroll

Gwen's godmother was Agnes Harries, Ellen Terry's companion, and on one occasion she took Gwen, when still a little child, to Ellen Terry's home where to her immeasurable delight she was given a rather large doll's tea-set. This was a present Gwen greatly treasured, and from the time in the early 1930s, when she settled into Tagley Cottage, pride of place in the dining-room was given to the display of this tea-set. When Gwen was fourteen years old, and showed no sign of wavering in her ambition to become an actress, her mother asked EllenTerry if she would see Gwen and assess whether the girl had the talent and the character to enter so hazardous a profession. The meeting duly took place in Ellen Terry's home. Gwen has described the encounter in detail. She had been asked to show her mettle, and she performed with unbridled passion Juliet's balcony speeches. She then collapsed into a chair and awaited the verdict. There followed a long silence, as Ellen Terry gazed into the distance, and after a pause said 'Yes'; and then after an even longer pause came 'Yes'. Yet another excruciating pause was followed by 'You'll do'. A great deal of very practical advice was then given regarding Gwen's reading, her movement, her observation of others, and the importance of her general cultural development.

Ellen Terry had urged Gwen to enter the profession directly without spending time at a drama school. No doubt she formed the model from her own experience of the theatre, in which she had made her début at the age of nine. Before Gwen made her début, at the age of twenty, she had over many years received private tuition and accustomed herself to a rigorous programme of exercises involving movement and speech. The first influential teacher she had was Mrs Louise Manning-Hicks, an American, whose musical and dramatic accomplishments were exhibited more on the concert platform than the stage. She helped to develop

Gwen's vocal and presentational powers, and established a regime of exercises for her which cultivated physical poise and vocal flexibility. Mrs Manning-Hicks was a Christian Scientist, and she inculcated in Gwen a belief that acting has a great power for good, and such a gift, rightly used, should lead to the betterment of the world. Gwen was never to lose sight of this doctrine.

When Louise Manning-Hicks left England for America, Agnes Platt took her place as Gwen's drama tutor. This new teacher was an advocate of the Delsarte method of drama training. Gwen gave a description of this method in the October 1988 television 'Omnibus' programme. Unfortunately this graphic section of the programme was cut and therefore not seen by the general public. When Nigel Hawthorne, who presented the programme, asked her about the Delsarte method this was her response:

'It was founded on the Greek idea of balance. You never stood equally on both feet, you had a balance on one foot so that there was always a sense of rhythm and you could move easily from one hip to the other without shuffling your feet. If your feet went one way your hips went another and your shoulder turned that way so it was almost like rhythm, like a wave of the sea. It made you have complete control over your change of position without shuffling your feet. If you have your balance on one hip and the other foot lightly, perhaps slightly with the heel, you can turn without shuffling. You look at Greek statues, nearly always the weight is on one hip and the body turns back and there is that wonderful sense of rhythm. All that I was taught by this lady at a very early age and it has stayed with me all my life. It's the same if you make a gesture. You want to raise your arm, you don't just sort of raise it straight, you raise it gradually from the shoulder, relaxed, the elbow goes relaxed, the whole thing is rhythm. It's without being self-conscious or thinking that everybody will think what a wonderful dancer I am or how marvellous I feel, you don't think anything at all, it is utterly real and becomes so much a part of you that you move like that. But it does have a certain grace. That's all I can tell you. It was the Delsarte system of expression based on the Greek idea of rhythm. There were exercises and you learned how to do it naturally until it became second nature.'

Gwen subjected herself to a routine of disciplined daily exercises to achieve poise of bearing; standing in significant attitudes; rising and falling; pivoting; spiral movement; rotation of head; and exercises of lid, brow, nostril, mouth. She had singing lessons with Reginald Dansie at Streatham, and she diligently widened the scope of her reading, as Ellen Terry had suggested, but above all she studied her Shakespeare, because it was in his plays that she hoped to achieve her greatest success as an actress.

Auntie Florrie had grave reservations about Gwen taking up a career as an actress, especially if it meant enrolling in a drama school such as Mr Tree's. The cost of training and the hazards of subsequent employment were additional problems that, she felt, her sister Annie could do without. Gwen was neither to be deflected from her course, nor was her mother anything but enthusiastic and wholly supportive in her daughter's ambition. However, securing employment as an actress

14

was a daunting procedure. It involved reading the advertisements for vacancies, queuing up endlessly at stage doors, and, if one got that far, almost inevitably suffering humiliating rebuffs at auditions. The breakthrough came in 1911, when Gwen was twenty. She had spotted a notice that Beerbohm Tree was planning a new production of *A Midsummer Night's Dream* at His Majesty's Theatre in The Haymarket. Singers were needed. With her usual thoroughness in doing her homework, Gwen discovered that the conductor was to be a German, Adolf Schmidt, and that Mendelssohn's music was to be used. She discarded her usual English audition piece, and chose one of Schumann's Lieder which she sang in German. She secured the engagement – as a singing fairy, mostly off-stage.

Gwen was very modestly paid for her first professional role, but at least she was now in a position to look after herself. Her sister Marjorie, on the other hand, had suffered something of a nervous breakdown after a heart-breaking love affair, and was being looked after by a guardian, whom Geoffrey, when he tried to visit his sister, described in unflattering terms. Geoffrey himself was making excellent progress at St George's, Harpenden. He was on course to becoming head boy. The threatening family financial crisis, which had put at peril his continuance at the school, had been settled by the generosity of Sir Crossley Rayner, his uncle. Sir Crossley had for some time tried to persuade his sister, Annie, to

Geoffrey Ffrangcon-Davies

visit him and his wife in the West Indies, where he held high Government office. Annie at last agreed. She rented out 18 Canfield Gardens, made arrangements for Geoffrey to spend school holidays with friends, and hoped that Marjorie would be satisfactorily looked after by her 'custodian'. Gwen found lodgings at the Three Arts Club, Marylebone Road. Annie set sail for Georgetown, British Guiana, at the beginning of November 1912 on the Royal Mail Steam Packet, S S *Magdalena*.

Annie wrote to Gwen of her time in British Guiana in vivid terms. Her brother was hospitable, keen to plan excursions, and for his sister to meet the local gentry and their wives. His wife, Agnes, to whom Annie referred as 'her ladyship', seemed cold in her welcome and sadly lacking as a hostess in both her personal and public duties. For the first part of her stay Annie was bored and home-sick. But within two weeks of her sailing for home, she wrote a letter, dated 24th February 1913, which was tumbling with news and excitement. She had been to many receptions and met congenial friends which included a fellow spirit, a Mrs Wieting; she stayed with much comfort and enjoyment with a Mrs Fowler; she attended a grand reception for the visiting MCC cricketers, and gave a glowing description of an adventurous journey up river, by steamboat on the *Essequibo*, which included an overnight stay at a luxurious hotel commanding a magical view of the surrounding countryside.

15

'...There is no roughing it here...We had five courses and after that the moon had risen and the beauty of it was indescribable...the great river and the silent impenetrable bush on either side – this will be an unforgettable memory...Mr and Mrs Wieting are delightful people – I enjoyed it *so* much more having her with me – She is much more like me than Auntie Agnes and understands and appreciates. Auntie Agnes grumbled much more at the heat than admired the view which made the rest of us forget all inconveniences and *she did not* come out into the moonlight ...'[10]

Annie, at the beginning of this letter, had sympathised with Gwen, who after working hard with the chorus on rehearsals for Puccini's *Turandot*, had heard that further plans for the production had been abandoned. In consequence Gwen had been approached to join the 'Gaiety', a group that specialised in musical comedy. The 'Gaiety Girls' did not enjoy a reputation for high moral probity. Gwen knew this, and in her last letter to her mother had described how some of the girls secured their roles through their dependency on an 'uncle'. Gwen had stressed to her mother that she had gained acceptance through a Mr Mackenzie 'who has been too splendid for words; he has given himself endless trouble to get me in and yet has not been "nasty", but has just done it, as he says, because he likes to help young artists who are really anxious to get on in their work.'[11]Annie began to feel alarmed for her daughter:

'I do hope yet that you need not go to the "Gaiety" – but I have every confidence in you, and know that *all things* will work towards good. When you wrote of the experience of those three girls in being thrown out at the manager's pleasure I felt that you *cannot* go on with this life but we must be ready for whatever comes and know that the right work is seeking us. Get into the Silences and develop your creative musical ability. Let it work in you – Try meditating for three minutes at a time on Harmony or Melody. Shut out as far as possible all other sounds and see the result...I feel I want to be home again and help you now to greater development. You must be free to give all your time to your work....'[12]

Annie here urges Gwen to give all of herself to her work, and to strengthen her endeavours by Christian Science methods. Later she is to say the same to Marjorie, but adding 'like your father'. She gives no hint that such total dedication from Ffrangcon might in part have been responsible for his breakdown. She wrote to her husband from British Guiana, and told Gwen in February 1913 that

'she feels she must get back to Father. In spite of going to Mr Dansie's he does not seem really better in himself – writes very gloomily and with distaste of the Hospital of course – and ends his letter by saying "well – if I am alive I may see you in April." He seems to like going to Streatham. I wonder how it is all going to end!'

Gwen, in her letter dated 22nd February 1913, tells her mother of her visit to her father when he was staying at Mr Dansie's. She writes 'He says himself that he feels like a broken man and does not seem able to look forward to the prospect of getting well.' But she also reports that Mr Dansie 'wants awfully to give a concert with me'. There is no evidence that such a concert took place, but Gwen is full of ideas for ways of earning her living at those times when roles in the theatre are scarce. One such idea, for staging in the 'Halls', she describes in a letter to her mother dated 29th December 1912 which was post-marked in British Guiana 24th February 1913.

> 'I thought of a rather novel setting for some songs, namely this: Call the turn a Singing Picture. Have a large frame, with a background of black velvet, and pose as some well-known picture, say Greuze's "Girl with the broken Pitcher." Then as the music starts gradually come to life, come out of the picture, sing your songs and perhaps do a little dance. At the end go back into the picture and resume the original pose; curtain.'

Gwen 'will ask Mr Kinsley tomorrow what he thinks of the idea'. And then she goes on to tell her mother of some significant work she is undertaking in the coming week: 'Next Wednesday is *Eager Heart*. It is being quite extensively advertised in the papers and even in the tube!'

Eager Heart was a play by A. M. Buckton, and was to be performed at Church House, Westminster. It was the story of Christ as a child appearing each Christmas Eve to discover what welcome awaited him. Eager Fame would greet the child with a fanfare of public acclaim; Eager Sense lays on a hearty banquet; Eager Heart, in simplicity and humility, offers the child all she has, and what she values most, her love. For Gwen this was her first straight acting role. The cast was not paid for this work, nor did their names appear in the programme, but the work received national coverage, and the reviews, especially for Gwen, were very encouraging: '...the acting perfectly devout and sincere, and in many cases – notably in that of the exquisite Eager Heart herself – exceedingly fine and affecting.'

There were many more accolades of this sort. They were important for Gwen. *Eager Heart* was to be performed on many other occasions, and one year Geoffrey pleads with his mother to write to his headmaster giving him special leave to see his sister perform in it. Gwen's identification with a role with such a spiritual dimension, might well have been influential in some future castings - *The Immortal Hour* for instance.

Gwen was at the threshold of her career. Her parts had been minor: dancing as one of a chorus; singing, but not always on stage. The speaking part of Eager Heart, although not presented on the professional stage, was something of a breakthrough. She had learned to look after herself on extremely low wages, but she had mixed regularly with theatre people, some of whom were destined for great things. For instance, the Nares were long-standing friends of the family with strong connections with the theatre, and Annie, from British Guiana, asked Gwen to give them her good wishes and let her know how Gwen was getting on with them. Gwen in her letter of 29th December 1912 listed her various Christmas presents which included a lovely evening scarf from Mrs Nares, and in her letter of February 22nd 1913, wrote 'Owen (Nares) has been engaged to play the leading part in Gerald du Maurier's revival of *Diplomacy*. He and Gerald and Arthur Mortimer as the three men, rather good this trio I think. Owen is lucky but of course he deserves to be.

His wife has made quite a bit in Marie Tempest's play[13] so now I hope they will get on better.'

Gwen was looking forward to her mother returning home from the Caribbean in April 1913. Annie had so encouraged her in her acting ambition, when so many others had been anxious, like Auntie Florrie, or deeply shocked, like Uncle Crossley, and even more so Aunt Agnes, especially at Gwen's association with the Gaiety. But Gwen would press on whatever the opposition. She wrote (December 29th 1912) 'Please give my love to Uncle Crossley; and tell him or not about my going to the Gaiety, whichever you think best. It doesn't matter of course whether he objects or not.' Annie was in touch with Marjorie, who had now recovered, about arrangements for the family to be living together again when she returned to England. But she was wise enough to leave her daughters to choose as they wished. Geoffrey at least would no longer be obliged to stay with school friends during holiday times. Annie thought of Geoffrey as a scallywag, and rebuked him for not having the same concern for letter-writing as his sisters. Gwen would leap to his defence and claim that his letters may well have been prevented from reaching British Guiana through the militant activities of the suffragette movement, one of whose aims was to draw attention to their cause by undermining the postal system. When Annie arrived back in England in the Spring of 1913 war clouds were already darkening the skies of Europe.

Geoffrey's War

In 1908 the payment of Geoffrey's fees at St George's, Harpenden had been beyond what Annie could afford. Through the good offices of the headmaster, Sir Crossley Rayner was approached and the financial crisis avoided. At the outset of his schooling Geoffrey had given cause for concern both with regard to his character, as a boy who seemed oblivious of the needs of others, and also in his academic work, which was weak. But he excelled at football and rugby. He liked the school and wanted to do well. His first pencil-written note from school to his mother reads:

> 'My Dear Mother
>   I have arrived quite safely. It is awfly nice here. I saw Dudley Wright. And Chubb showed me round awfly well....
>   Your loving son Geoff

He threw himself into any number of school activities such as helping to plan the school bazaar, joining the scouts and the chapel choir, and steadily becoming more integrated with the community. He desperately wanted his mother and sisters to visit him, and this they did. When they failed to on occasions he thought important, he did his best in his letters to hide his disappointment. His letters are strewn with requests for postal orders, kit, and, of course, for food. On the eve of his fourteenth birthday he wrote:

> My dearest Mother
>   I am nearly fourteen now think of it. It is on Tuesday please send me a nice big cake, iced you know. I am allowed to have it on my birthday

also 2 6d boxes of devonshire cream caramels please do, get cook to make the cake and marjorie to ice it...It is lovely here now all the trees are out and it is perfectly beautiful the brown shoes are all right. Could you also send me a puppy collar for my puppy...I am sorry this letter is so full of wants do not worry to get them all at once but can I have the cake and caramels by Tuesday...'

Towards the end of his schooldays Geoffrey had progressed remarkably. He became chairman of the Debating Society, editor of the school magazine, captain of football, and head boy. When his mother went to the Caribbean, it was Lucy Grant, the headmaster's wife, who took responsibility for ensuring that his holidays were spent with hospitable and welcoming school friends and their families. One such family lived at 15 The Turl, Oxford. From here he wrote to his father in hospital:

'...I expect you will remember the street very well as it is so near your college. We are just opposite Lincoln...I have been round most of the colleges already; I think up till now my favourite is Jesus, it seems such a quiet compact little place, a great deal nicer than the huge 'quad' of Christchurch or Trinity...[he then goes on to tell his father of the various school offices he fills, and proceeds with details of the choir's programme – a degree of detail which does not appear in his letters to his mother]...We did the Christmas parts of the *Messiah* on Carol Sunday the Choruses "And the Glory of the Lord", "O Thou that tellest good tidings" and "Unto Us", and the solos "Comfort ye", "Every Valley shall be exalted" ...We are doing the *Crucifixion* next term to sing on Good Friday... I hope you will be able to enjoy Christmas better than last year. I expect I shall have a very quiet time.
I must end now. I always think of you and pray for you
                    Good night
                    From your loving son
                    Geoffrey'

While mother was in the Caribbean all the children made a point of writing to their father and visiting him either in hospital or when he was staying with Mr Dansie. On one occasion Geoffrey wrote of Gwen and himself making a visit together. Geoffrey looked to Gwen also to visit him at school and, as in earlier days, take him out to tea.

When war was declared in August 1914, Geoffrey lost no time in volunteering, and by September he was heading for the front. In the train on his way to Southampton, the embarkation port, he pencilled a note to his headmaster. It is on a half piece of writing paper, bearing the school's name.

'Dear Sir
                    We are in the train on our way to the front so I am now writing to say Goodbye and God bless the dear old school. If I do not come back you will know that I have tried to do my best for the credit of St George's.
                    Yours affectionately   GFfD.'

His first letters home from the front were jolly and jokey. He was improving his French; he was, when given short periods of leave, enjoying the cuisine of the French cafés; he met up with some of his school acquaintances, and even encountered his cousin Harold Daniels, Auntie Florrie's son. But, oh, he could have done with so many more food parcels: chocolate, mince pies, potted meat, marmalade. And as winter drew on he was asking for boots, extra underwear, cigarettes and candles. He gave a desperate account of life in the squelching mud, and when his mother suggested that he should put in for a commission, he replied that 'looking like absolute children' the new officers were the first to be picked off

Marjorie Ffrangcon-Davies

by the German snipers. Time and again he wrote home asking for news of Millie, his girl friend, as he had not heard from her, and he begged Marjorie to ring her on City 1491. Millie did eventually get in touch with Geoffrey and sent him a parcel which included a stylo with which he wrote a letter to Marjorie on 6th May 1915. As the weather improved so did the intensity of the battle. However, when relieved from front-line duties, Geoffrey formed a glee club of six, from which he and his friends derived much fun, even giving a concert for the Brigade, which the Brigadier and all his staff attended. But back once again in the trenches Geoffrey found himself moved from the reserve sector to the firing line. In a letter to his mother dated 4th May he bemoaned the horror of poison gas and its effects. He was toying with the idea of taking a commission in the Gurkha regiment, and continued:

'There was a nightingale in a wood just behind our trench and it was singing all night the last time we were up. It's extraordinary because the wood is full of stray bullets all night as when the Germans miss our trench the bullets fly over and hit the tree. At dawn we hear the lark and very nice it is too. Please tell Father that I am writing to him next week.'

On 6th May Geoffrey writes to Marjorie ('Dear old Barge') thanking her for her 'topping' parcel. And on 7th May he writes to his father. On that day he was hit by a stray bullet in the back of the head, and died forty-eight hours later without regaining consciousness.

Geoffrey was buried in a nearby churchyard in Clytte, Belgium. A friend of the family and one of Geoffrey's comrades wrote in pencil to Marjorie, heading his letter

'Trench, 3.30 am, 24/5/15:
My dear Marjorie,
         Lionel Gates and I went over three days ago to Geoff's grave. We found it quite easily. The cross is rather crude but the lettering has been

20

burnt on so it ought to last a long time. When we got there it had only just been finished but all the other finished graves looked very nice with flowers etc and I have no doubt his will be the same in a short time. We intend to go over again if we can get leave. Ever yours   Clive'

Annie received an official note which read:

'The King commands me to assure you of the true sympathy of His Majesty and The Queen in your sorrow.
Kitchener'

In 1922 the Imperial War Graves Commission let her know that the inscription she had chosen THERE IS NO DEATH had been engraved at her expense on the headstone, but that there would be room for only G.FFRANGCON-DAVIES and not his full Christian name.

On Geoffrey's death it was Gwen and Marjorie who went together to the hospital to tell their father the sad news. The religious sensitivities of the family led each of them to wonder whether this tragedy had come about through their own spiritual deficiencies. A letter from America dated 12 July 1915, written by Louise Manning-Hicks, the Christian Science friend of long-standing, greatly helped Annie and the girls to cope with Geoffrey's death within the context of their Christian belief. And it was partly this that encouraged Annie to choose the words that were to be engraved on Geoffrey's headstone.[14]

On Tour

Geoffrey admired his sisters and depended on them, not just for taking him out to tea, or for icing his birthday cake. When at the front, he asked them to send photographs of themselves so that he could show them to his comrades, and he warned that some of them might want to strike up a correspondence with his sisters. He was especially proud when he heard that both were giving concerts to the troops at home. Both sisters took part in concerts performed before troops about to leave for the front. Marjorie was in great demand, singing in Liverpool and Manchester, and being pressed for repeat performances. Geoffrey wryly wished that she could come and sing to the men in his outfit. Marjorie was later sent to entertain the troops in Egypt. She gave concerts in the Cairo Opera House, and even performed the part of Candida on stage. It was in Egypt that she met a handsome young officer, the Hon. Malcolm Norbury and, despite his family's opposition, married him there. Annie and Gwen set to and made Marjorie's wedding-dress themselves, and it was shipped out to her in the middle of the war. The wedding was a grand affair, with the Bishop of Jerusalem officiating.

Gwen sang for the troops when she was 'resting' between professional engagements. Her work in London was spasmodic. She had been chosen for the chorus of *Turandot*, but that project had fallen through. She was employed as part of the chorus for *Bonito*, a Portuguese light opera, directed by Granville-Barker. She learned a great deal from this particular director but, alas, the production met with scant success, and was soon taken off. Wartime seemed to be inimical to straight drama on the London stage; musical comedy was more the vogue. In 1914 Gwen left the Gaiety and found employment with a theatre group that was to tour with the farce *The Glad Eye* an adaptation from a French comedy *Le Zèbre*. The part of Niki, a shop-girl, was given to Gwen. The play had already been a success in the West End, and now it was scheduled for an extensive tour of the provinces. Gwen's part was small, but sufficiently significant for the critics to single her out in a number of reviews, referring to her performance as 'chic and irresistible'.

Marjorie's wedding in Cairo in 1917. Gwen made the wedding dress.

Soon after the tour of *Glad Eye* came to an end Gwen was taken on for a chorus part with the group that was to tour with *Tonight's The Night*, presented by George Grossmith and Edward Laurillard, which was still running as a success at London's Gaiety Theatre. A non-speaking chorus role was not exactly what Gwen was hoping for, but she was not only wise enough to accept the part to keep her in the theatre milieu, but she offered to take on the role of an understudy; and she was told to understudy for Maidie Andrews who took the leading female role. When the touring company was playing in Nottingham, Maidie Andrews was indisposed, and Gwen was asked to step in for the Monday and Tuesday performances. She was in digs at 74 Shakespeare Street, Nottingham, and from there she wrote home on the Wednesday:

'My dearest mother

I know you will be glad to hear that I played again last night and everyone said I was excellent and that it was better even than the first night. But what was so extraordinarily lucky was that Mr Laurillard came down from town to see the show, whether he came down especially to see me or not I don't know and it doesn't matter – Anyway he came and brought Mr. Blackmore (the greatest London theatrical agent) with him. They both came round to my dressing-room after and were awfully nice. Mr. Laurillard said he was very pleased indeed. He asked me out to supper afterwards, just a little exclusive party, myself, the two other leading girls, and the principal men. I felt quite honoured! Anyway every-one says I've done most awfully well, of course having the management down from town was the most terrific bit of luck. I wonder if this at last is Estelle's prediction? I do hope it will lead to better things. As I left Mr. L. said "I shan't forget you." So I hope he wont! I am awfully pleased it has gone off so well and frightfully grateful to Science, because I wasn't a bit nervous yesterday. To-day I return to the back row of the chorus again as the girl is coming back. Still I mustn't grumble as I've had my chance...'[15]

In fact Maidie Andrews did not resume the lead role, which Gwen filled for the rest of the tour. Her letter underlines the element of chance, which all actors have to come to terms with: chance of being noticed by a person of influence; chance that a good review might lead to further advancement; chance that a bad review might not drag one down. That reference to Estelle's prediction had also to do with chance. Gwen's mother was given to listening to fortune-tellers, having her horoscope read, and was ready to give her ear to the visions of clairvoyants. Estelle, a reader of horoscopes, had told her that Gwen was destined for great things. Gwen and her mother were consequently quick to associate that week in Nottingham when Gwen by chance first played the lead in *Tonight's The Night*, with Estelle's pronouncements. When the tour of this musical comedy was extended in 1916 because of its warm reception wherever it was put on, Gwen found herself playing opposite Jack Buchanan, who had taken the male lead. But there was still some way to travel between the leading female role in musical comedy and the great classical roles on which Gwen had set her heart. That goal seemed still so very far off, and her progress along that road, oh, so slow. Her patience and steadiness in pursuing her ambition were fortified by her religious belief and by the time she dedicated to reading and meditation, which 'Science', that is Christian Science, prescribed for her.

During the war years Gwen spent the greater part of her time touring in the provinces in a variety of musical comedies. But there was another significant development beyond her strictly professional work, which, like her role as Eager Heart in that 'mystery-morality play', pointed towards her future. In 1914 the first annual Glastonbury Festival had been planned. Rutland Boughton, who had been one of David Ffrangcon-Davies's most gifted accompanists, had written an opera, but not yet completed the work. It was called *The Immortal Hour*. In 1914 at Glastonbury it was Marjorie Ffrangcon-Davies who sang in the concert version of this opera. At a subsequent Glastonbury Festival the Whitsun play was the medieval morality *Everyman*. Gwen, as the only professional in the cast, took the leading role. Her annual appearances at the Glastonbury Festival became important spiritual events, as well as acting opportunities, in her life. And it was at Glastonbury that she first sang, in the role of Etain, the completed version of Rutland Boughton's *The Immortal Hour*.

Letters from Gwen to her mother, written when on tour, from cold and comfortless lodgings, give a graphic and rather grim picture of the life of the young actress during these war years. The company travelled on Sundays from one town to another. Long distances were traversed on the day that the railways performed at their lowest efficiency. There were fewer trains and more repairs; the carriages were unheated and the interminable waiting on station platforms was dispiriting. But Gwen was not given to complaining. She stressed the camaraderie; the help given her particularly by Peter, one of her travelling companions. He helped her with her luggage, saw her to her lodgings, and on one occasion even acted as her secretary in writing to her mother at Gwen's dictation. She valued this attachment, but it came to an abrupt end when Peter told his wife of this relationship. Another close friend was Freddy, not touring with Gwen, but on another circuit, making a success of Iago in a touring production of *Othello*. Gwen was urged by her mother to let Freddy down lightly. This interesting exchange of most personal matters was a characteristic of their mother-daughter relationship, and would be even more marked in the critical years immediately ahead, with the mother harmonising with her daughter's feelings, not trying to frustrate them, or being censorious on moral or religious grounds.

Ellen Terry had advised Gwen when she was fourteen years old to widen her experience, observe people closely, and extend her reading diligently. The letters to her mother written during this touring period show quite clearly how conscientiously Gwen is following that prescription. She moved from Stoke to Middlesborough from where she wrote that she had sent her mother a simnel cake from Hanley. As she knew that she had to spend some time in the Potteries, she and Peter had set themselves the task of reading Arnold Bennett's novels about the Five Towns. On leaving that area both she and Peter were of the opinion that Bennett could 'keep his Five Towns'! In Stoke she went to the Gaiety Theatre with Peter to see a performance of J. M. Barrie's *Alice-Sit-By-The-Fire*. They were both very impressed and moved by the performance, and, in a letter, she burst out 'But oh! how discontented it makes one feel with musical comedy...[we] had the hump all evening.'[16] While in the Potteries Gwen had taken up the offer of being guided round the Wedgewood factory, and she gave fascinating details of the manufacturing process from beginning to end:

'...some of the finer ware is still made on the old-fashioned potter's wheel and it was simply marvellous to see the old man working it and with the touch of a finger turns it from a shapeless lump into a long-necked graceful vase'.[17]

This habit of learning as much as she could from whatever environment she found herself in, persisted throughout her life. On tour a few years later, when playing in Leeds, the secretary of the Bronte Society asked her out to lunch and then drove her to Haworth Parsonage. She wrote to her mother:

'I went and very much enjoyed it. The parsonage is now a museum, which is a pity because one loses the sense of the place having been lived in; but it is full of their m.s. and some of their old furniture and clothes. One mouse coloured taffeta dress which was Charlotte's "going away" gown I tried on! Made by the little village dressmaker, but very quaint and charming. Her shoes are minute. I am sure Doreen (Gwen's small niece) could not get into them – so very very narrow, one wonders how she could have traipsed the moors as she did and thought nothing of marching to Keighley and back, a matter of eight miles! I am now reading Mrs Gaskell's Life of her, and having

24

seen the place can visualise it very clearly. I think there is a play in these tragic sisters. I must speak to Berkeley about it. The bleakness and coldness of the place make me realise where Emily got her amazing terror and gloom in *Wuthering Heights* from.'[18]

Imagine a visitor to Haworth Parsonage today being allowed to try on Charlotte Bronte's taffeta dress which she wore after her wedding to the Reverend A. B. Nicholls in 1854!

Gwen's attentive friend, Peter, was a member of the stage management staff, and accustomed to look after the needs of others. Certainly, his help given Gwen on tour, especially when her lodgings were far from the theatre, was greatly appreciated. In a letter to her mother written from Bradford, Gwen reveals her debt to Peter, but also includes an account of an interesting visit to Rutland Boughton in Doncaster. His good news was that his music drama *The Immortal Hour* was to be granted special publication through the Carnegie Awards. However, during the war Boughton had been forced to relinquish his work for the Glastonbury Festival to his partner, Christina Walshe, and become a military bandmaster, a role which he filled without relish.

'7 Manneville Terrace
Bradford
Monday
My dearest mother
      Many thanks for your letter on Saturday. I am sorry it still continues so very cold with you, but I suppose it is the same everywhere. You say I told you nothing about myself in my last letter. There was nothing much to tell. I was quite all right on Sunday, and played Saturday night, tho' felt pretty rotten. Have been perfectly well since then and I really don't need a 'tummyband'! I went over to Doncaster yesterday to see Rutland. He has a very nice room there and a decent piano. We had a good old talk and some music. I think it did him good, but poor dear, he is fearfully fed up with it and no wonder. He says his mind is stagnant and he has lost interest in everything. It will come back tho' I am sure. One thing it has done for him, he says, shown him what a wonder Chris is. I am glad for he needed to be reminded – but just at present he is rather muddled...Forgive this scrawl but I am writing in front of the fire on my knees. My rooms are miles from the theatre and poor Peter will feel it very much I fear – He was a lamb about yesterday, brought my suitcase here for me, saw me off in Sheffield, met me at 10.11 and brought me here. I don't know what I should have done without him. I'm so tired that I'll rest a bit before the show so good-bye dear...
      Ever so much love
        From Gwen
PS My bill was most reasonable only £2.15.'[19]

The PS must refer to payment for her last weekly board and lodgings at Sheffield. Gwen was performing in a musical comedy, *The Arcadians*, a revival of a popular London success, staged with striking designs and costumes. She played the part of an Arcadian maiden, Sombra, who takes a fairy-like human form, one of those parts prefiguring her role of Etain in *The Immortal Hour.* Her acting and particularly her singing gained many plaudits.

Marjorie and Gwen were not the only members of the family on tour. Annie, too spent the war years travelling. After Geoffrey's death in May 1915 she spent most of the remaining war years in various parts of the country, mostly visiting her sisters. She had a twin sister, Rose Eaton, who was married with six children; an older sister, Helen (Nellie) Williams, married to a minister, who had one son, Jack; and a younger sister, Florrie Daniels, married with two children, Harold and Audrey. A fair amount of Gwen's correspondence comprises letters to and from these aunts. As Annie went from one sister's home to another's she passed on to her daughters some trenchant comments. For instance she admired Nellie's magnificent house near the north Welsh coast, but deplored its position in the middle of a noisy town. When she left her younger sister's home after a lengthy stay she wrote to Gwen of Florrie, that had she stayed any longer 'I would have killed her'.

Geoffrey, from the trenches, had written to his family mentioning his cousins, speculating that Harold would probably marry Rosie, one of Rose's daughters. He had said how misguided Harold was to seek a commission.[20] Harold eventually joined Geoffrey in France, but was later posted to Mesopotamia, where he was killed in the summer of 1916. Annie wrote commiserating with Florrie on her loss. Gwen, too, had written, more than one letter, giving her aunt news of Harold's fate as she had gleaned it from the Civic League. Florrie replied at length in a letter dated 16 July 1916. It is a remarkably graphic account of the way a bereaved mother tries to cope with the news of her son's death in battle.[21] She was deeply shocked by the overall loss of life, and when standing on a railway platform and seeing two young officers, boarding a train on their way to the western front, she was overwhelmed with anxiety for their fate. She was bewildered by the conflicting news that was sent her. There was no official notice of Harold's death. The Privates in Harold's Company reported to her by letter how they saw him advancing, leading his men towards the Turkish lines, and that he was shot in the head. Lt. Col. Talis wrote to her 'I would accept all information given by private soldiers with great reservation as it is usually inaccurate. There is on the other hand another report that Lieutenant Daniels reached the Turkish lines, and so may have been taken prisoner.' Florrie, sad and confused, wondered what she should do about wearing mourning clothes.

It was at this time that Ffrangcon was making what appeared to be a miraculous recovery from his state of mental depression. He had been allowed periods of leave from the hospital. He had attended a few concerts, begun to sing in public once more and to give poetry readings. He had been staying with friends and family, and Florrie had to confront the possibility of his wanting to stay with her. The prospect made her even more nervous:

> 'Rose said in her letter to me that Ffrangcon did not seem to be normal – and that John Evans said he was "certainly not normal" – He sang "very dramatically". I do hope you can prevent him leaving the hospital. I feel sure it will only be the same thing over again. I don't want to put Ffrangcon off coming, if you would like him to come, though we are a little bit afraid of what we shall do with him, or how we shall get on with him – so if you are not very wishful for us to see him – or he to come – *we* won't press it.'

26

Her letter ends with reference to the great comfort that she and many other anxious and bereaved relatives derive from the 'Quiet Day' at the Cathedral on Thursdays:

'I could only go afternoon and evening – it was very peaceful and helpful. I liked the "Fellowship of Silence" we had'.

Yet another cousin, Jack, Nellie's son, also perished in the war. Each of three of the Rayner sisters had lost an only son.

Florrie was proved right about Ffrangcon's temporary recovery. In 1916 Ffrangcon seemed to be regaining his confidence and his love of music and poetry once more. He resumed his correspondence with Elgar and other former colleagues, all of whom responded with great hopes of his return to his former achievements. His hospital records for this period read as follows:

'July 1 He has been granted a month's leave of absence.
July 22 He was brought back from the Cheadle Asylum, Manchester, where he had had to be confined to a padded room, having become maniacal while arranging with Manchester agents for singing engagements.
July 29 Since his return he has had to be detained in a padded room because of violence and general restlessness...He is abusive and threatening. Says his wife is a whore and has been guilty of immorality with various members of staff.'[22]

A report later in the year speaks of his being more resigned. In 1917 there is an entry indicating that he is taking no further interest in playing the piano or singing, and that he seems quietly resigned. In 1918 he suffered a heart attack and died on 13 April.

Of the Ffrangcon-Davies family the two men had died: the three women survived. With Ffrangcon's death a great burden had fallen from Annie's shoulders. A freer and less care-worn life awaited her. Marjorie was married to Malcolm Norbury, who also survived the war. She had achieved considerable success as a singer, with a repertoire of songs both light and classical. She had performed at the Glastonbury Festival with acclaim, and on many other concert platforms in England and, of course, in Egypt. Her personal and professional life promised well.

At the end of the war Gwen, twenty-seven years old, had achieved an occasional lead role in touring companies performing a repertoire of musical comedies in the provinces. During the last year of the war, when her stage career was in the doldrums, Gwen improved her skill as hat-maker, and thereby secured a small income. Because of her fluent German, she was offered employment by the Censor's Office, to read and translate the letters that the prisoners of war were sending home to Germany. Her ambition, nevertheless, was as bright as ever; her personal preparation as rigorous; but the clock was ticking away, and the offer of those classical roles on the London stage seemed as far off as ever. There were, however, glimmers of light. The press and public had greeted with acclaim some of her non-professional performances, such as Eager Heart and her role in *Everyman*, which had demonstrated those almost ethereal qualities in her acting which moved hearts and lifted spirits. Her performances at Glastonbury had had the same effect and it was from Glastonbury that her career eventually took wing – with a song.

Chapter Two: The Wings of the Morning (1919-25

'The great baritone's daughter'

Reviews of farces such as *The Glad Eye* (1914) and musical comedies such as *The Arcadians* (1917) frequently included words of praise for Gwen's performance, but never associated her with her father. On the other hand, reviews of her performances after the war at Glastonbury and as a singer on the concert platforms of Bristol, Bournemouth, London and elsewhere, often referred to her parentage. She bore her name proudly, and the accolades she received were no less warm than those conferred on her father twenty or so years earlier. The programmes of her recitals included Irish and English folk songs, some set by Hubert Hughes and Gustav Holst, the 'Willow Song' from *Othello*, a selection from Debussy, and groups of German songs, favourites among which were the works of Hugo Wolf and Robert Franz. A particular song, for which she was repeatedly extolled, was a new setting of a medieval lyric. *The Daily Telegraph* reviewer of her recital, given in the Aeolian Hall, London, wrote:

> 'The most delightful of all her songs, and perhaps the most original was the setting of the twelfth century "I synge of a Mayden", by a composer at present unknown to us - Mary Macnair. A quaintly beautiful song this, in the antique manner, fragile but intimate, formal but charming. It was sung twice, and the singer might well have been excused for singing it again at the end of a delightful programme.'[1]

When asked for an encore, Gwen wisely chose the modern setting of the medieval carol. Listening to the same concert, the music critic of The *Westminster Gazette* pointed out her limitations, but stressed how she worked within them:

> 'Some charming songs delightfully sung were heard at the recital given in the Aeolian Hall yesterday. This is a young artist who steadily advances. Her voice is of limited volume, but the quality of it is very pleasing, and what is more noteworthy still is the skill with which she uses it. In the purely technical sense her production and control are exceedingly good, and the taste and understanding which she brings to her interpretations are no less conspicuous. She showed excellent judgement, too, in the composition of her programme, which included among other things, a group of folk songs (Irish and English), which she did particularly well - with just the right lightness of touch and simplicity of style which such things - even the emotional and pathetic ones - require.'[2]

The discipline, learning and craftsmanship, with regard to movement and diction, which Gwen acquired as an actress, she applied with equal diligence to the cultivation of those qualities which were to make her so distinguished a singer. Although her father had no hand in her training, Gwen was greatly helped by two

Rutland Boughton

of her father's closest friends, each of whom had been excellently placed to absorb her father's command of technique and teaching skills: Rutland Boughton, who had acted as her father's accompanist during Ffrangcon's teaching sessions, and Reginald Dansie, who had been taught singing by Ffrangcon, and in turn taught Gwen.

In 1919 the Glastonbury Festival was held once more, and one of the items on the programme was *Cupid and Death*, a seventeenth century masque, written by James Shirley and performed in 1653, during the Commonwealth, before the Portuguese ambassador. It was reported that 'the antique music of Matthew Locke and Christopher Gibbons, which Mr. Edward J. Dent has brought together for this occasion, is perfectly exquisite...Mr. Sheerman Hand and Miss Gwen Ffrangcon-Davies were among the principal singers.'[3] The last work of the Festival that year was Rutland Boughton's *King Arthur*, an opera whose story is of Arthur who, wishing to distract his knights from their internal quarrelling, urges them to seek the Holy Grail. Gwen sang the part of Nimue, who effectively lured Merlin, a malign influence on events, to his death. A reviewer refers to her performance as follows:

> 'Miss Ffrangcon-Davies had not much in the way of opportunities, but the lightsomeness and sweetness of her singing were the outstanding feature of the lake scene. In the encounter with Merlin...her acting was intensely realistic - in fact, she displayed emotional powers to a degree seldom attained on the stage.'[4]

Also, as part of that year's Glastonbury Festival, but performed just before Christmas, was Rutland Boughton's musical adaptation of the Nativity from the medieval Coventry Mystery Plays. In this production, which was performed first at Glastonbury and subsequently in many other places, Gwen sang the part of the Virgin Mary. She was, as usual, especially selected for praise, but the reviewer here goes on to pay tribute to the chorus in meeting such a musical challenge:

> 'For the leaders there is much singing, and the music calls for experts. In this respect the company is well chosen. Miss Ffrangcon-Davies gives a beautiful performance. Her voice is of the penetrating character that carries well in a hall, and her acting was beautifully pathetic...A great deal of the choral music is sung unaccompanied, and the extent to which this severe test is borne by the singers is at once pleasing and a testimony to their excellence as vocalists.'[5]

At the 1919 Glastonbury Festival, however, it was the production of *The Immortal Hour*, that proved the main attraction. Rutland Boughton's original presentation of this work had been at the first Glastonbury Festival on August 26,

1914. The timing was not propitious; the war had begun on August 4. Rutland Boughton, himself, played the part of Dalua. The text of this opera is based on the play and the poems of Fiona Macleod (William Sharp). The story is shot through with Irish mysticism, fairy folk-lore, and an evanescence that exasperated the practical-minded and enchanted the idealists. At the end of the First World War, when *The Immortal Hour* returned to Glastonbury, the idealists were only too ready to harness their aspirations to such a presentation. The carnage of the last four years had created a yearning for a better world. Could it be built on ideals which the world of spirits might unlock? The opera became the focus of a cult. Letters to Gwen testify to some of the audience having seen it twenty or thirty times, and some even more. It was taken up from Glastonbury by Barry Jackson in 1919, to be staged by his famous repertory company in Birmingham in 1920, and then in London's Old Vic in 1921. In 1922 it was presented at the Regent Theatre near King's Cross, London. Revivals occurred regularly in the following ten years: audiences never failed to support the productions wherever the opera was performed.

The Celtic myth on which the story is based is set in a land of dreams that bears no resemblance to the world of common life. The first character to appear is Dalua, whose touch, William Sharp explains, is madness or death for any mortal, and whose falling shadow even causes bewilderment and forgetfulness. A dialogue takes place between him and the off-stage mocking voices of the forest spirits. Etain, daughter of 'Shee', the Hidden People of the Isles, enters. She is in a strange mood, wondering whether to return to her own folk or wander among the children of men. Then Eochaidh (pronounced Yokkay), King of Ireland, weary of his earthly possessions and seeking the kingdom of dreams, appears. He recognises Etain as the woman he is seeking, and they embrace. The first act ends with Etain hearing more clearly the call of the fairy folk and as she moves in response, the curtain falls. The second act takes place in the king's palace. The Druids enter, singing in chorus, followed by a courtly procession, hailing Etain as their queen; but she is restless and abstracted. A young stranger enters, takes the old minstrel's harp, and sings. Etain, who now has cast aside her royal robes, recognises the song of the fairy folk of the forest, and the singer, Midir, their prince, her first love. She follows Midir. Dalua moves towards Eochaidh, and touches him with the touch of death. And so the opera ends.

What is 'the immortal hour'? One interpretation is that it is that one hour which the earthly king spends with the elusive Etain. The story is banal when set against the music which transforms it. Productions of the opera reached their peak with the staging facilities available for its presentation by Nigel Playfair, who ran the Lyric Theatre Hammersmith from 1928-1932, and Barry Jackson, at the Regent Theatre in 1922. The Birmingham Repertory Company, under the strict direction of Barry Jackson, was renowned for its rigorous rehearsal schedules and its attention to detail. The costumes and set had been magnificently designed by Paul Shelving, and the orchestra came under the baton of Appleby Matthews, who had first drawn Barry Jackson's attention to the opera, and taken him to see it at Glastonbury. From this visit in 1920 two important decisions were made that radically affected the direction of Gwen's career. The first was that the Birmingham Repertory Company would itself present *The Immortal Hour* in Birmingham; and the second was that Gwen would be offered the job of juvenile leading lady with the Company.

What made the performances of *The Immortal Hour* such an extraordinary phenomenon? Its presentation in that post-war period seemed to meet a need for an other-worldly mysticism. However much it drew on the Celtic twilight, there was an Englishness that fostered a sense of patriotism. Time and again it was referred to as the first English opera. Boughton was a Buckinghamshire man, from the heart of England. The English were becoming a little chary of being so dependent on German music. Was not Edward Elgar, whose music formed such a linchpin of the Malvern Festival, showing the way? The essence of the opera's success lay in Boughton's music, its engaging tunefulness and pervading sense of mystery, the striking setting and costumes and perhaps, above all, the impact on the audience of Gwen's performance as Etain. E. J. Dent, in 1922 for *The Illustrated London News* wrote:

'Mr. Boughton has succeeded in conveying this atmosphere of poetry and dreams with a singular simplicity of resource. The tale is told quietly, and the reticence with which he has treated the love scene at the end of the first act gives it a most unearthly beauty. What makes the appeal of the opera - and its appeal is singularly haunting - is its invariably melodious and vocal character. It is not based upon folk-songs, but it has many turns of phrase which one recognises at once as Irish in character. The most beautiful of these is the melody associated with the King's love for Etain, which recurs in various places, and it has a worthy companion in the songs of the faery folk.

The part of Etain is taken by Miss Gwen Ffrangcon-Davies, whose father will be remembered as one of our most impressive oratorio singers. She has sung the part in almost all the performances of the opera which have been given, and her interpretation of it is a remarkable accomplishment. She is an actress as well as a singer, indeed one almost forgets that she is a singer, so little show does she make with her voice. She sings the whole part in a delicate mezzo voce that exactly suggests the remoteness of Etain's personality. Every word comes through perfectly, and every note is exquisitely sung - it is the most striking example of that art which conceals art....'

Like most actors and actresses Gwen kept scrap-books of press-cuttings which referred to her work. The references to *The Immortal Hour* abound. So far as Gwen is concerned, apart from one instance, the reviewer writes in admiration of her accomplishment. In most cases she is picked out as the star of the performance. The papers and journals in which these 1922 reviews occur, some of them at great length, are as follows: *Daily Telegraph, Morning Post, Times Daily News, Daily Express, Daily Chronicle, Daily Mail, Pall Mall Gazette, Westminster Gazette, Daily Mirror* (which also lists the names of the titled ladies and gentlemen who were observed in the audience), *The Star, Reynolds Weekly, Daily Graphic, The Observer* (which includes a large section on the musical notation), *Sunday Times, The Referee, The People, Sunday Express, Sunday Pictorial, Sunday Herald, Illustrated London News, The Weekly Dispatch, Era, The Lady* (which gives in great detail an account of Etain's costume), *Toronto Weekly Star, Daily Herald, Evening Standard, Musical*

Gwen as Etain in *The Immortal Hour* 1922

As Newly Born in *Back to Methuselah* 1923

Times, Birmingham Gazette (a long article on Gwen, headlined 'A Birmingham Actress in London'), *Time and Tide, Punch, Musical Standard, New Witness, Vogue* (full-page pictures), *Tatler* (full-page pictures), *Sphere* (full-page pictures), *Daily Sketch* (picture), *Eve* (picture).

Gwen had become a star. The press coverage of the 1921 Old Vic and the 1922 Regent Theatre performances of *The Immortal Hour*, had blazoned the name of Gwen Ffrangcon-Davies throughout the English-speaking world. Her life was being lifted up, and changed, on the wings of the morning. And yet another change came to her. Gwen was in love. A married man had stayed at her lodgings overnight, and on more than one night. In a state of rapture she wrote to her mother of her ecstasy. Her mother replied in a letter dated 7 April 1921:

'Beloved Gwen,

That I can call you this after your letter yesterday proves what a very extraordinary mother I am from the world's point of view! But I am trying to learn to keep my hands off other people when they are no longer children, and only to "stand by" in case of need. You know as well as I do that this rapture of happiness may need its price - all good things do in this most imperfect world but that it will be worth it in the tremendous expansion of consciousness and the completion of your physical make-up I do not doubt ...I thought of Browning's "In a Gondola" where the lover when he is stabbed says "Think not of them they never lived, but I have lived and so can die" - The world is "made over" for you and you are lifted "off your feet"! I wonder how many legally married people experience the depths and heights of true "passion". This is not to say but that you must most carefully guard your secret. You have a tell-tale face, people always jump to one cause and if you cannot give it out they immediately expect that it is "illicit" - so be very wise.

This ought to result in the making of a "masterpiece" by...turning the Life-force into a work of Art and then there is no waste. Your work ought to be greatly enhanced and will be in my eyes the greatest justification for this momentous step.'[6]

Annie was writing to Gwen in April 1921. The first London production of *The Immortal Hour* took place in June of that year. Gwen's mother might have been right in believing that Gwen's rapture of love would lead directly to stardom.

Shavian Interlude

Annie, in her reference to the Life Force in her letter to Gwen, is using a current Shavianism, which GBS was to explore dramatically in a number of his plays, no more so than in *Back to Methuselah*. The play had been written long before its publication in 1921, the year of its first presentation in New York. It is a massive work in five parts. The New York company put on each of the five plays for a three week period, which enabled them to rehearse each of the succeeding plays in turn.[7] The Birmingham Repertory Company in 1923 was set the mammoth task of presenting the whole of *Back to Methuselah* within the one week. For Gwen, who had substantial roles in the first and the last parts, the rehearsals of twelve hours a day, and the exacting performances put her under one of the greatest strains of her acting career. But this challenge came at a time when she was in the third year of her Birmingham contract, and when she had, as a member of that company, a string of considerable successes to her name. Among her many repertory roles, she had played Phoebe Throssel in *Quality Street*; Lady Mary in *The Admirable Crichton*; Queen Mary in *Mary Stuart*; Lucy in The *Professor's Love Story*; and Queen Isabella in Marlowe's *Edward II*. Many of these plays were presented first in Birmingham and then transferred to the London stage. Following the artistic triumph and great financial success of *The Immortal Hour* at the Regent Theatre, other London theatres, such as The Kingsway and The Court Theatre were eager to offer hospitality to this famous provincial company. In the case of *Edward II*, for instance, the London staging took place at The Regent Theatre and subsequently at The Court. Duncan Yarrow played Edward II and Gwen Queen Isabella. Most reviews refer to Mr Yarrow's bronchial affliction, both in rehearsal and performance. Edward Shanks was in an ill-humour when he wrote his review for *The Outlook* on 24 November 1923:

> 'Miss Gwen Ffrangcon-Davies was not at all good as Queen Isabella: her realistic sobs and groans were hopelessly out of the proper key...Perhaps every one was rattled a little by fear of collapse of Mr. Duncan Yarrow: it is disturbing to have on the stage an actor who may not be able to continue his part to the end. (By the way, did Mr. Yarrow so very unexpectedly grow a beard during the second interval in order to protect his throat?)'

Ralph Wright, on the other hand, for *The New Statesman*, although he commiserates with Mr Duncan Yarrow on his attack of laryngitis, is disposed to be more generous to Gwen:

> 'One figure alone stands out, that of the Queen. I had never seen Miss Gwen Ffrangcon-Davies act before, and was immensely impressed by the dignity of her performance. She has excellent gesture, a musical voice, and she looked most graceful and finished. But better by far than this she spoke intelligently, as if she realised the meaning and the measure of the words she was speaking. While she was acting one could remember how supremely Marlowe could write.'

When ten years later the artist, Walter Richard Sickert, wanting to paint Gwen's portrait, asked for a photograph of her in one of her stage roles, she gave him a snapshot of herself as Queen Isabella, 'the she-wolf of France'. This painting still hangs in the Tate Gallery.

Gwen, always meticulous in the selection of her costume, worked with designers who were sensitive to period settings and period costume. *The Saturday Review* comments:

> 'The queen of Miss Ffrangcon-Davies was a beautifully firm piece of work and as good to look upon as a portrait of the Flemish school.'

That sense of matching her stage appearance, where appropriate, with classical art models, was nurtured by Gwen throughout her professional career, and became of great significance for her productions in South Africa twenty years later.

Before appearing in *Back to Methuselah* Gwen was required by the Birmingham Repertory Company to give further performances in London of both *The Immortal Hour* and *Bethlehem*. Both were again great hits. *Bethlehem*, brought to the London professional stage just before Christmas 1923 and continuing well into January 1924, earned many fresh plaudits for its composer, Rutland Boughton. Gwen, playing once more the Virgin Mary, won golden opinions. The reviewer of the *Cork Weekly Examiner*, asked Gwen about her costume and reported as follows:

'She lived the part in her simple robe of palest blue with a light veil of snowy white. "I have consciously modelled all my gestures on the pictures of the Virgin, by Bellini, which I studied during a visit to Venice," she said. "My favourite Madonna, however, is the little Botticelli in the National Gallery. I now no longer use these poses consciously. Mary is the easiest part an actress can play, because she embodies a spiritual truth. Utter simplicity is required. I try to bring out her spirituality and at the same time her exquisite maternal love, as when, for instance, she bends over the Child in the manger fearing that it might be cold. It is no use endeavouring consciously to portray this. I try to relax my mind and let the feeling possess me. The playing of the part then comes easily." '

Gwen's role in the extended run of *Bethlehem* came between the Birmingham and London performances of *Back to Methuselah*. Her parts in this cycle were that of Eve in the first part, *In The Beginning*, in which she ages from the second-created to the older Eve, intent on cherishing the Life Force, and The Newly Born in the last part, *As Far as Thought can Reach*. The enterprise brought her into close contact with Bernard Shaw, which developed into a lasting friendship. Gwen had met Shaw earlier on many occasions because as a champion of so many theatrical innovations he had warmly supported the Glastonbury Festival from its inception. Gwen and her sister Marjorie had both been involved. In a broadcast talk she gave in South Africa nearly thirty years later entitled 'I Remember Shaw', she spoke about those early meetings, and of how Shaw, who was a keen photographer, would take snapshots of the performances. He was a great walker and would often have her accompany him over the hills.

One of her earliest parts with the Birmingham Repertory Company was that of Cleopatra in Shaw's *Caesar and Cleopatra*, with Cedric Hardwicke as Caesar. Shaw came to her dressing-room afterwards and declared himself well-pleased with her performance. When Barry Jackson asked Shaw for the rights to present *Back to Methuselah*, Shaw on one of his famous postcards had written 'are your wife and children provided for?' Gwen was surprised to find how old-fashioned Shaw was in some of his staging notions, such as wanting real grass used in the first part. He was tactfully frustrated by Paul Shelving, who had more modern techniques to explore. At the production in Birmingham, but not in London, Edith Evans played the Serpent in the first part. Shaw had maintained 'that there should be a 'prop' serpent coiled around the tree of life, opening and shutting its mouth by means of some mechanical device with Miss Edith Evans speaking the lines in the wings, 'but,' Gwen wrote 'Edith soon put a stop to any nonsense of that kind.' Gwen's work with Edith, and the warm and wonderful friendship that developed between them, lasting until Edith's death in 1976, was the most significant outcome for Gwen of this production of *Back to Methuselah*. This was how Gwen, writing to her mother, described the beginning of that friendship:

> 'Shaw came on Monday (to a dress rehearsal) and was rather devastating about it, but I was assured by the fact that he went for Edith Evans even worse than he did for me! She says that is just his way – If he thinks anything of you as an artist he will bully you unmercifully or rather lash you with the whip of his humour – It is when he is kind and patient that you have to despair because that usually means that he thinks the job is hopeless, and resigns himself accordingly! He was nice about the old Eve, the one I had been most fearful of and I have since been through it with EE who has given me some helpful hints. We have become great friends – We have so much in common – on almost all subjects and she is also a student of C.S. We are sold out for the first night and the rest of the booking is going very well. Have you got your tickets yet?'[8]

Edith Evans had been cast as Millamant, for a London production of Congreve's *The Way of the World*. She therefore relinquished her part of the Serpent, for the London run of *Back to Methuselah*, to Caroline Keith, whom, the critics noted, played it with less distinction. 'Miss Caroline Keith' says Ivor Brown 'knew too much about the mechanics of elocution.'[9]

The run-up to the Birmingham production and its subsequent presentation in London created a great sense of anticipation in social and cultural circles. A significant theatrical event, and indeed a considerable endurance test, for both actors and audience, was about to take place. Gwen writes to her mother from 37 Duchess Road, Birmingham, on the eve of this event:

> 'Lady Londonderry is coming down for the Saturday matinée of part 1. I had a nice letter from her in which she said her cousin the Duke of Sutherland was always enquiring after me and wanted me to go and stay up there – I don't remember a Duke of Sutherland at all – Argyll and Northumberland are the only two I remember!...I was reading through some old letters this morning and came across such a nice one of yours – written to me just three years ago when the cloud seemed very dark and the future very obscure – When I look back on that time I am filled with gratitude to God for the wonderful way things have unfolded - and I don't regret the hard times or disappointments at all – Because as you say in your letter, easy success might have been the worst possible thing for me - I am sure it would have been – because I should have got proud and thought I had done something – whereas now I know that any so called success only comes from God.'[10]

Not only Dukes and Duchesses sought Gwen's acquaintance, but members of the royal family as well. Queen Victoria's granddaughter, Princess Marie Louise, who said she had seen *The Immortal Hour* fifty times, regarded Gwen as a personal friend, and wrote her very many letters, expressing the warmest sentiments, usually heading them 'Dearest Etain'. The way Gwen managed these friendships - and there were many - over a great number of years testifies to her sense of balance and charm, with no hint of arrogance. As the latter part of the letter to her mother, quoted above, indicates, she had a keen sense of dedicating her art to a spiritual end. To help her achieve this she would seek the support of Christian Science practitioners, whom she and her mother mention from time to time. When facing the strain of rehearsing for and presenting *Back to Methuselah* she went to see a Mrs Harrison, and after the successful performance, ascribed her own achievement in no small part to the support she received from Mrs Harrison. She writes again to her mother after the first performance:

'Dearest Mother,
I did not write yesterday because I felt too tired and limp – It was a great night but also a great strain! I was so grateful for Mrs Harrison's help and I know it did wonders – The notices are good on the whole – a few of the *Daily Mail* variety have not got eyes to see of course and must try to be funny! You will have seen the *Daily News* notice – I was so glad he got what I tried so hard to bring out in the second act – What he objects to and calls "finnicky" in the first is not really my fault. Shaw wanted it played like that – rather matter of fact and almost modern in contrast to the Serpent - I had great difficulty in altering my conception of the part at the last minute so that probably it did not quite "come off" - I expect it will be better next time – Shaw is wildly pleased apparently – thrilled to death about it all which I am ever so glad about – and every-one has been awfully nice about "Eve". Ayliff (the producer) stopped me on the stairs yesterday and took hold of my hands and said "everyone is simply raving about you!" Of course it was only to be expected that the critics would give the notices to Edith and she deserved them. She was magnificent! You will like her she is such a dear – A friend came round and told me after that Mrs Shaw was delighted. She said when I first came on "Oh I am sure that little thing can never do it." And at the end she said it was one of the most beautiful performances she had ever seen. Wasn't that lovely? Shaw wouldn't make a speech tho' they cheered and clapped for nearly ten minutes. But he said after it was the finest first night one of his plays has ever had – He couldn't say much more could he – of course he didn't say anything to me, not even to Edith – he never does apparently but one hears from other people.'[11]

At the end of the first week at Birmingham, when the great cycle had been completed, Shaw did at last speak to Gwen about her performance:

'Shaw seemed pleased and came up to me to see me after and said – "When I was misguided many years ago to write this play there is no doubt that Providence caused you to be born especially in order to play the part" which was great praise as he has never before said anything to me of an encouraging nature, and I was very grateful.'[12]

Back to Methuselah maintained its fascination for the theatre-going public, partly as a unique theatrical event, the dramatisation of Shaw's extraordinary Pentateuch, partly as a test of endurance for actors and actresses, and partly as foremost topic of discussion in town. It continued to flourish into March of 1924. By the beginning of April Gwen was again playing in London: Cordelia in *King Lear*, staged by the Phoenix Society at the Regent Theatre. This society was founded to present plays by the minor Elizabethan and Jacobean playwrights. That *King Lear* had been chosen brought some protest from certain parts of the press, but commentary on Gwen's performance was unflinchingly supportive. Within the first week of her portrayal of Cordelia at The Regent Theatre, the *Daily Express* and the *Westminster Gazette* praised highly her performance of Desdemona in a dramatic reading of *Othello* given at the Haymarket Theatre.

Gwen's greatest ambition was to play Juliet on the London stage. She had played the part in Birmingham. In April 1922 she had sent a telegram to her mother: 'Just heard I'm to play Juliet next month am nearly crazy with joy'.[13] In this production Ion Swinley played Romeo and Barry Jackson the Chorus. Two years later *Romeo and Juliet* was presented by Barry Jackson at the Regent Theatre London, with Gwen as Juliet and John Gielgud as Romeo.

Heart's Desire

S. P. B. Mais, the drama critic of *The Daily Graphic*, and subsequently the prolific author of a great number of books on literature and travel, attended the first night of *Romeo and Juliet* at the Regent Theatre in London, on 23rd May 1924. His article, which appeared on 29th May, read as follows:

> 'My mind this week is full of one thing only, the acting of Gwen Ffrangcon-Davies, whose superb interpretation of Juliet at the Regent, where the curtain now rises at 8 instead of 8.15, has earned for her the high dignity of having a leading article all to herself in a London newspaper. She is there rightly described as "Shakespeare's Juliet made concrete on the stage." Praise can go no higher. It seems impossible, when you see her, to imagine her doing anything else. She does not play Juliet; she is Juliet come to life, both in her personal beauty, frail porcelain-like physique, and in the exquisite, love-drenched timbre of her voice.
>
> Usually the Juliet of the stage is either lovely and can't act, or a skilled actress, too mature in years or girth to satisfy our physical senses of an ideal interpreter. Miss Davies' Juliet is as near flawless as any Juliet has ever been or is likely to be. She has achieved a success of so rare a kind as to defeat criticism.'

Praise indeed! But Mais was holding back what he really felt about Gwen's performance. He felt himself shackled from saying what he felt by the convention of his craft and the expectations of his editor.

Romeo and Juliet is one of Shakespeare's longest plays. It was presented at the Regent in almost its complete form. The audience was treated to a text that had rarely been acted before, and although the performance, as Mais remarked, started fifteen minutes earlier than usual, many had to leave before the end to catch their last train home. Mais was one of them. He left just before the end. In the train taking him home, he wrote his account of the performance which appeared in The *Daily Graphic* a few days later. While still on his journey to his home in Sussex, he wrote a remarkable letter to Gwen.

'22A, First Avenue,
Hove, Sussex.
23 May 1924

Dear Miss Davies

What I have said about you in print in *The Daily Graphic* today in no way represents what I feel. For a critic to be suspected of knowing Shakespeare is more than dangerous – it means instant dismissal.

For a critic to rhapsodise over an actress argues in the mind of his Editor that he is intimate with if not passionately in love with her. So what I said in print doesn't matter a damn.

Now listen to what I really think. *Romeo and Juliet* is almost intolerable upon the stage, because one's dream-creations are so much more real than the poor players with their protuberant bodies –

But you, my dear, gave us last night the love scenes exactly as we have lived love in our dreams.

Love of the Shakespeare kind untrammelled by psychoanalysis lies in the magic of the voice and in truth your voice as you leaned over the balcony was so vibrant with love that you seemed so suddenly to take on the loved accents of everybody's lover in the theatre.

Oh Lord! Words beat me here. What I mean is that people go sloppily wandering through loving a tiny bit here and a tiny bit there, spilling their [?] from the cup until it is all wasted. Once – and once only the cup can be poured out in one hectic giving – a young girl waking to a new heaven and a new earth – a young man driven almost to madness by the pain of parting, delirious at the touch and so on.

That divine drunkenness you gave us as I believe no other living actress would and I want to thank God for you.

But above all I want to thank you for playing the part as Shakespeare saw it, as a sort of infantile paralysis, with a completely unsophisticated child's abandon.

"Men have died ere now, but not for love." Perhaps, but youth has often died for love - and it is your youth that makes your performance so memorable. I wish I could say what I mean.

We live in a perpetual state of old age in England: you restored to us the first flush of adolescence when we were mad and rightly mad.

In *The Immortal Hour* I loved you for acting the part of my own spirit which refuses to be tamed by this sickening world of fat old men and unimaginative ugly clever women of no age at all. But I feel like a prostitute in selling my initials to a newspaper to say not what I feel but what they pay me to pretend that I feel. This is a disjointed letter written in a train at white heat.

I shall never forget the Balcony Scene or the scene in your bedroom when you take fright at the potion.

I then had to leave. I hope that I may be permitted to come and see the rest of it soon. But my imagination is good enough to let me know how you interpreted those closing passages.

You are lucky in your Romeo. That is probably more than half your fault.

All I really have to say is Thank you for being you. I am the better for your having lived as I am the better for having heard larks sing and for a high dive into the clear Cornish sea. I am perhaps more than anyone
Gratefully yours
S.P.B. Mais'[14]

What a cry from the heart is here! Is he drunk with Gwen's performance, or is he just drunk? There is a cogency in his writing that lends little support for the latter supposition. Mais, in this letter, accurately reflects the views of many journalists at this time, and perhaps after nearly a hundred years things have not altered all that much, in that they were required to respond to the precise requirements of their editors or their jobs would be at hazard. He also reflects the public's penchant for farces, musicals, and melodramas, performed by stars, rather than classical drama performed by a dedicated ensemble of actors. Some of the reviews of *Romeo and Juliet* especially praise Barry Jackson for his boldness in bringing this play to the Regent Theatre, as though in doing so he is taking a great risk. The predominant note in the reviews stresses the youthfulness of the two taking the main parts, as though this too is a vastly risky undertaking. The general expectation had been for middle aged, established actors to take these parts. Gwen was thirty-three years old when she played Juliet in 1924; John Gielgud, born in April 1904, was twenty. Gwen looked much younger than her age, even off stage, and in this part her whole intention was to present Juliet as a young adolescent. In this she succeeded gloriously:

> 'Miss Ffrangcon-Davies never forgets that Juliet is a child. She keeps intact the child's unconsciousness of self, the child's passionate sincerity, the child's unstained ideal of love...we think her Juliet adorable. She fascinated us, quite as much as she did Romeo in the balcony scene without a garden and without a visible moon...The "potion" scene too was a thing of real beauty: the frightened child struggling to heroism by the faith of her love. Then came the death scene so tender...It was a poem that Shakespeare conceived, and it is a poem that the actress gives you.' (*The Times*, May 1924)

The dozens of reviews, almost without exception, applauded the production and the other actors, but above all they treated Gwen to their most glowing tributes. This was John Gielgud's first major Shakespearian role. Gwen had previously seen him perform in *The Insect Play* by the brothers Čapek. Gielgud played the part of the Poet Butterfly, wearing a laurel wreath, white flannels and pumps. She was unimpressed. It was only when she was standing in the wings during a rehearsal that she first heard him speaking Romeo's lines in the scene with Friar Lawrence, and she then knew all would be well.

An Actor and His Time was published in 1979, written by John Gielgud in collaboration with John Miller and John Powell. It was the outcome of a series of

Gwen as Juliet in 1924

With Barbara Golt as the Nurse

interviews given by the actor for transmission by the BBC. In writing to Gwen about the launch of this book, which has a section on the 1924 production of *Romeo and Juliet*, Gielgud wryly compares the launch of a book with the launch of a play:

'Lots of tiresome promotion sessions about the book – thank God we don't have to stand outside theatres where we act with sandwich boards round our necks to encourage passers-by!' [15 December 1979][15]

In his reference to the *Romeo and Juliet* production, he acknowledged his debt to Gwen, in the support she gave him in playing this most exacting role, 'she taught and encouraged me', and also mentions what devoted friends they have been since, but he is silent about her performance of Juliet.

'She set such a good example, never playing the spoilt leading-lady, even though the costumes were clumsily made and she was sewing her own dresses in the wardrobe twenty-four hours before the curtain went up. At the dress rehearsal we were both so full of pins we could hardly embrace. I had no say in how I was to look, and had to suffer a black wig with a centre parting and white tights with soles sewn onto them – very difficult to move in. Romeo is a very long and arduous part and I was no good at sword-fights. Scott Sunderland, one of Jackson's favourite actors, was playing Mercutio in a very violent style. He used to knock me about on the stage which made me nervous and threw me off balance. I spoke the lines not too badly, I think, but I was so inexperienced that it must have been very hard on Gwen.'[16]

Gielgud then explains how he and Gwen were engaged at the Coliseum for two or three weeks, with top billing, to enact the balcony scene. The love-scene was preceded by Teddy Brown, a huge man of twenty stone, who played on the xylophone, and it was followed by the Houston sisters. As the revolve took away the fat man to the screams of the crowd's delight, the garden scene came into view with Gwen standing in what seemed to be a pink bath. When the Houston sisters came on, as the revolve took the lovers out of sight, one of the sisters would speed them on their way with 'A thousand times goodnight' spoken in a broad Scottish accent.

In 1953 when John Gielgud's name appeared in the Honours' List of those awarded knighthoods, Gwen was among the first to congratulate him. He replied from South Pavilion, his home near Aylesbury:

'Darling Gwen – so sweet of you to write. If only you had been on the list with me it would have given me so much more pleasure. You have been such a guiding light and great artist and dear friend, over these (many?) years –
Fondest love from your
Once skinny Romeo'[17]

Although Gwen, as an actress, had fulfilled one of her heart's desires in playing the part of Juliet on the London stage to rapturous applause, she was never to play the part again in its entirety. But in the volumes of fan mail she received from 1924 until her death in 1992, much of it recalls her 1924 portrayal of Juliet and also her performance in *The Immortal Hour*. During the last years of her life this fan-mail never seemed to slacken, because her public was reminded of her Juliet through her radio broadcasts, in which she gave extracts from the play, and the 1983 BBC television programme about her, 'Life in the Theatre'. There were also the 1988 programmes: her two appearances with Terry Wogan; her Desert Island Discs with Sue Lawley; and the BBC Television 'Omnibus', 'A Juliet Remembered'. Even those who had never seen her 1924 Juliet, wrote to her saying how much they had been moved, and how well they could imagine her being so splendid in that role. Of particular interest is the consistency with which her correspondents write how deeply affected they were by her portrayal of Juliet, and how moved to tears. In 1988 Gwen was 97. What extraordinary power could she still exert over her audience? With regard to one of the radio programmes some writers commented how they were in the middle of washing-up, or doing the ironing, when they were caught up in this young girl's passion, and found themselves, involuntarily, weeping copiously. A husband, coming in from his studio, having heard the same programme, had tears in his eyes, as he looked at his wife, with her hands still in the washing-up bowl, her eyes streaming. Many of them who had never written a fan letter before, wrote to Gwen to thank her for bringing such beauty and truth into their lives. S. P. B. Mais might have been the first to thank her for her Juliet, and for having enriched his life, but he was by no means the last.

From Juliet to Tess

In 1924 *The Immortal Hour* was once again performed at the Regent Theatre with Gwen singing Etain. As usual it ran to full houses. This certainly helped to ease the financial burden under which Rutland Boughton laboured because of his complicated domestic circumstances. In 1924 he was still the driving force behind the Glastonbury Festival arrangements. The Festival offered music and drama performances at different times throughout the year, and had secured the support of such eminent backers as Bernard Shaw, Sir Edward Elgar, and Sir Thomas Beecham. When Barry Jackson had offered to present *The Immortal Hour* on the London stage, Boughton had at first refused, feeling his work was conceived for the historic Glastonbury setting, and that it would somehow be defiled by a London presentation. Barry Jackson thought that Boughton was looking for a higher fee rather than holding to a point of principle, and so he increased his offer. It was only at the persuasion of the Glastonbury company, who had been so faithful to Boughton, that the composer at last agreed. But the phenomenal success in London of *The Immortal Hour* was not altogether to Boughton's liking. He was a prolific composer, and as new works were ready for performance he began to feel irritated that *The Immortal Hour* had become popular in a way that was proving disadvantageous to his other works. When he read of Gwen's great success in *Romeo and Juliet*, he read also of the interviews she had given to a number of newspapers wanting to publish the background to her present position as toast of the theatre world. He wrote to her, not primarily to congratulate her on her performance, but to urge his own role on her path to fame.

'Dear little Gwen. It did my heart good the other day to read that you had in public interview just mentioned Glastonbury as a place that had been of some service to you. I have two letter of yours which very emphatically say the same thing, and one of the things that has hurt most has been that two or three times when you had the chance you did not say just that word...whereas rumours reached me that you spoke on the contrary of "all you had done for me" – Well, you have, my dear, - It is a great thing for a maker of music to find exactly the right person to remake it properly- [then there is a short passage in which he hoped that Gwen would perform in some of his more recent music-dramas.] Meanwhile our love to you, and very true congratulations on your reaching the goal of your ambitions in Juliet in London.

Yours very sincerely   Rutland B'[18]

While Gwen was performing in *Romeo and Juliet* she took lodgings once again at the Three Arts Club, as she had done ten or so years earlier. Then all she could afford was a cubicle at fifteen shillings a week including all meals. Now she could afford a good bedroom at twenty-seven shillings a week. When, after *Romeo and Juliet* came to the end of its run, Gwen returned to her repertory work at Birmingham, she and John Gielgud still had their duet to perform at the Coliseum, which had to be fitted in, journeys as well, with their other work. The stretching of personal resources of actors and actresses in such a way was nothing new. And for Gwen it continued during the second long run of *The Immortal Hour* at the Regent Theatre. She was committed to appearing nightly at the Regent, but she also played two afternoons a week as Eve in Shaw's *Back to Methuselah* at the Court Theatre. John Gielgud attended these matinée performances and was awed by her versatility. He wrote to her on 20th September 1924:

'Dear Gwen,
I must just write this line to thank you again for your wonderful performance yesterday. I can't tell you how much it moved me from beginning to end, and with one kind of emotion after another. After seeing it, I feel as if I don't believe I could have survived Juliet at all if I'd seen it from the front - of course this is a fine part too, and gives you a wonderful chance of a tour de force, but what thrilled me so much was the way you kept the character going all through with the same elements - the striving after knowledge, the primeval sense and appreciation of beauty, and the alert common-sense and, I would almost say, shrewishness on occasions - and then you developed it all like a lovely pattern and roughened out the edges in the old woman, with her amazing experiences vividly in her memory, her body hard but tired, and her soul and intelligence both striving after the fine things and the dreams which she knows she could entirely wrap herself in but for the need of work and the jarring everyday commonplaces that continually drag her back to earth against her will. Of course I always have had a dreadful weakness for old ladies on the stage - but I refuse to excuse myself for adoring you as one - and your tragic moments were as simply and surely placed - with absolutely perfect precision - as your comedy ones were - and I loved your little touches of character with elbows and head, and the way you roughened your voice

44

sometimes and then let it soften again in the big speech. The healthy purity of the first scene, and the Madonna-like purity of the second, I shall always remember - the first much more of the body with occasional glimpses of the real soul coming through, and then the second, with most of the body feelings over and done with - except as mechanical utensils. And the mind which knows itself better than any other minds round it, and has had to reflect on itself, so to speak, because it has no one to exchange its ideas with - levelly smoothing its path towards the end of life, and making up for its hardness and loneliness by a yearning towards exaltation of spirit...I look forward to tomorrow, but fear it is impossible that it can be as magnificent as yesterday.....

Ever yours   John'[19]

There follows a long postscript. This letter by a young man of twenty illustrates the intricate skill and dedication which Gwen devoted to her acting, in this case a part she had performed the previous year at Birmingham, and Gielgud's extraordinary perception in his analysis of Gwen's portrayal of her role of Eve, from the new-created to the aged and burdened mother of mankind. He writes not only with that degree of observation which will enhance his career to become one of our greatest actors, but also with that deep understanding of the craft which will help him develop into an outstanding director.

A Midsummer Night's Dream was produced at the Drury Lane Theatre Royal for the Christmas season of 1924/25. It was presented by Basil Dean as family entertainment, an alternative to pantomime. Mendelssohn's music was used, as well as ten compositions from the conductor Herman Finck. There was an extensive chorus of dancing fairies, drilled in the Russian style by Michel Fokine. The cast glittered with stars, who, in the words of *The Observer* reviewer 'have often carried whole plays to success on their own shoulders'. [1924 December 28th][18] The pantomimic presentation and the production paraphernalia diminished the playwright's role and led some reviewers to insert 'Book and Lyrics by William Shakespeare', or 'Librettist - William Shakespeare'. The scenery, too, with its rocks and boulders for the forest of Athens, rather than green swards, presented great hazards for the dancing fairies, both earthbound and airborne, which the critics were amused to point out. All the immortals were airborne from time to time, including Puck who, 'being jerked up by his hinder parts', collided with the scenery on several occasions. The Fairy King, Oberon, was played by Robert Harris, and his Queen, Titania, by Gwen, who recalled that it was at Drury Lane that her father had begun his professional career. She was warmly commended for her performance, part of which was singing Oberon's lines 'I know a bank where the wild thyme blows' to the melody 'On wings of song'. *The Manchester Sunday Chronicle* reviewer much regretted that his belief in fairies had been shattered because, when Titania flew, her wires shone brightly in the limelight. The critics clearly had their festive fun in reporting this production, but they also reflected the great enjoyment that the audience experienced. They found Miles Malleson, playing Snout, extremely funny. The lovers' quadrille of Helena and Demetrius, Hermia and Lysander, was performed by Edith Evans, Frank Vosper, Athene Seyler, and Leon Quartermaine. Cicely Hamilton writing of the production in *Time and Tide* says:

'If there were nothing else in the performance but Edith Evans as Helena and Gwen Ffrangcon-Davies as Titania it would be worth going some way to listen to them. I say "listen" advisedly - because it is not often that in the course of an evening's entertainment one can hear two players speak verse with a perfect command of its rhythm. Is there any other actress who could swing out Helena's couplets as Miss Evans does - swing them out to their full length and accent, with never a quiver in their sense? And it says much for the art of Miss Ffrangcon-Davies that her delicate Titania gets over the footlights of an outsize theatre; her touch may be silken but there is plenty of grip behind it.'

At this time Gwen's mother was clearly concerned that her daughter should keep as firm a grip on her personal life as she so apparently had on the direction of her professional career. On New Year's Eve 1924 she wrote a solemn letter to Gwen with her good wishes for the coming year tempered by some strong cautionary exhortation, drawn directly from the Book of Common Prayer:

'New Year's Eve.
1924.
My dearest Gwen,
        I must wish you a very Happy New Year! The best possible in every way. You have had so much to give thanks for in 1924, opportunities for fine work and success after success. It is a rather giddy path isn't it? So many temptations to pride and self-congratulations that you need to be very stern with yourself to be able to "carry the corn" safely. Success is a great testing of the foundations of character for pride is the most insidious of all the seven deadly sins, and so many fall from their first big successes through pride and are never heard of again - You know many such as well as I. It was your father's deadly enemy and got him in the end. So forgive me if at the beginning of a new year I ask you to take stock of yourself and look backward over the year past and into the new year coming, and make some resolutions as regards money, "language", real study, duties and influences upon those you meet, not to be turned from the path by lesser gods but to hold your high gifts most sacredly as a charge. If I did not know that in your heart you desire right I should sometimes be afraid for you, but if you keep the words "Humility" and "Service" ever in mind you cannot go far wrong. It was want of Humility which ruined your father and left him at the last friendless and alone and a heritage of suffering to his family. There is one inexorable law "as a man soweth that he shall reap".
        You and I have been companions and friends, I value your confidence more than I can say. I want to help you always. You cannot think the joy it is to me that you can express yourself, can be and do the highest you dream of, no one can stop you but yourself. You can transcend all early fears and transmute "natural" failings into positive virtues. All of Love and Good is waiting to pour itself through you out to the world. What a joyful task to bring beauty and gladness even for a few hours to these heavy hearts...Let everyone be better because they know you, and more anxious themselves to

give of their best to the world's service...I am going to add the quaint words of the old Baptismal service which was said over you and no doubt they are lying in your unconscious mind still. "O merciful God, grant that the old Adam may be so buried that the new man may be raised up in her. Grant that all carnal appetites may die in her and that all things belonging to the spirit may live and grow in her. Grant that she may have power and strength to have victory and to triumph against the devil the world and the flesh..." God bless my dear dear Gwen in 1925! Her loving Mother'[21]

What did Gwen make of this? An actress, who after twelve years of professional anonymity, now finds herself, on the verge of her thirty-fourth birthday, at the peak of her career, with written reports and photographs of her various stage triumphs, as both singer and straight actress, published in all the English-speaking countries of the world, and here her mother, in a finger-wagging, puritanical way, is urging her to eschew the world, the flesh, and the devil! Were there particular temptations to which Gwen was succumbing, about which her mother felt pressed to be so cautionary? Annie's tone here is very different from that when she wrote to Gwen in April 1921, supporting her daughter who had formed a passionate liaison with a married man. Ffrangcon is twice referred to in this letter: his tragedy brought about by his lack of humility, and the burden of that tragedy carried by the rest of the family. The family shared in that tragedy in a material and also deeply emotional way. One of the darker thoughts that must have lurked in their minds was whether the father's madness might in some way be inherited by either of the daughters. In the medical records kept at the Bethlem Royal Hospital, Beckenham, under the heading 'Insanity or other Diseases of Nervous System', is the entry 'Maternal cousin died in Denbigh Asylum from Religious Mania'. Annie had reason to be anxious, as her daughter's fame was beginning to outstrip that of her famous father. But she need not worry on those counts of 'humility' and 'service'. Her daughter was to live for a further sixty-seven years and, apart from her exquisite craftsmanship, humility and service were her salient qualities.

On 1st January 1925, in the New Year's Honours List, was the news that the King had bestowed upon Ellen Terry the title of Dame Grand Cross of the Order of the British Empire. On 2nd January, to celebrate this honour, Dame Ellen attended a performance of *A Midsummer Night's Dream* at Drury Lane, a play in which, as Titania, she had made a name for herself many years ago. It was in this play, too, that Gwen had made her début in 1911 as a not always visible member of the fairy chorus. Now she was the Queen of the Fairies. 'Dame Ellen', *The Daily Chronicle* reported, 'is a great admirer of Miss Ffrangcon-Davies, who takes her old part of Titania. "I saw her in *Back to Methuselah*," she said, " and I think she is very good. I knew her father very well, and therefore take a special interest in her.""

There is no doubt that Gwen would have been conscious of the presence of Dame Ellen in the audience during that evening's performance. Inevitably her mind would have reverted to the time as a teenager, when her mother had taken her to see Miss Terry, seeking confirmation as to whether her daughter had the ability and personality to risk dedicating her life to the stage. Miss Terry had then stressed to her the importance of the three 'I's: Industry, Intelligence, and Imagination; of which the greatest, she added, is Imagination. That night Ellen Terry would have witnessed to what extent Gwen possessed those attributes. As she had already seen Gwen's performance as Eve in *Back to Methuselah*, she would have been as convinced, as was the twenty-year old Gielgud, of being in the presence of an actress of rare imaginative gifts.

Barry Jackson brought another Shaw play, *Caesar and Cleopatra*, to London in 1925, opening at the Kingsway Theatre on 21st April. It was produced by H. K. Ayliff, and starred Cedric Hardwicke as Caesar and Gwen as Cleopatra. Gwen, once more, captured the reviewers' main accolades:

'Certainly Miss Ffrangcon-Davies is that piece of mischief to which Mr. Shaw has given the name Cleopatra. See her rise from between the paws of her favourite sphinx to interrupt Caesar's moonlit meditation; her red hair is a challenge to the moon, her dress an echo of it. It is a gay, a gracious and enchanting performance she gives. She lets the child grow into the spiteful and pettish woman without provoking, in a mind once subject to her convention, a challenge at any point of transition... on the stage Miss Davies banishes controversy. You may lean back, comfortably own yourself a pedant, and yield to the enchantment of comic acting that creates its own conditions of credibility and draws all else into its peculiar atmosphere.'[21]

There was, however, an interesting reservation to Gwen's performance voiced by S. P. B. Mais in the *Daily Graphic*. He applauded her portrayal of the petulance, waywardness, cunning and cruelty of the sixteen-year old Cleopatra, but then offered his one criticism:

'There is just a slight danger lest Gwen Ffrangcon-Davies should be modelling herself too closely on Edith Evans. I have never noticed it before. She is beginning to drag some of her syllables.'[23]

In the light of Gwen's letters to her mother explaining how helpful Edith had been during rehearsals of *Back to Methuselah*, it is more than likely that Mais's keen ear had indeed detected a borrowing from the older, more experienced actress. Certainly Gwen's dragging of some of her syllables became very pronounced in her later playing of Gwendolen Fairfax in *The Importance of Being Earnest*.

The choice for the London theatregoer in the middle of the 1920s was grand opera, an occasional play by Shakespeare, a regular diet of Bernard Shaw - *Caesar and Cleopatra* and *St Joan* were being performed in London at the same time – or domestic and musical comedies. Noel Coward was making a name for himself as playwright, actor, and composer. *The Vortex* had been performed in 1924 and *Fallen Angels* and *Hay Fever* in 1925. These were plays with themes that threatened, however amusingly and light-heartedly, the structure of contemporary society. Gwen's next play was mildly in this category, rather than in the line of classical drama. It was *The New Morality* by Harold Chapin, a vacuous entertainment, set on house-boats, moored on a river bank, and categorised as 'an airy trifle'. This play opened at the Kingsway Theatre in July 1925 and was cast from the stalwarts of the Birmingham Repertory Company, which included Louise de Lacy, Scott Sunderland, and Cedric Hardwicke. It was well acted, well reviewed, but recognised as 'a puff of air'. There were sterner things to come.

Thomas Hardy's *Tess of the D'Urbervilles* was published in 1891 to a very hostile reception. When *Jude the Obscure*, published in 1895, received even harsher treatment, being vilified, and denounced from the pulpit, Hardy gave up writing novels altogether. He did, however, before the end of the century, make a dramatised version of *Tess of the D'Urbervilles*, which was produced in America and later made into a film 'in which Tess frequents a cabaret in diamonds and leaps in and out of automobiles', an American exuberance Hardy felt powerless to suppress.[24] In 1924 the first performances of Hardy's dramatised version of the novel were given in England: in the Town Hall of Dorchester, and later in Bournemouth. Some of the London reviewers had seen the Dorchester production and reported favourably on the deep-bosomed actress, the daughter of a local farmer, who played Tess. For the first London presentation of the play in the following year much preliminary work had been undertaken. Philip Ridgeway, who was the manager of the recently opened Barnes Theatre, south-west of the city, had agreed with the author some modification of the original script. He visited Dorset to discuss the production with Thomas Hardy at Max Gate, and he took with him his leading lady, Gwen Ffrangcon-Davies. Hardy whole-heartedly approved this choice and, almost as important, so did Hardy's second wife, Florence. *The Daily Express* reported that meeting:

> 'He was glad that the choice had fallen on Miss Ffrangcon-Davies, because this young actress came nearest, he said, to his ideal of Tess as depicted in the famous sketch which hangs on the wall of his favourite room...She seemed to him, he said, to possess all the qualities of the tragic figure of his imagination - youth, beauty, and simplicity of mien.'

There developed a friendship and deep affection between the Hardys and Gwen as their correspondence testifies. But there were serious problems with the play. Gwen could see that large portions of the dialogue required rewriting, and when she very tentatively approached Hardy on this delicate subject, suggesting that borrowing dialogue more directly from the novel might enhance the play, Hardy, a little surprised that an actress should have so close an acquaintance with his novel, readily agreed. The revisions were undertaken collaboratively, with Hardy in the end giving Gwen a fairly free hand to exercise her judgement. Many of Gwen's suggestions were filtered through Florence Hardy, who often wrote to Gwen on behalf of her husband, who was then eighty-five years old.

When the play was advertised to be staged in September 1925 at the Barnes Theatre there was a sensational scramble for tickets for the first night. All seats were sold three weeks in advance. Many of the 'titled gentry' were disappointed. Mr. Gossip of the *Daily Sketch* commented on those who were present:

> 'Lady Walpole had the one available box, and among others present I noticed Dame May Witty, Ada Crossley, Dennis Eadie, Godfrey Tearle, and Angela Baddeley.
>   Sir Barry Jackson was delighted. It was he who discovered Miss Davies and "lent" her for this play. Nigel Playfair was there, deeply interested.'

Gwen as Cleopatra in Shaw's *Caesar and Cleopatra*, 1925

In 1925, as distinct from 1895, Thomas Hardy was regarded as the greatest living literary figure in the country. *Tess of the D'Urbervilles* was his most widely known book. Managers of many West End theatres, noting the magnetic attraction of the public to the production at the Barnes Theatre, competed for the play to be performed at their theatres. That at least accounts for some of Nigel Playfair's 'deep interest'.

The critics on the whole turned against the Barnes Theatre production. They were scathing about the play not reproducing the novel's spirit, its diversity, and its detail of local colour. They argued that the character of Tess was too well known and too well-loved by so many of the audience that disappointment was inevitable. There was also a substantial lobby that recalled that deep-bosomed Dorchester milk-maid, and felt that the frail, pathetic character given by Gwen was woefully inadequate. And from Dorchester came the claim that Thomas Hardy should never have allowed any but a Dorset actress to take the part of Tess. There were other reviews that referred to Gwen's triumph in the title role, and few critics - and particularly West End theatre managers - could ignore the prolonged, almost tumultuous, ovation given to the actors, mostly directed at Gwen, at the end of the play.

Florence Hardy saw the play at the Barnes Theatre on the Thursday of the first week, and the press reported her presence and recorded her pleasure with the performance. A few days later she wrote to Gwen:

'Dear Miss Gwen:
    I shall be so *very* very much obliged if you will autograph this sweet portrait. Since last Thursday your *wonderful* performance has been in my mind the whole time. I feel that everyone in London ought to see you. And it is so delightful to know that besides being a great artiste you are also the greatest dear.
        Yours affectionately
        Florence Hardy
PS. Addressed envelope for return enclosed.'[25]

Florence Hardy wrote a number of letters to Gwen with news of the comments about the play which had come to her husband: Harley Granville-Barker's enthusiasm for Gwen's performance and for the way Alec D'Urberville has been played; that more than one friend has been disappointed that Felix has been made rather a comic character, 'which T.H. said he never intended'; that she hoped 'that the reporters will restrain themselves a little when they write about T.H. because he cannot bear being called an "old gentleman" or his years alluded to, for he does seem so young in his mind that one forgets the actual years.'

Henry Arthur Jones, the playwright, who was in his seventies, saw the first London performance of *Tess of the D'Ubervilles* and wrote a long letter to Hardy whom he had known personally for very many years. He had some criticism of the structure of the play, but when he came to the performance he wrote:

'Miss Gwen Ffrangcon-Davies won my heart in the third and fourth acts. My daughter and I found ourselves with streaming cheeks. Miss Davies was so unforced, so sincere and restrained. There was not one wrong note in her performance. I cannot remember when I have been so touched. She must not be judged because she did not render those parts of the character which are in the novel but not in the play. She played unerringly those scenes which you gave her to play. I am sure the play would have lost immensely its beauty and pathos if Tess had been acted by a robust wench in a robust way. That character is not in the play you have written.'[26]

51

Jones sent a copy of this letter to Philip Ridgeway, and by the same post a letter to Gwen, praising her for her beautiful and poignant performance of Tess, and inviting her to tea with his daughter and himself.[27]

The play was transferred to the Garrick Theatre and the correspondence between Hardy and Gwen continued, regarding revision of the scenes, in preparation for the West End presentation. Gwen had sent Hardy her suggestions, and he showed his confidence in her judgement in his reply:

'17th October 1925.   Max Gate,
                                            Dorchester.

Dear Miss Ffrangcon-Davies:

My best thanks for the photograph, which has come safely. You look more thoughtful and pretty in it than in any other that I can remember to have seen.

I note what you say as to the suddenness of the transition to the lodging-house in Act V, after Angel has left Tess in Act IV, and the desirability of showing more clearly the stress to which she was put before she went back to Alec, and I have been searching for an old draft of the play in which this was shown by a scene or two combining the swede-hacking with the bailiff coming for her mother's furniture. But this was omitted as making the play too long, and the effect was endeavoured to be obtained by substituting Alec's call on Tess on the evening of her marriage, and the discussion of her poverty by her mother and Angel, which I thought made her situation sufficiently clear.

If however, you do not think the situation emphatic enough the arrangement you send in outline fulfils the same object, and nothing better can be done than that you should adopt it, in consultation with Mr. Filmer (the producer) - The words pencilled you can use or not as you choose. - The removal of the play to the West End might be a good occasion for inserting the scene, if Mr. Ridgeway approves, as he no doubt would. Unfortunately I cannot find my old draft, though I could reconstruct it I think. But yours has the same effect, and does not require more scenery, as my arrangement would have done.I think you are quite right in wishing to retain the diamond scene, if Alec's call is omitted.

I return your draft, in case you may not have kept a copy. I hope you do not feel the daily strain to be excessive.

Yours most sincerely
Thomas Hardy

P.S. We have heard from Mr and Mrs Granville Barker how much they were moved by your presentation of Tess. Also from other experts in drama. T.H.'[28]

On the same day Florence Hardy also wrote to Gwen:

'...How *wonderful* you are. I am so grateful to you for suggesting those essential alterations in the play. They were what were always wanted. I do hope the play will be altered without delay.

Gwen as Tess....... and with Thomas Hardy 1925

"TESS"
in THOMAS
HARDY'S
DRAWING
ROOM

Keystone.

"TESS OF THE D'URBERVILLES"
GOES HOME TO DORCHESTER.

The entire "Tess" company visited Mr.
Thomas Hardy at Max Gate last week to play
the great D'Urberville drama before its
creator. The picture shows Tess and Angel
Clare in the "Confession" scene. It was
a memorable and perhaps pathetic occasion.

Theatre

Extract from *Theatre World* in Gwen's scrapbook

It was good of you to write such a kind and tactful letter to my husband. It always does him good to hear from you, and at his age attentions of that kind give so much pleasure, and I am so anxious that he should have interests in his life outside Dorset. I should be grateful if you could write to him whenever you have time - but I know how busy you are....'[29]

Once the play had been successfully launched at the Garrick, Florence promised Gwen that she would come to see it at the earliest opportunity. She hoped that Gwen would have the success there

'that you deserve, for there isn't an actress in London who is doing anything to touch your performance as 'Tess'. I feel that T.H. and I owe you more than words can say - The financial part of the business means nothing - absolutely *nothing* - to us, but it would have been grievous for T.H. to have had a failure in this play at his age.'[30]

There had been much interest shown by the press and the public concerning when Thomas Hardy would come to the Barnes Theatre to see the play. Florence Hardy came, but not Thomas. That interest was renewed when the play moved to the Garrick Theatre. Faced with the likelihood of the great man never feeling quite well enough to journey to London, the whole cast volunteered to present the play in the spacious drawing-room of Max Gate. The play was performed there in December 1925. The audience comprised Mr and Mrs Hardy, the servants, a local friend, and a member of the press. There is a photograph of the scene in which, on Tess's wedding-night, she confesses to her husband, Angel Clare, her previous enforced liaison with Alec D'Urberville. It shows the two actors performing their parts. Angel is in a chair, Tess at his feet, within two feet of where Thomas Hardy is seated himself. It was reported that as the play came to an end it was noticed that tears had filled the author's eyes.

Gwen's correspondence with the Hardys continued long after *Tess of the D'Ubervilles* had completed its run at the Garrick Theatre. Florence Hardy wrote to Gwen on 2 January 1928, when her husband's health was failing:

'Many thanks for your kind letter. *Must* just let you know that T.H. was talking about you this morning - about 2.0. am and asking me where you were, and what were you doing. He was greatly pleased with your letter. He is still very weak, but another specialist is coming to see him this afternoon and I have great hopes for his recovery. He is so wonderful. He sends his love - and so do I.

Ever Affectionately - F.E.H.'[31]

Thomas Hardy died on 11th January 1928.

When Gwen was ninety-seven years old and completed the Television 'Omnibus' programme with the recital of a poem, she chose Thomas Hardy's 'The Oxen'.[32] There could have been no fitter ending to that incredible programme. There was such a reaching towards beauty and truth, the artistry of the speaker catching the spirit of the poet, that one could not but think back to that earlier loving and understanding relationship between the great man and the actress.

Chapter Three: Meridian (1925 to 1936)

Loving, losing, finding

Gwen's success as Tess, at both the Barnes Theatre and at the Garrick, had been achieved in spite of the critics' disparagement of the play. The tenor of the initial criticism had stressed the impossibility of conveying in dramatic form the range, feeling, and subtlety of background found in the novel. Furthermore the close knowledge of the book, cherished by so many readers, the critics argued, would lead those readers to be sadly disappointed by any dramatic adaptation. In the event these were not the main problems encountered by audience or players. The play of *Tess of the D'Urbervilles* proved thoroughly unsatisfactory as a piece of theatre craftsmanship. That it succeeded in filling the theatre at Barnes and being successfully transferred to the Garrick, was in some measure due to Gwen's adaptation of parts of the original Hardy text, but mainly due to her outstanding performance as Tess. Gwen had acquired a strong and growing theatre-going following. Ecstatic and prolonged applause followed as the curtain fell on the last act of *Tess of the D'Urbervilles*. Her fan mail was considerable, and among those who admired her performance and wrote to tell her so were George Bernard Shaw, Henry Arthur Jones, and James Barrie.[1] At this stage of her career, with such successes as *The Immortal Hour* so often repeated, and with her triumph in a series of Shakespearian parts, notably Juliet, audiences were being drawn to the theatre primarily to see Gwen Ffrangcon-Davies perform. The play in which she appeared was of less importance. Her first entrances on the stage were met by enthusiastic and prolonged clapping. The issue of *The Sphere* dated 20th February 1926 indicated Gwen's standing with her public, and her fellow professionals:

'You cannot measure an actor's popularity from the noise provoked in the stalls by a first entry at a first night. The friends-in-front may be few, but they are always persistent; which is why at an opening performance, Miss Tallulah Bankhead is cooed as much as players of first-class merit - Miss Gwen Ffrangcon-Davies, for instance.

But when the pit, the gallery, and the upper circle hold up the action for two minutes with hand-claps, it means that the actor or actress has a real "following". I can think of only six performers on the so-called legitimate stage whose personalities can attract in London good audiences to an indifferent play for longer than a fortnight - Sir Gerald du Maurier, Miss Irene Vanbrugh, Miss Gladys Cooper, Miss Sybil Thorndike, Mr. Ivor Novello, and Miss Gwen Ffrangcon-Davies.'

Her popularity in the late 1920s increased further when she starred in a wide variety of plays, including those of Strindberg, Ibsen, and Shaw. In the early 1930s her fame seemed to reach its peak with the public's unstinting acclaim of her roles of Elizabeth Barrett in *The Barretts of Wimpole Street*, and Anne of Bohemia in *Richard of Bordeaux*. However, the years between 1925 and 1936, marked by professional success, brought personal turmoil. Her mother, whose constant support had been so instrumental in her own personal and professional success, towards the end of this period began to fail in health. She died in 1936. Gwen's sister Marjorie, who aspired to be a first-ranking concert soprano, struggled despairingly with a failing marriage, the care of her two daughters, and her professional ambitions. Gwen played an exacting and exhausting role in encouraging Marjorie, showing practical concern for the children, and vainly trying to reconcile her mother to Marjorie's point of view.

In the letters exchanged between Annie and Gwen at the beginning of April 1921, Gwen had told her mother of the rapture she had experienced in the arms of a married man, and Annie had responded, not castigating her daughter for committing adultery, but stressing how important this experience would be for her personal and professional fulfilment. In these letters the name of the man had not been given. He was cryptically referred to as C.

Gwen's intimate relationship with C lasted for nearly six years, from 1921 to the beginning of 1927. When the future of their relationship was very much in doubt, Gwen wrote to her mother on 25th January 1926 'we are going to the zoo to see the new aquarium. It is not perhaps the most suitable place for a heart to heart talk but perhaps I shall manage it.'[2] Gwen told her mother that she had been helped by Mrs Bovet, presumably a Christian Science practitioner, who had promised to continue 'to work for her'. Gwen summarised her position: '...perhaps if I don't see or hear from him for a month or so I may be clearer in my mind about things - anyway it's the best I can do at the present.'

C's letters of 1926 and 1927 reveal that his intimate relationship with Gwen was drawing to a close, but a close that was hard to finalise. In his letter to her of 30th January 1926 he refers to his attending a rehearsal of *The Immortal Hour*, and to his intention of sending her flowers for the first night. He is self-deprecatory, ashamed of himself, 'giving silver for your gold', and categorising his affair with Gwen as a 'married man's dalliance'. He recognises her genius and wishes that it might flourish 'unmolested'. Later that day he left at the Stage Door of the Kingsway Theatre, a sonnet for Gwen, which he entitled 'Before the First Night of *The Immortal Hour*'. It is cunningly wrought in the Shakespearian mould. Gwen's Cecil was no mean wordsmith.[5] On 2nd February 1927 he wrote to her with finality, disparaging himself as selfish, inconstant and beastly, but feeling reassured that Gwen had such a friend as Marda, 'who is a good woman, and just the sort of person to keep you on an even keel'.

The next letter from C is dated 1st December 1930. At the end of this letter he describes himself as emerging from obscurity to praise Gwen. He had just seen *The Barretts of Wimpole Street*, and been bewitched:

'Your performance in *The Barretts* is nothing short of miraculous, and places you definitely on the pedestal that you once, as I remember, told me that you hoped to reach - of being the first actress in our tongue, of our time.

In those days Edith had a sort of halo that somewhat eclipsed you, but even in your performance as Lady Herbert, the scales were more than tipped in your favour, for, although the part was a feed, you put her in the shade.

I am not saying that to disparage Edith; but simply to compare you with your only serious rival.'[6]

The comparison of the parts played by Edith Evans and Gwen in *The Lady with a Lamp*, will be taken up later. In his enthusiasm for Gwen's portrayal of Elizabeth Barrett, C was not expressing a view coloured by his former relationship, but echoing public acclaim. Gwen replied to his letter with her customary innate generosity, thanking him for the inspirational support he had given her during the years of their intimacy. In his response he conveyed the feeling of relief that the burden of guilt and wretchedness had been eased.[7]

No further letters from C are to be found in the Frangcon-Davies archive. In 1927 C had referred to Gwen's friendship with Marda Vanne implying that perhaps Marda could take over where C left off. Such an assumption seemed extraordinary, but turned out to be justified by the passage of time. Marda Vanne's relationship with Gwen was also close and loving. It was a friendship that lasted from the 1920s until Marda's death, late in 1970. Gwen's relationship with Marda was the most significant in her life, but it was fraught with problems. Marda was born on 27th September 1896. She was five and a half years younger than Gwen. South African by birth, she was the daughter of Sir Willem van Hulsteyn, a prominent lawyer, whose own birthplace had been Holland. She recalled her mother as 'beautiful, and kind, and headstrong'; her father as 'very pious, intelligent, and headstrong', and added 'never those twain did meet.'[9] The quality that Marda inevitably inherited from her parents was that of being headstrong. From an early age she had been determined to become an actress. This goal she achieved with distinction. She was young, beautiful, talented, and well launched into her career, when she married. Her husband was Johannes Gerhardus Strydom, a successful lawyer. The marriage was very short-lived, lasting barely a year. Strydom pursued a political career and in 1954 became the Prime Minister of South Africa, an unabashed protagonist of the apartheid cause. He died in office in 1958. Among the mass of Marda's papers, left in Gwen's keeping at the time of her death in 1970, there is scarcely a mention of Johannes Strydom. She studiously avoided reference to that brief episode in her life. She never wished to be known by her married name and for professional purposes changed her unmarried name from Marda Van Hulsteyn to Marda Vanne. In 1918 she took up residence in London intending to establish her acting career in England. However, it was not until 1965 that she applied for and was granted British citizenship.

Marda Vanne was a prodigious letter-writer, versifier, and journal-keeper. Among the papers inherited by Gwen's nieces were Marda's letters, poems, journals, contracts, leases, and a copy of her will, dated 25th June 1965, in which she left everything to Gwen, her sole executrix.[10] It is from this cache of information that a great deal is revealed about Gwen's own life, which was so closely interwoven with Marda's from 1926 until Marda's death, forty-four years later. Even after that, Gwen ensured that the anniversary of Marda's death was remembered by a requiem mass sung as close to 2nd December each year as possible. In her own writing Marda marked her close relationship with Gwen as having begun on 18th November 1926. This was a date she would annually mark as though of sanctified significance. Yet, however much she loved Gwen, her nature was promiscuous, which created turmoil for herself, her partners, and Gwen.

In 1934 Gwen and Marda jointly bought Tagley Cottage, an eighteenth century building with later additions, at Stambourne, about five miles north east of

Gwen with Marda Vanne

Finchingfield, Essex. They paid for the property jointly, but it was registered in Gwen's name. Gwen took the precaution of writing a letter formally accepting Marda's right to half the proceeds in the event of the property being sold, or in the event of her dying before Marda.

The Finchingfield area was at that time becoming a retreat for actors, authors and artists who had regular commitments in London, but who appreciated an escape to their country retreat. In March 1934 John Gielgud, riding on the crest of the wave with the success of *Richard of Bordeaux*, bought himself an old farmhouse, set in four acres of land, just outside Finchingfield for £1000. Gwen, who shared that success in fame and fortune to a lesser degree, bought her property in the same area. Other friends including Dodie Smith, the playwright and novelist, and Diana Wynyard, the actress, also bought houses in the neighbourhood. A few years later, Marjorie, Gwen's sister, was to make her home in Finchingfield.

Tagley Cottage became a staple of Gwen's life. She lived there for nearly sixty years; she died there, and was buried in the grounds of the church nearby. The cottage became for Gwen and Marda not only a place of refuge, but also a source of physical and spiritual refreshment, both for themselves and the very many friends who over the years enjoyed the hospitality and fellowship so generously offered. These friends invariably wrote to express their heartfelt thanks for the revitalisation they had experienced.

There were, however, significant periods in Gwen's life when she was away from Tagley Cottage. Her role as an actress obliged her to undertake extensive tours in the provinces and sometimes abroad. In the summer of 1936, she and Marda spent a few months in South Africa. Ostensibly, this visit was planned as a holiday without any association with their future acting careers. Yet this holiday was to prove seminal to both of their professional futures. A few years before Gwen experienced her first South African adventure, an adventure of a very different sort had absorbed her for the best part of two years. The artist, Walter Richard Sickert, had become infatuated with her.

Walter Richard Sickert: an Interlude

On April 7th 1932 Gwen first met Walter Sickert, the painter. She wrote to her mother about this encounter. Annie's immediate response was to give Gwen a leather-bound notebook, and urge her to record her impressions of the great man. Sickert was regarded as the leading English painter of his day. Gwen wrote many letters about her meetings with him and much later gave radio talks in South Africa and England of her impressions of Sickert, but in her leather-bound notebook there are only two entries. The first is dated the day of her initial meeting, and the second July 31st 1932. An extract from the first reads as follows:

'April 7 1932

Met the great Walter Richard Sickert and his wife at lunch. He looks like a rather disreputable old bookmaker, as Cedric Hardwicke would play one - in a plaid suit, with swallow-tailed coat and a grey billycock hat - He has a finely-cut sensitive face with untidy white hair falling all over the place, but withal a great distinction. One would say at once "Oh, who is that?" He spoke much and very flatteringly of my work, for which he professes an extravagant admiration, but was very disappointed, so he said, to find me so *young*! He talked of his early days when he was a super at the Lyceum and of his friendship with Pinero who from the heights of a small part gentleman condescended towards him in a friendship that has lasted all their lives [Pinero died in 1934.] - He is an old man 72, but full of life and sparkle tho' I fear he drinks too much - consuming the best part of two bottles of champagne at lunch, after which he became a little vague but still very courteous, charming...He says he is the crowned head of the artistic world, as King George is of England....'

Sickert, who deplored any show of modesty in the creative artist as a hamstring to his work, was scarcely exaggerating his position as leader of the English school of painting at this time. He was prolific in his output, greatly varied in his style, which accorded with the precise nature of his work in progress. As personal friend and acquaintance of such as Whistler, Dégas, Camille and Lucien Pissaro, he could recall the revolutionary development of painting, drawing and etching through the formative years of the last quarter of the nineteenth century and the beginning of the twentieth. Above all, certainly as far as Gwen was concerned, he was a brilliant conversationalist. Duncan Grant in a letter to Richard Stone dated 14th April 1971 wrote:

'I always used to believe that Cocteau's was the most brilliant conversation I ever heard but I'm now inclined to think that Sickert's was unbeatable when he was on form.'[11]

From April 1932 until January 1934 Sickert and Gwen met on numerous occasions: at his home with his wife, Thérèse Lessore, who was also a painter; at restaurants, also with his wife; at one of his three studios, where on one occasion Thérèse, at her husband's request, took photographs of Gwen. There were various excursions which Gwen and Sickert made together: to the Ellen Terry annual festival, directed by Edith Craig and Christopher St John at Small Hythe, Tenterden, Kent; to Kenwood, and to Margate. During this time Sickert wrote many letters to Gwen that were delivered, not by the postman, but by taxi. He also sent her a stream of telegrams, some many pages long. He asked her not to write letters to him in reply. At a time of financial hardship Gwen sold all of Sickert's correspondence addressed to her. They were snapped up by a private purchaser, but Gwen has left transcriptions of a handful of these letters. They testify to his adoration of Gwen, and to his absorption with his art, which was given new life through this friendship. A skipping rejuvenation has come to him that compels him to make Gwen and her stagecraft the centre of his own creative output.

Sickert had seen Gwen at St Martin's Theatre in March 1932 as Prue Sarn in *Precious Bane*, a dramatised version of the novel by Mary Webb. He invited Gwen to join his wife and himself for lunch at the Station Hotel, King's Cross. He told Gwen how impressed he had been by her stage business in which she had carried out her household chores including beating an egg and making a pudding in a pudding basin, as though she had personal day-to-day experience of such things. He wanted very much to paint a portrait of her in one of her stage roles, but he had no wish for her to sit for him. What he required of her was a photograph, not a studio photograph but a snapshot. Later, when he was looking

Gwen with Walter Richard Sickert

through a collection of her photographs he came upon one that immediately attracted him. It was taken by Bertram Park of Gwen when she was playing Queen Isabella, the she-wolf of France, in Marlowe's *Edward II* (1923).

Rather than have his subject pose in his studio, or use a studied photographic portrait, Sickert often chose to paint from a snapshot in order to catch the unguarded moment. His paintings of King George V (1927-8), the young King Edward VIII (1936), and Hugh Walpole (1929) are examples. His absorption in painting Gwen Ffrangcon-Davies was part of his life's devotion to the theatre. In the first decade of the twentieth century some of his most striking and original work depicted scenes in the theatre, which were more concerned with the audience than the performance of the actors on stage: scenes from the upper circle or 'the gods' of a behatted group, men and women, some standing some sitting, all responding to that moment on the stage. Among the many actors and actresses he painted were John Gielgud, Nigel Playfair, and Edith Evans. Peggy Ashcroft he painted a number of times, always from photographs; in her bathing-suit and on holiday in Venice, but also on stage, performing as Kate Hardcastle in *She Stoops to Conquer* (1932-3), and with Paul Robeson in *Othello* (1935-6). His friendship with Gwen, however, generated a creative excitement that spilled over from his life into his art.

In a letter to her mother dated 23rd July 1932, Gwen describes how Sickert 'rushed home to lunch the other day exclaiming "Gwen's dry and she's on the operating table." "Great heavens" said Mrs Sickert, "poor girl, what is the matter with her?" But he was only referring to the canvas, which was stretched on a table for him to do some stippling.'[12]

The painting was exhibited at the Wilson Galleries, 24 Ryder Street, St James's, during the week ending Sunday, September 18th, 1932. It was over 8ft high and 3ft wide. Sickert acknowledged his debt to Bertram Park by painting his name onto the canvas. Frank Rutter, the *Sunday Times* art critic wrote:

'...But for this scrupulous acknowledgement of the artist's indebtedness, nobody would imagine that the portrait has any photographic basis, for it is carried out in a very broad and freely handled manner, and though the colour scheme is severely restricted, the style of the painting may fairly be described as a Rembrandtesque impressionism.

'Indeed, excepting the flashing green note of one solitary jewel, the painting is, practically a monochrome, Indian red, black and white being almost the only pigments used throughout this eight-foot canvas. The gamut of tones, from the loveliest pinks to the deepest reds, which Mr Sickert has obtained with this very simple palette, amounts to nothing less than a *tour-de-force*, and he has never shown his wonderful mastery of light and shade more completely and brilliantly than in this painting.'[13]

The *Daily Mail* reported, at the time of the exhibition in the Wilson Galleries, that the work was hailed as Sickert's greatest masterpiece, and that the critics described it "as a picture far better aesthetically than anything achieved or likely to be achieved by any other living artist". *The Morning Post* related the magnetism of the painting to Gwen Ffrangcon-Davies's genius as an actress:

'The poise of the figure has a Tintoretto like monumentality, but the face and eyes suggest the latent powers of expression that make her supreme on the stage.'

That same week Gwen, interviewed about the painting by a reporter from *The Evening Standard*, quoted Sickert as saying:

'I have made it quite clear by painting "Bertram Park phot" in a corner of the canvas that the portrait is copied from a photograph.

'Painting a portrait is like catching a butterfly. I have painted portraits with my subject before me. But it is seldom absolutely satisfactory. Your sitter, particularly if a woman, dislikes keeping regular appointments. She is often late. The artist resents his time being wasted.'

This edition of the *Evening Standard* describes the painting as 'an acclaimed masterpiece'. In one of her letters[14] Gwen explains how Sickert insisted that the portrait, which he entitled *La Louve* (the She-wolf), should be the sole exhibit in the room in the art gallery where it was to be displayed. This request was granted. He then painted for display on the opposite wall, in tones of blue to contrast with his major work, a small snow scene featuring a prowling wolf, as though having devoured an unfortunate traveller. He wrote beneath 'Gwen, when she had finished with her audience.' The picture was inscribed to Gwen's mother. This painting mysteriously disappeared.

La Louve now hangs in the Tate Gallery. It was by no means the only work of art for which Sickert used Gwen as his subject. He made a number of etchings of her which he gave to her. He also painted another full portrait, again taken from a photograph. In it he shows her as Florence Nightingale in *The Lady with a Lamp* (1932-4). Gwen's original role in this play had been that of Lady Herbert to Edith Evans' Florence Nightingale in January 1929, but she had subsequently been cast as the lead when, in the autumn of that year, the play was taken on tour.

Sickert had some of the characteristics of a chameleon. Certainly, he changed his colours in his paintings in the different phases of his work, but he also changed his clothes, like an actor, to assume a different persona. He changed his lodgings frequently, and was always changing his studios. Usually he had at least three different studios. This he explained to Gwen as a device to avoid his creditors. He changed his name too. In 1927, when he was sixty-seven years old, he decided that he should from then on be known as Richard Sickert. It was as Richard that Gwen invariably referred to him.

Sickert's Danish father, Oswald, was a gifted artist and musician. His mother, Elinor, was partly of Irish stock. Walter Richard Sickert was born in Munich, where he spent the first eight years of his life before coming to England. In the relationship with Gwen there were some Celtic affinities and also a mutual appreciation and understanding of the German character and German music. Sickert was not only insistent on meeting Gwen's mother, but also attended with Gwen a concert given by her sister, Marjorie, when the programme comprised mainly songs by Mahler.

In the summer of 1932 Gwen took Sickert on various excursions in her car, including a visit to the parish church at Hackney, a building of which Sickert was particularly fond. After their visit they could not remember where they had parked the car, and so they asked help of a passing policeman. Before putting the question, Sickert introduced Gwen, with a flourish as 'the greatest actress of our time'. Gwen commented in her letter, as she tells this story to her mother, 'The policeman was polite, but obviously thought the poor old man a mental case and me his nurse.'[15] They had another outing to Kenwood together when, after they had had tea, they went to sit on the terrace. An incident then happened not dissimilar from one described by E. M. Forster in *Howard's End*. Gwen writes:

'I noticed a female hovering near - So I thought, oh someone has recognised him and is going to gush. But what she said was "I'm so sorry but I think you have my umbrella" - and sure enough we had walked off with a brown parasole - impossible to explain "this is the great R. S. and he's a little vague, but not a kleptomaniac". She left looking distinctly suspicious.'[16]

During the period of their friendship Sickert lived in Islington and when Gwen visited his house, she was shocked at its bareness and absence of normal creature comforts. Sickert seemed completely indifferent to the ordering of his financial affairs to his advantage. Although he could acquire significant sums of money for most of his paintings, he had been known to cut through any number of canvases and throw then away to make more room in his studio. In January 1932 he wrote to Gwen that he had been ill, and that his wife's mother was also ailing. He moved with his family to St Peter's-in-Thanet, near Margate in Kent, and began to teach at the Thanet School of Art in Margate. From this point until his death in 1942 there appears to have been no more correspondence or meetings with Gwen. They had come together at a time when Gwen was enjoying one of her most successful periods on the stage. In 1930 *The Barretts of Wimpole Street* had been an unqualified success, and was to be revived in 1935. In 1932 *The Immortal Hour* was staged yet again, with Gwen singing the part of Etain, after which she played Prue Sarn in *Precious Bane*. June 1932 saw Gielgud's triumphant production of *Richard of Bordeaux*, which was repeated in 1933 and ran for over a year.

This two-year period of her friendship with Sickert was a particularly fulfilling time for Gwen. She repeatedly refers to the stimulation she derived from the vigour and brilliance of his conversation, and how he could make the personalities of forty or fifty years earlier live as though they were inhabiting the room where the conversation was taking place: Henry Irving, Aubrey Beardsley, Max Beerbohm, Charles Keene, Edgar Dégas, and James Whistler were all brought to life. In *A Free House*, (Macmillan 1947), Osbert Sitwell wrote a very perceptive study of Sickert as an introduction to the artist's writings. Referring to the last phase of his painting, Sitwell concludes his introduction as follows:

'Sickert proved himself to be a splendid and audacious innovator in colour, and the canvases of his last years blaze with a richness that indicates the ultimate fulfilment and fructification of a painter's genius, owing to decades of perseverance in practice and experiment.'

That brief friendship with Gwen Ffrangcon-Davies surely played some small part in the painter's genius being fulfilled.

Performances: Peaks and Troughs

The period, 1925-1936, was for Gwen a time of great achievement, when playhouse managers, her audiences, and the drama critics were, for the most part, prepared to fête her as one of the brightest stars in the theatre firmament. Gossip magazine journalists wrote articles, fully illustrated, about Gwen in her Hampstead home, Holly Place, Gwen and her furniture, Gwen cooking, Gwen grooming Snuffles, her pug dog, Gwen with Walter Richard Sickert, Gwen with royalty. There were also during this period keen professional disappointments, anxiety about unemployment, or employment in plays she deemed sub-standard. She had set her heart on another production of *Romeo and Juliet* with John Gielgud. Gielgud had spoken to Gwen of this possibility, but when he came to choose his next Juliet it was Peggy Ashcroft and not Gwen Ffrangcon-Davies. Gielgud was somewhat shame-faced about this decision, and the way the news was conveyed to Gwen made him ill at ease, but it left Gwen feeling badly let down. Gielgud chose Peggy Ashcroft for his Juliet both for the 1932 O.U.D.S. production, when Edith Evans played the Nurse, and also for his 1935 New Theatre season, when he alternated with Olivier, as Romeo and Mercutio.

In 1935 and 1936 Gwen was feeling that her professional career was being 'stymied'. Her family was in crisis: her mother's health was failing; Marjorie's marriage was near breaking point; some weight of responsibility for Marjorie's two girls had fallen on Gwen; and Marda was pressing her to go to South Africa with her. In the event, Gwen spent two months in South Africa with Marda in the summer of 1936. Here the seed was sown for her future theatre work in that country. Soon after her return to England her mother died, and she alone took on her shoulders all the necessary arrangements for the funeral and the settling of her mother's estate. Marjorie remained out of the country. Gwen at this stage could not see her future in the theatre with any clarity. She could, however, look back and wonder how the great successes of the past eleven years could have led to the professional uncertainties with which the year 1936 closed.

In 1923 and 1924 Gwen had performed in *Back to Methuselah* to universal acclaim. Her grasp of the Shavian style received rare plaudits from the playwright. Her success as Cleopatra in *Caesar and Cleopatra* (1925), was followed by her playing Mrs Dubedat in *The Doctors' Dilemma* (1926), Eliza Doolittle in *Pygmalion* (January, 1927) and Ann Whitefield in *Man and Superman* (February 1927). However, apart from the 1926 (January/ February) revival at the Kingsway Theatre of *The Immortal Hour*, the play that drew most critical attention was the production of *The Marvellous History of St Bernard*. Barry Jackson, during a holiday in Savoy, had been greatly impressed by seeing Henri Gheon's adaptation of a fifteenth century play about Bernard of Menthon, a young man of a rich and powerful family, who escapes from his parents' castle on the eve of his wedding night, leaving a sorrowful note saying he would henceforth devote himself wholly to God's purposes. Violence between the bride's family and Bernard's is only prevented by Marguerite, the bride-to-be. She, it seems, is the only one capable of understanding the imperious call to which the young man has subjected himself. Barry Jackson translated the Henri Gheon prose and verse text, and presented the play first at Birmingham, and subsequently at the Kingsway Theatre, London. He had as usual assembled a very strong cast with Robert Harris as Bernard, Valerie Taylor as The Virgin Mary, and Gwen Ffrangcon-Davies as Marguerite, with Scott Sunderland, Dennis Barry and George Howe in supporting roles. The design of the setting and the resplendent costumes was undertaken by Paul Shelving. One reviewer remarked that some of the stage scenes looked as though they had been modelled on the illuminated pages of a medieval missal. Such a simile was repeated by Ivor Brown a few years later when he reviewed *Richard of Bordeaux* (1932). Gwen, from early in her career, in *The Immortal Hour*, for instance, had been noted for the elegance with which she managed spectacular costumes, often designed by Paul Shelving. Included in *The Lady*'s review of *The Marvellous History of St Bernard* is the sentence 'Miss Gwen Ffrangcon-Davies, as Marguerite, wears her voluminous and gorgeous robes with that air of wistful fragility that is characteristic of her. 'Corisande' of *The Evening Standard,* commenting on the richness of the colour of the production, drew attention to 'Miss Margaret Chatwin's black and ruby velvet gown with its golden tissue sleeves' and to the fascination of 'Miss Gwen Ffrangcon-Davies's wonderful robes of turquoise blue velvet and silver in one act, and ivory and gold wedding draperies in the other.' This 'Mystery Play' as it was called, gripped the 1920s audiences by its dramatic content as well as by its scenic

As Bella in *Maya* in 1927

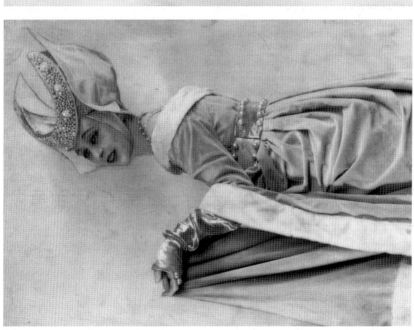

Gwen in *The Marvellous History of St Bernard*
at the Kingsway Theatre 1926

delights. Apart from some of the cast walking through the auditorium, which critics found disturbing, the play received a rapturous response. Its religious theme was met without cavil or cynicism. The London audiences seemed relieved to turn aside from the current Noel Coward theme, costume and décor, and instead be entertained by a play with a spiritual dimension in a setting of medieval splendour. A significant part of that splendour was not only the robes that Gwen wore and they way she moved in them, but also her array of medieval head-dresses: wimple, coif, chaplet and henin.

The Marvellous History of St Bernard had been presented at the Kingsway Theatre in April 1926. In November of that year The Riceyman Steps was staged at the Ambassadors Theatre for six matinées only. This provided Gwen with a part as different as possible from the stately Marguerite. The play was an adaptation by Michael Morton of Arnold Bennett's novel of the same name. The story is of a miserly Clerkenwell second-hand bookseller, Henry Earlforward, who marries Mrs Arb, the sweet-shop owner on the other side of the road. Earlforward's niggardliness indirectly accounts for both their deaths. A charwoman cleans both premises. This step-scrubber servant-girl is hungry, flat-footed, and passes between the two establishments, forgoing her own chance of happiness through an inarticulate and dim devotion to the Earlforwards. Christopher St John, writing in Time and Tide, recorded 'Riceyman Steps in general, and Miss Gwen Ffrangcon-Davies in particular, gave me more happiness than I have experienced in the theatre for some time.' Gwen played the part of Elsie, the char, the limping undernourished go-between. The Evening News reporter commended the play for its quality, and then spoke of Gwen in particular:

'Gwen Ffrangcon-Davies's performance as Elsie, the charwoman and general servant, was above all ordinary acting. As I looked at her shapeless dresses, her ugly shoes and thick stockings, her steadily turned-in toes, her spiritless, untidy hair, I wondered if there were another actress of her standing in London who would so thoroughly make herself graceless.'

Few actresses, indeed, renowned for their grace and elegance in the playing of princely parts gorgeously arrayed, would have hazarded their reputation in such a part as Elsie. In Pygmalion Eliza Doolittle, a role Gwen was to play two months later, develops from a sluttish, dirty, cockney flower-girl into a young lady that 'can be passed off as a duchess'. Audiences and actresses find such transformations delightful. The part of Elsie in The Riceyman Steps enjoys no such metamorphosis. The drama critic of The Morning Post wrote:

'But The Riceyman Steps has its own distinction, and perhaps the greatest ingredient of it is the character of the maid-of-all-work, Elsie, so charmingly acted yesterday by Miss Gwen Ffrangcon-Davies. It is not Henry Earlforward, the predestinate miser, nor Mrs Arb, the miser by adoption, who fill The Riceyman Steps with humanity: they nearly empty it of that quality; it is Elsie, the golden-natured girl who makes kindliness and affection flourish wherever she goes.'

Gwen had played before parts that were concerned with the moral and spiritual dimensions of life. A few months before playing Elsie she had acted in *Everyman*. She had taken the lead in this medieval morality play many years earlier; and in 1912 she had played the main part in A. M. Buckton's *Eager Heart*, a Christmas morality play. As she amply manifested in her playing of Etain in *The Immortal Hour*, there was in Gwen's acting an otherworldly quality that could profoundly move audiences. It was apparent in her role of the noble Marguerite in *The Marvellous History of St Bernard*; it was as evident as the limping charwoman in *The Riceyman Steps*. Such quality was to be found even in her most controversial role, that of the prostitute, Bella, in Simon Gantillon's *Maya* (November 1927).

Although *Maya* had been performed recently in Paris without censorship problems, there was no chance of the Lord Chamberlain licensing the play in London for public performances. If performed at all it would have to be at a private theatre, open to club members only. The Gateway Studio Theatre, 'under' Charing Cross Station, was in Villiers Street. It had 196 seats; membership cost 5s. 6d; a full house took £25. Its very first production was *Maya*. The play is in fourteen scenes, all set in the dingy bedroom of a brothel, which is run by Bella, a girl from a rich family, who has chosen this way of life. The location is a dockside port in the south of France. Seamen of all nationalities frequent the brothel. Bella, Gwen's role, receives her clients in this bedroom. There are also scenes in the bedroom with some of the other prostitutes. *The Daily Express* reported:

'Episode after episode deals with her (Bella's) daily life of degradation, and the men who pass in and out of her life. Although one or two scenes are written in beautiful language, most of the incidents, which take place in the same bedroom, are so sordid and so brutal that only the lesson of their truthfulness condones their performance before even the most brazen person of the audience. Zola's frankest work is baby-like compared with this. It cannot even be described.'

The Times reporter, less shocked, found much to commend in the play, and detailed some of its strengths:

'She (Bella) is, to be plain, a harlot in a dockyard port, and her clients are the scourings of the world. Each of them discovers in her, not perhaps a representation of his desire, but a compensation for it. There is a stoker who finds consolation with her before going out to drown himself, a Norwegian sailor who likes her to be audience of the tales that quiet his homesickness; there are men of all kinds and their characters are indicated with firm dexterity - who though they may find a harlot in her, find also more than that. The women of her own profession are not less skilfully drawn, and there is one scene in which she sees a girl innocently in love going out joyfully to what may be disaster, that is written with beautiful strength and economy...Through all her experiences Bella's character increases in interest and subtlety until we know her well in Miss Ffrangcon-Davies's dignified and imaginative portrait.'

The reviewers are at pains to praise the strength of the supporting cast, which included Gillian Lind, Derrick De Marney, and Norman Shelley. Peter Godfrey, who produced the play, took the part of 'An East Indian'. As a producer he is praised for his imagination and resource (*Daily Telegraph*), and as the Hindu in the final scene, who dealt throughout with symbolism, he was remarkably effective. 'Maya' is the Hindi word for 'illusion'. While both *The Times* and *The Telegraph* reporters were prepared to praise the production, the players, and the power of the writing, they were both reluctant to ascribe to the play the symbolism that seemed to be claimed for it in the final scene. Bella's transforming power, amounting almost to spiritual reform, over the characters that passed her way, remained less than wholly credible.

While *Maya* was being performed at the Gate Theatre Studio, Noel Coward, who had been highly praised for *The Vortex* (1924), *Fallen Angels* (1925), and *Hay Fever* (1925), had a number of subsequent failures, such as *Home Chat* (1926). One of the London critics belaboured Coward for his habit of laughing at audiences behind their backs. The same critic had seen *Maya*. He deplored the slightness of Coward's themes and machine-made plays which he declared

'...shows something to be wrong with the dramatic conscience of our critics. Strindberg's *The Father* had to fight its way by sheer merit into the public esteem, and most of our critics are so dense that only one or two of them have told the public of the poetic realism and dramatic skill of the remarkable play *Maya*, produced this week at The Gate Theatre Studio.'

Gwen was clearly a risk-taker. She accepted the part of Elsie in *The Riceyman Steps*, which involved considerable work for a limited run of only six matinées, and then she portrayed Bella in *Maya*, for which the preparation would have been intense but the monetary return negligible; in addition she might well have been inviting public opprobrium. On the whole she showed excellent judgement in the plays she chose to take part in. The part of Elsie extended her range of character performances; and the part of Bella, with a touch of sensationalism, was not without moral pretension, and certainly earned for Gwen a good deal of publicity which mostly was without venom.

In October 1928 Gwen was involved in another play performed to a club audience. This was Strindberg's *Easter* at the Arts Theatre Club. The play is about the family of a middle-class man who has been sent to prison for embezzlement. His son, Elis Heyst, lives in fear of his father's creditors, and he suspects Kristina, the lady to whom he is engaged, of being unfaithful. His sister, Eleanora, has just returned from a period in a lunatic asylum. Other characters within the home are his mother and a student lodger, Benjamin. The landlord and chief creditor is Lindkvist, whose approach with demand for payment, is dreaded most of all. The play begins on Maundy Thursday and ends on Easter morning. It is a story of suffering followed by redemption. This message of redemption, which involves a change of heart in Lindkvist, is carried mainly by the character of Eleanora, who is touched with insanity. The part was played by Gwen. James Agate writing for *The Sunday Times* commented on the play and in particular on Gwen's part in the production he saw on October 10th:

'The point, you see, is not how much or how little Eleanora's arguments weigh in the scales of reason, but that, being pure spirit and imponderable,

68

they elude those scales altogether. Strindberg's genius was never proved more firmly than by the fact that by the end of her first scene we accept Eleanora as the touchstone of the finest kind of truth. It is very much hit or miss with writing of this order, there being nothing but the thinnest line between the larger lunacy and the greater wisdom. Much, too, depends upon the actress. There must be no doubt, not only about Eleanora, but also about her impersonator. There was none whatever about Miss Ffrangcon-Davies, who brought to the shadowy delineation a certainty and assurance which approached the miraculous. This player's art may have the defects of its qualities, but when sensitiveness and other-worldly communion are the things supremely called for there is no actress on our stage to excel her. To Miss Ffrangcon-Davies, then, as well as to Strindberg, belongs the credit of making us willingly accept the final pronouncement of the mother which is the whole play: "Eleanora, this child of sorrow, has brought joy, though not of this world. Her unrest has been changed to peace. Sane or not, for me she is wise, for she knows how to bear the burden of life better than we do." It is Eleanora, and Eleanora alone, who gives the play beauty of content and texture.'

The part of Kristina in *Easter* was played by Peggy Ashcroft. None of the many reviews gives any prominence to her performance. In most she is not mentioned at all. Peggy Ashcroft was nearly seventeen years younger than Gwen; she died about seven months before Gwen in June 1991. She had made her début at the Birmingham Repertory Theatre as Margaret in *Dear Brutus* in 1926, and her first London appearance was in 1927. When she appeared with Gwen in *Easter* she was on the threshold of her very famous career. She was to share the stage with Gwen on many occasions, the most celebrated of which were the Gielgud productions of *The Importance of Being Earnest* in 1939 and 1942. In these productions they starred and sparred together. Their friendship endured until Peggy Ashcroft's death, but not without an undercurrent of gentle sparring.

Eminent Victorians by Lytton Strachey was first published in 1918. It was a scholarly work, which shed fresh critical light on four revered nineteenth century figures, one of which was Florence Nightingale. Reginald Berkeley's play *The Lady with a Lamp* draws much material from Strachey's account. Florence Nightingale was born in 1820 and died in 1910. Strachey charts these years in some detail; the playwright follows suit. Consequently the play deals with this indomitable character from her youth until her extreme old age. It follows the career of Florence Nightingale and her dependence on Sidney Herbert, who became Secretary of State for War, and fought her cause in Cabinet. His championship of such a cause was to the detriment of his health and he died prematurely. His wife, Lady Herbert, lived on, grieving for her husband and bitterly resenting Florence Nightingale's ruthless manipulation of him, to the point of precipitating his early death. The two actresses playing Florence Nightingale and Lady Herbert were required, on stage, to age together. The playwright compounded his problems by introducing a Captain Henry Tremayne, a former suitor to Florence, who dies at the hospital in Scutari in Florence's arms. This part of the story was definitely not to be found in Strachey's account. The critics took Berkeley to task for the structure of his play, in particular the weakness of the first act in its almost comic portrayal of Florence's parents, and for the gratuitous sentimentality of Tremayne's death. But they were neither dismissive of the play as a whole nor of the distinguished cast. The play was produced jointly by Edith Evans, who played Florence Nightingale, and Leslie Banks, who played Henry Tremayne. Mr Nightingale, Florence's father, was played by Richard Goolden, and Mrs Nightingale by Muriel Aked. Sidney Herbert was played by Neil Porter, and Lady Herbert by Gwen Ffrangcon-Davies. Almost at the bottom of the cast list one reads 'A German Diplomat...Leslie Mitchell'. Leslie Mitchell in the 1930s became one of the first presenters of BBC Television News.

Edith Evans received abundant praise for the range of her portrayal of Florence Nightingale, from young girl at her family estate in the New Forest, Hampshire, to the old lady of eighty-seven years old, receiving the Order of Merit, within the fortress of her London home, with the mumbled words 'Too kind, too kind!' The *Times* reporter, referring to Gwen's role, wrote 'And there is a study of Lady Herbert by Miss Ffrangcon-Davies which in its subtlety, overshadows any other performance of the evening.' The play proved a great success, and the London run was followed by an extensive tour in the autumn. Edith Evans left the cast at that stage, and Gwen took over the role of Florence Nightingale. Gwen wrote to her mother on November 16 from Glasgow,[17] telling her of the reception of the play in Edinburgh. She speaks of very appreciative but not large audiences. On the Sunday she was asked by the minister of a congregational church, who was to focus his service on *The Lady with a Lamp*, to take part in the evening service. One of the cast read the lesson, and then Gwen ascended the pulpit and spoke of the influence of Florence Nightingale on the modern woman, and what was owed to her and other pioneers. Gwen also tells her mother of the sightseeing she has done in Edinburgh, including the castle and Holyrood House, and the relatives, friends, and scholars she has met, who all in different ways help her to understand a little more the character and sad history of Mary Queen of Scots. Gordon Daviot, at Gwen's request, had written a play on this theme especially for her friend, but it was not to be staged for another four years. After portraying Florence Nightingale in *The Lady with a Lamp*, Gwen, in the early months of 1930, found herself rehearsing three parts almost simultaneously: Nora in Ibsen's *A Doll's House*, Lady Macbeth, and Ophelia.

Macbeth was produced by the president of the O.U.D.S., Brewster Morgan, during the second week in February 1930. One professional was invited to join the Oxford University cast, Gwen Ffrangcon-Davies, who played Lady Macbeth. The cast list reads like a Varsity sports occasion, where the name of the player is followed by the name of his College. For instance:

  'Macbeth..........V. Dyall (Christ Church)
  Macduff...........E.E. Sabben-Clare (New College)
  Fleance............O. Holt (Merton)'

James Agate demolished all aspects of the production in his review in *The Sunday Times*. Apart from one individual, he did not bother to go into any detail of how the performers acquitted themselves, and completed his article with 'I find that I have omitted all reference to the O.U.D.S actors proper. But, alas! That is because I would rather not allude to them. It is a lean year at Oxford.' The one performance which he did treat in detail was that given by Gwen. He totally refuted her inter-

With Cedric Hardwicke in
The Barretts of Wimpole Street **in 1930**

Gwen as Lady Herbert in *The Lady with a Lamp*
with Edith Evans as Florence Nightingale 1929

pretation of the part of Lady Macbeth, especially in the early scenes. Perhaps he thought that he was being merciful to the rest of the cast, having ridiculed the inadequacies of the producer, by turning, with a stinging attack, on the one professional. It was in substance the same attack that he made on her performance of Lady Macbeth twelve years later in February 1942, when she partnered John Gielgud. On both occasions there were other critiques of the performances that were supportive and commendatory. A powerful and influential drama critic such as James Agate might have little influence on a one-week run at Oxford, but a destructive review of a production by a professional company on tour on its way to a London opening could spell disaster for that unfortunate group. The nub of Agate's objection to Gwen's playing of the part was her physical inadequacy. He argued that the part called for feminine dominance from a wife that had the size and muscle almost to enforce it. He wrote:

'...in this part this distinguished and charming actress seemed to me to resemble the dime-exhibit who claimed to be the World's Smallest Giant. Frankly I have never considered Lady Macbeth as wistful, and I could not for a moment believe in Miss Ffrangcon-Davies's assumption of the character. It was incredible that she should ask for the daggers, incredible that she could have killed the old man, resemblances or not, incredible that she could compute the amount of blood left in him. But Miss Ffrangcon-Davies is a very clever artist, and by sheer brain-power convinced us that she had skirted physical defeat, even turning fragility to success by giving a most moving rendering of the Sleep-walking Scene.'

Another view of Gwen's performance as Lady Macbeth in this OUDS production was given many years later by Oliver Holt, who had doubled as Mentieth and Fleance. In a letter to Gwen[18] he explained that he had felt com-pelled to watch each performance of the Sleep-walking Scene from as close as he could get on the stage without being seen by the audience. He was gripped by her sighing, her breathing, her walk, the movement of her hands. He thought it all magical and masterly. He became from that moment a devotee and, during the last years of her life, a valued friend.

Shakespeare's birthday was celebrated, a day early, on 22nd April 1930, with a matinée performance of *Hamlet* at The Haymarket. An all-star cast had been assembled for this special, sole, performance. The director was Sir Johnston Forbes-Robertson. Henry Ainley took the lead; Claudius was played by Malcolm Keen, Gertrude by Irene Vanbrugh, Ophelia by Gwen Ffrangcon-Davies, Horatio by Godfrey Tearle, and the First Gravedigger by Cedric Hardwicke. Among the rest of the cast were Richard Goolden, Robert Speight, Austin Trevor, Ernest Thesinger, Baliol Holloway, and Margaretta Scott. Reviewing the production in *The Daily News*, E. A. Baughan found Ainley 'too robust' in the part, and wondered why the Ghost should have been invisible until *Hamlet* met him face to face. Of Gwen's performance he wrote: 'At first she seemed to me unpoetic and undistinguished, but she acted the mad scene with beautiful simplicity and haunting pathos.' He noted that the applause of the audience at the end of the play was thunderous, and in his curtain speech Henry Ainley announced that the King and Queen had commanded a repetition of *Hamlet* on May 19th. 'With more than common modesty Henry Ainley added "God save the King".'

James Agate deliberately began his *Sunday Times* review of this *Hamlet* with a paragraph praising Godfrey Tearle for his distinguished portrayal of Horatio. There followed a crushing analysis of Henry Ainley's sad inadequacy in his interpretation of the title part, despite that actor's fine physical presence and resonant voice. One can imagine Gwen's growing anxiety as she scanned this review for the passage which referred to her performance. It read as follows:

> 'Miss Gwen Ffrangcon-Davies gave a lovely performance of Ophelia, as one little detail will show. At the end of the mad scene Ophelia came down-stage towards Laertes with recognition on her face. But before she could take shelter in her brother's arms her mind clouded again so that she found herself confronted by a stranger. And it was a stranger to whom she said "God be wi' you!" This was most touching, and if it be a part of tradition, why then, Miss Ffrangcon-Davies recreated it so that it seemed new.'

Gwen had explained to Agate how this stage business associated with Ophelia had been related by his father to Godfrey Tearle, who in turn had passed it on to her. It is clear from Agate's reference that her performance profited greatly from this hint, achieving the poignancy of losing that moment of love and recognition by lapsing back into insanity.

One of the parts Gwen played between her Lady Macbeth and Ophelia was that of Nora in Ibsen's *A Doll's House*, promoted by J. T. Grein and produced by Henry Oscar at The Arts Theatre Club. The reception of the play was unreservedly enthusiastic. Gwen's performance was hailed in the headlines as 'Another Great English Nora' (*Morning Post*). The play was planned to celebrate the 102nd anniversary of Ibsen's birth. The Norwegian Minister was present on the first night, 20th March 1930, and at the end of the play read a message from the stage from King Haakon of Norway, expressing his personal appreciation of this tribute to the dramatist, also paying tribute to Mr J.T. Grein and the Cosmopolitan Theatre for their valuable work in promoting international goodwill.

A strong cast helped carry the intensity of the play. Henry Oscar played Torvald Helmer, Harcourt Williams Dr Rank, Frederick Lloyd Nils Krogstad, and Mary Barton Mrs Linden. Many amendments had been made, with advantage, to William Archer's original translation. The great challenge to the actress playing Nora is to make credible her change from Torvald's 'squirrel' or 'singing-bird', fluttering and silly, in the first part of the play to the enlightened and determined woman of the final act, who can leave her husband and, above all, her children, to seek a new life. The critics were of a mind that the actress managed to bridge that divide. Harold Hobson, writing in *The Observer,* referred to Miss Ffrangcon-Davies's 'inspired performance'. W. A. Darlington for *The Daily Telegraph,* recognising the challenge facing the actress, indicated how Gwen dealt with it:

> '...Miss Ffrangcon-Davies solved this problem successfully, but could not make us forget its existence. She can never help giving the impression of intelligence, which informs every expression and gesture in her remarkable

73

range; but she did manage to make us feel that Nora's intellect was in abeyance...it was with Nora's awakening to knowledge of Torvald that the actress rose to her full stature. This Nora was drawn so firmly, so clearly, with such confident strokes, that it was only by virtue of that impression of dormant powers in the earlier Nora that we could believe in them as the same woman. Miss Ffrangcon-Davies has done some fine things in her time, but I think this deserves to rank as her best achievement.'

In May 1930, Gwen played the name part in Sudermann's *Magda*, presented by J. T. Grein in German at The Arts Theatre Club. The play was then performed in an English translation. Many critics referred to the great number of parts, in so short a time, that Gwen was playing on the London stage, and there was some question of whether there was a deliberate policy of promoting her as one of the most popular of national actresses. 'There seems a conspiracy on foot in the theatrical world' wrote the drama critic of *The Sunday Pictorial*.

'It is a conspiracy, if I am not mistaken, to raise Miss Gwen Ffrangcon-Davies to a higher position in the theatrical hierarchy than she has hitherto occupied...The plan of the campaign is apparently this: to present Miss Ffrangcon-Davies in a series of famous parts which can only be satisfactorily tackled by a supremely fine actress, thus proving what a supremely fine actress Miss Ffrangcon-Davies is. Which, ladies and gentlemen, she is.'

The part of Magda, played previously by Sarah Bernhardt and Mrs Patrick Campbell, is that of a gifted daughter rebelling against her authoritarian father, leaving home, and making a name for herself as a famous opera singer. On her return, her Prussian father is horrified to learn that during her absence his daughter has not led a wholly chaste life. Gwen's fluency in German allowed her to play the role as convincingly in the original as in the English version. There was some similarity in the theme of rebellion, and running away from home, to *A Doll's House*. Such a theme was inherent also in her next great success.

When Rudolf Besier's *Barretts of Wimpole Street*, with Gwen playing Elizabeth Moulton Barrett, was first presented by Sir Barry Jackson in Malvern in August 1930, it was well received, apart from the overt stress on the incestuous feelings that the tyrannical father felt for his favourite daughter. This element was very much diluted before the play reached the London stage. It opened at The Queen's Theatre in September 1930 to the warmest of receptions from both audience and drama critics, and seemed certain to have a long run. The Barrett family, however, of which there were twelve surviving grandchildren, protested at the distortion in the play given to the character of their grandfather. The theatre manager was asked to reserve fourteen seats in the front stalls for the opening night. It was thought that this booking was for the Barrett family. He was relieved to be able to reply that all seats for the opening had long been taken.

The play was produced by H. K. Ayliff and the design of costumes and set by Paul Shelving. This was a tried and trusty team, and they were working with actors whom they knew well. Apart from Gwen, the leads were Cedric Hardwicke as Mr Barrett, and Scott Sunderland as Robert Browning. Cedric Hardwicke made an indelible impression as the domineering patriarch; Scott Sunderland was less successful as the lover-poet. Gwen, writing to her mother, a week or two into the run, tells her how well the play is being received:

> 'We took over £2000 last week...we might get quite a run...The booking extends well into January...Scott varies very much, some nights he is quite good and again he'll be so bad as to make me despair. But I don't think the general public find him so trying, and anyway it's got to be faced, so we must just make the best of it. He is very sweet and nice in himself and I think does try. He has got a new wig which suits him better, but of course he'll never be R.B. in a million years!'[19]

It was Gwen's custom to study the parts she was playing in great detail. If the part was historical, she would not only read whatever literature she could find on the subject, but also, as in the case of Mary Queen of Scots, seek counsel from established academics. The poems and letters of Elizabeth Barrett Browning shed for her fresh light on the father's character, which made her believe that Besier had 'only shown one side of Barrett's character'.[20] Among her archival papers is a copy of the marriage certificate of Robert Browning and Elizabeth Moulton Barrett, dated 12th September 1846. It shows the signatures of the married couple and the two witnesses. The marriage took place in the parish church of St Mary-lebone, in the County of Middlesex.[21] Gwen's possession of such a document emphasises the pains she took to study and understand the characters she portrayed. She was rewarded by the accolades she received for her performance as Elizabeth. *The Daily Telegraph* pronounced

> '...this is the most beautifully fitting achievement yet set to the credit of this finely accomplished actress. Her every intonation, movement and gesture is instinct with a sort of quiet inspiration; she has steeped herself in the personality she depicts to the point of complete identification; here is the superlative imperceptibly attained. Her scenes, whether with her family or her lover, bear equally and delicately the imprint of the truth which is akin to genius.'

The Barretts of Wimpole Street proved so popular that it not only had a long run, but enjoyed a revival at the Piccadilly Theatre in January 1935. Between these two productions, 1930-1935, Gwen appeared in a number of plays and also in another performance in February 1932 of *The Immortal Hour*. The outstanding success of this period was John Gielgud's production of *Richard of Bordeaux*. The play was written by Gordon Daviot (Elizabeth Mackintosh), a very close friend of both Gwen and Marda. It was in modern prose, and took the story of King Richard II from his late teens, 1385, to his imprisonment in the Tower of London in 1400. Richard, the advocate of peace, courageously opposes the hawkish policies of his overbearing uncle, the Duke of Gloucester, and the clique of noblemen who clamour for yet another invasion of France. As Richard matures in years and achieves a temporary advantage over the self-asserting nobles, his judgement becomes tainted. The love of his wife, Anne of Bohemia, had been a calming and healing influence. When she dies of the plague, the self-willed king is finally crushed by the death or desertion of friends, and the ambition of Henry Bolingbroke, the Earl of Derby. The play was first staged at The Arrts Theatre Club in June 1932. The set and the costumes were designed by three young ladies who went under the name 'Motley'. In preparation for the second presentation of the play in February 1933, the central theme was strengthened, and many of the scenes sharpened. The larger stage at The New Theatre offered more scope for the action, setting, and pageantry. John Gielgud, as producer, was able both to make alterations to the text in consultation with Gordon Daviot, and also to advise 'Motley' on colours and style of the costumes. In a letter written to Gwen, dated 28th December 1932[22], he tells her that he is in a panic about the casting: Robert Donat is a possible stand-in if one of his first choices fail him. He then describes some colour and staging effects:

'You are to have a light pink dress for your death scene if that will please you - and I am in white - against a white scene. I have planned a new ending for it, with you on the stage, the doctor and all the nobles shrinking back into the cloister, when the doctor tells me you have plague - then from this curtain with the stage full of people - a tableau in the same set of me above with your coffin - as she originally wrote - and then the same room bare with a bare tree outside instead of the blossoming one. This does not really concern you, but I do believe it will all help to heighten the effect, and build the tremendous sense of loss *for me*!! And I want to end the second scene by putting a torch to the brushwood piled round the walls, which will burn down the palace as soon as I leave it! I expect also that you will have to sing Robert's (Robert de Vere, Earl of Oxford) song for him now. I must say I rather hope so.

Much love to you darling, and thank you so much. It is nice to be working with you again - and we *will* do Romeo once more before we die.'

To Gwen's disappointment, they never played opposite each other again in *Romeo and Juliet*, but their triumph in Gordon Daviot's play made an even greater impact. *Richard of Bordeaux* was a chronicle play and frequently compared with Shaw's *St Joan*. Richard's friendships and enmities were played out with great intensity. The late fourteenth century colour and grandeur of costume and style were an endless source of delight to the eye. Gielgud received adulation such as he had never enjoyed before, nor would ever enjoy after. As the same people repeatedly had flocked to *The Immortal Hour*, so they came to *Richard of Bordeaux*. Jean Scott Rogers, who at one time was the Administrator of the British Theatre Museum, wrote to Gwen, after hearing her reminisce on her 'Juliet' on Radio Four in 1988. She confessed herself a life-long fan, having seen her first in *The Immortal Hour*, and in practically every play she had appeared in since, including two dozen or more visits to *Richard of Bordeaux*.[23] Gwen was greatly lauded for her Anne of Bohemia. Ivor Brown wrote:

'The lovely picture of his queen, Anne of Bohemia, composed by Miss Ffrangcon-Davies, is like something out of a missal reproduced with self-conscious delight by a modern amateur of medieval beauty.'

76

**Gwen as Anne of Bohemia with John Gielgud as Richard II
in Gordon Daviot's *Richard of Bordeaux*, 1933**

James Agate, 2nd February 1933, would not demur:

'Here is the place to say succinctly that if Miss Gwen Ffrangcon-Davies is not the best actress in England there is certainly none better. Her performance is a little miracle of sensitive perception; she creates the woman and sets her in her period as definitely as she created Mrs. Herbert and set her in the age of Victoria, and since critical memory is long, created and rightly dated that Egyptian kitten, Caesar's Cleopatra.'

Handsome as the praise was that was showered on Gwen, it was very much less than that conferred on John Gielgud, both as star performer and producer. As far as the theatre-going public was concerned Gielgud was King. Gwen tells this 'kingly' story about him. It appears, not in a letter, but on a torn page from an accounts book:

'Many years ago King George and Queen Mary came to a gala performance of *Richard of Bordeaux* in aid of the King George's Pension Fund. John and I were to be presented in the interval. In some agitation he came to my dressing-room to ask if I thought he should wear his *crown*. I said I thought he should and he *did* - and has worn it ever since - "the observed of all observers" and greatly beloved.'[24]

The gala performance, referred to above, was the second occasion on which Queen Mary had seen *Richard of Bordeaux*. Gwen had written a number of letters to her mother about the production: the first night reception of the audience[25]-'I never heard such shouting except at the *Barretts* and all the Old Vic enthusiasts were there in full force'; the party on the first night which had been hosted by Dame May Whitty,[26] when John van Druten told her that she was his favourite actress, and that he hoped that one day she would appear in one of his plays;[27] she hoped that the success of this play would encourage Bronson Albery, one of the most influential theatre managers, 'to put on some Shakespeare for John and me later - that would be heavenly'; and she tells her mother of the visit to the play of Queen Mary. Her mother responds

'What a thrilling time! What excitement there must have been "behind". I am very very glad and congratulate you all. I hope Her Majesty will give the King such a glowing account that he will want to see *Richard* also, but perhaps the poor dear is not allowed out at night! I will send your letter on to Marjorie so you needn't write to her, she and the children will be very excited that you really saw and talked with the Queen face to face!'[28]

Annie shared with Gwen the hope that out of *Richard of Bordeaux* further opportunities would develop. She writes 'I think you are sure of a longer run than you were expecting and is there a chance now for *Romeo and Juliet*?'[29]

Annie was right: the run lasted for a whole year. Following its first showing, the improvements found in the 1933 production of the play were warmly welcomed. Frequent mention was made of the excellent cast which, apart from the two leads, included Ben Webster, George Howe, Frederick Lloyd, Margaret Webster, Donald

Wolfit, Walter Hudd, Richard Ainley and Ralph Truman. For Gwen, however, there was to be no *Romeo and Juliet*.

In 1932 Gwen had taken Sickert to Small Hythe to attend the annual celebration in honour of the memory of Ellen Terry in 'The Barn'. These occasions were organised by Ellen Terry's daughter, Edith Craig, and her friend Christopher St John. During the 1932 event, when John Gielgud, Peggy Ashcroft, and Old Vic friends had performed scenes from *Twelfth Night*, Edith Craig had asked Gwen whether she would be kind enough to participate in the 1933 celebration. Gwen agreed, and, in the middle of the run of *Richard of Bordeaux*, in July, was the main contributor. Edith wrote to her the following letter of thanks:

'July 25. 1933
Dear Gwen
            I can't tell you how grateful I am to you for the exquisite performance you gave in the Barn here last Sunday. It would be difficult to find the right words. I can only thank you for all the trouble you took - Chris has reminded me that after seeing you as Eve and Newly Born in *Back to Methuselah*, mother said, "Wonderful girl! She can do anything." So somehow your appearance here in honour of her has a special value for me. That you absolutely enchanted everyone in the audience goes without saying. It was dear of you to come - and I hope you will come again.
                        With love
                        Edy
Chris has written this from my dictation as I can't spell well and am an ignorant cuss.'[30]

Gwen honoured the memory of Ellen Terry throughout her life, not just by her performance at the 'Barn' in 1933. She cherished in one of her scrap-books[32] two photographs of Ellen Terry: one taken by 'W. N.' when Ellen, at the age of nine, appeared on the professional stage for the first time in 1856 in the part of Mamillius in *The Winter's Tale*; the other of Ellen, at the age of eighteen, with her mother in 1865, photographed by Lewis Carroll.

J. T. Grein, who had done so much to promote Gwen's career during the late 20s and early 30s, contributed an article about her in the 7th July 1934 edition of *The World of the Theatre*. *Queen of Scots*, the play that Gordon Daviot had written particularly for Gwen at her request, was being performed at The New Theatre. He begins and ends his piece entitled 'The Versatility of Gwen Ffrangcon-Davies' as follows:

'You have but to quote her creations of the last five years to appreciate the wide range and versatility of Miss Gwen Ffrangcon-Davies - Nora, Elizabeth Moulton Barrett, Anne of Bohemia, and now Queen of Scots...In the rich record of Miss Gwen Ffrangcon-Davies, this many-sided portrayal of the Queen of Scots is yet a great manifestation of that remarkable versatility which kindles speculation as to the infinite possibilities of this gifted actress.'[32]

The substance of the article deals with the play itself, an analysis of the Queen's character, her relationships with Rizzio, Darnley and Bothwell, and the author's failure in her treatment of Bothwell. Consequent upon this last weakness, the love scene between Bothwell and the Queen 'went for nothing'. Darnley, for whom the Queen showed such contempt, was brilliantly played by Glen Byam Shaw. Ralph Richardson had originally been cast as Bothwell, but when he withdrew a replacement had to be found at short notice - Laurence Olivier. Securing a place with The Birmingham Repertory Company had been as treasured an aim for Laurence Olivier as it had been for Gwen. This he had achieved eight years earlier, when he appeared as The Minstrel in *The Marvellous History of St Bernard*. He had thought that his contract also included his understudying the main part, played by Robert Harris; but to his chagrin he discovered that because 'he was thought to be lacking in pure religious feeling' this task had been passed on to a more experienced actor, Denys Blakelock.[33] This early professional association of Laurence Olivier and Gwen Ffrangcon-Davies developed into a life-long friendship, and although in later life they seldom starred together, that friendship was marked by the many letters in the archive from both Olivier and Vivien Leigh.

When Gwen asked Gordon Daviot to write a play for her about Mary Queen of Scots, the author had told her bluntly that she felt little sympathy for that particular queen. In the event, it was perhaps that lack of sympathy that resulted in a less than satisfactory play. Marda Vanne kept a detailed diary from April 1935 to the end of January 1936. She cherished Gordon Daviot as one of her dearest friends, and she resolved that she would chronicle her own life and thoughts for this year and possibly send the diary piecemeal to her friend, who lived in Inverness. The following extract touches on three disappointments recently suffered by Gwen: her not being chosen by John Gielgud as his Juliet; the relative failure of *Queen of Scots*; her being offered the lead, following Flora Robson's withdrawal, in *Close Quarters*, only for Flora Robson to insist that the play should come off on her leaving the cast.

'September 15th, morning, rainy
John Gielgud is putting on *Romeo and Juliet* at the New and has not asked Gwen to play Juliet. Next to Mary of Scotland Gwen dreamt of Juliet. She played it to John's Romeo some years ago. They have talked often of doing another production together. Now Peggy Ashcroft will be his Juliet, and Gwen feels that her hour has passed, and she will never play it again. She is so courageous in sorrow that I go into the lavatory to cry for her in private. You should have known better than to write Mary of Scotland for her out of some emotion other than your own enthusiasm. If your hatred for Mary had been robust you might have done a better job, but you merely disliked the woman, but there again your affection for Gwen marred your integrity as a playwright. You are not among those who can write to order. I wish you had left her her dream that a play could be written about Mary, and that she could play that tiresome, glamorous woman. Now that's gone, and her hope of ever playing Juliet again, and the little creature feels like a shrivelled acorn...Flora Robson was leaving *Close Quarters* because she said Homolka was ill-treating her...Ronnie Adam had rung up yesterday to find out whether Gwen would take over Flora's part and open at the Savoy on Monday week.

Gwen said she would. This little sop from Fortune may help her bear the loss of Juliet'.[34]

Despite Flora Robson's condition that *Close Quarters* should close when she left the cast, Gwen took over the role of Liesa at The Savoy before the end of that September. Towards the end of the year Gwen wrote to her friend Margaret Drew:

> '...This has been such a "stymied" year for me - all my plans seem to have gone awry - all my plays postponed or frustrated in some way - so let us hope that 1936 will be better. I have on the other hand had great joy in the cottage and country which have been heavenly!'[35]

It might have seemed that with such a series of great stage successes, which included Elizabeth Barrett and Anne of Bohemia, Gwen had reached the meridian of her career. She had yearned, however, for the opportunity to perform more classical roles, especially Shakespearian, partnered by John Gielgud, whom she classed as the finest actor on the English stage. 1935 had ended, therefore, with Gwen in the dumps, but she was not quite that 'shrivelled acorn' described by Marda. 1936 would provide for her the wonderful, enlightening experience of visiting South Africa. This experience would lead Gwen to return to South Africa during the war years, and elicit from her a range of extraordinary gifts which she herself was scarcely conscious of possessing.

1936: The First South African Adventure

Gwen was a royalist. Her scrapbooks are full of pictures of the royal family; of royal births, royal marriages, many letters from the various queens' ladies-in-waiting, royal events, in some of which she appears herself, and royal funerals. On 20 January 1936 Marda noted in her dairy that when Gwen came home she had brought with her a special edition of *The Evening News*. It contained a stop-press; 'The King's life is moving peacefully towards its close.' Marda's comment was: 'God knows why I who am a Dutchman should have a lump in my throat.'[36] Her entry for 28th January tells of Gwen and Ethel, the maid, leaving home at seven o'clock that morning and standing for hours to see the King go by. Marda and Snuffles slept on at home, but Marda said a prayer during the minute's silence for the dead King, and for King Edward and Queen Mary.[37]

This was a time in both Gwen's and Marda's life when they were finding that suitable and satisfactory jobs within their profession were hard to come by. Marda had been urging Gwen to mend her extravagant ways, and Gwen was complaining to friends that she was obliged to accept second-rate roles in poor plays to pay off her overdraft. In the correspondence with her mother at this time there is an undercurrent of anxiety about the possibilities of another world war. In addition, the death of the reigning monarch and the uncertainties forecast for the reign of his successor most probably heightened Gwen's sense of insecurity. Annie's letters underline this. She passes on to Gwen some royal gossip derived from her niece, Rosie, who, 'brought the information presumably from her army husband that two crowns are ordered for the coronation!! So His Majesty intends to marry! I wonder whether it *will* be the lady first mentioned, Lady Helena Gibbs. One never sees her name anywhere as being at functions, so it will be a surprise. Mr Baldwin is reported to be finding the King difficult to advise. He will go his own way.'[38]

The world was shortly to discover that Mr Baldwin's difficulties had nothing to do with Lady Helena Gibbs, but were focused on the King and Mrs Wallis Simpson.

Annie wrote to Gwen after a short visit to her at the end of January. From her cottage in Beaconsfield she expressed her concern for her daughter's problems:

'I have been feeling for some time as if you had come to a sort of crisis in your career, as if you were up against a wall you have to climb over before you can enter into a new "kingdom"... all this skidding along on the surface only gets you to the same place again, it is all a dead level, there is no effort in it, it is drifting with the stream. Gwen dear I feel that somehow you have got to get out of that swim *with* the tide if you are to do all that you can and ought to do.'[39]

Annie compares Gwen with Marda, and wonders why Gwen should be so much more restless than her friend. This restlessness was resolved by Gwen agreeing to accompany Marda on a visit to South Africa, lasting from the end of May until the beginning of September. For some time Marda had been entertaining the idea, rather nervously, of returning to South Africa to see her father before he died. She had been estranged from him for very many years and was beginning to think that it was more than time that a reconciliation should be sought. For his part Marda's father, Sir Willem van Hulsteyn, had for a long time been pleading with Marda to return to South Africa. Marda had been reluctant to do so, because from her childhood she had been aghast at the way her father had treated her mother. She recalled her mother being confined to a wheelchair as the result of her father's ill-treatment. While she maintained a close and lively correspondence with her mother until her death in 1929, she wished to distance herself from her father. Now she planned to make that journey of reconciliation and was infinitely pleased when Gwen agreed to accompany her.

The friends left England on 25th May, sailing in a small Dutch ship. Details of the voyages and the adventures in South Africa are derived from Gwen's letters to her mother at that time, and from press-cuttings. Gwen described her fellow-passengers on the outward journey as being interesting without being exciting. They were mostly parents with their children who were returning to schools in South Africa. There was a single man who spent some time with the friends. He was a doctor from Pretoria. The seas were calm, even in the Bay of Biscay, the weather warm and getting warmer, the swimming pool used twice a day, and the food abundant: sleep came readily. It was almost an enforced regime of relaxation that Gwen found congenial. She writes to her mother of the variety of books that she is reading with great enjoyment: Winifred Holtby's *South Riding*, Edith Sitwell's *Victoria*, Negley Farson's *The Way of a Transgressor*, and Mikhail Sholokhov's *Quiet*

Flows the Don. A salient characteristic of the mother/daughter correspondence is the exchange of information about their reading, not just titles but mini reviews, each encouraging the other to broaden her interests.

When their ship reached Cape Town, Marda's relatives and friends came on board to greet the travellers, and they all stayed on board for dinner. When they disembarked the next morning Marda's godfather had arranged for the head of immigration to see them through customs like royalty. Before they were able to begin their train journey to Johannesburg they were surrounded by reporters and photographers, anxious to please their editors and readers with news of these two celebrities. Gwen, during her first few days in South Africa, was astonished at the great number of Marda's relatives, and at the reporters' up-to-date and accurate knowledge of the London theatre world. She was even given a present of flowers, sherry, and South African liqueur from an unknown friend and admirer who wished to thank her for the pleasure she had given him on the occasion of his first visit to a play at the Birmingham Repertory Theatre. Once again in Johannesburg they were the target of the press with their cameras. They were given a grand tour of the city, and then travelled by train for a further hour's journey to Pretoria. On arrival they were taken to their rondavel accommodation in the Pretoria Country Club. Gwen described these rondavels as little circular, thatched bungalows, each having another rondavel behind it for bathing and Elsan facilities, but all scrupulously clean. She found herself waited on 'by coal-black gentlemen in white duck suits who do all the house-work and bring you your breakfast in bed. One hears them chattering their guttural Zulu outside the window and they laugh uproariously among themselves as they are a merry folk.'[40] Her use of 'gentlemen' changes as she travels. She will soon be referring to her 'boy' who is sixty years old.

It was at the Pretoria Country Club that Marda's father met them. Gwen thought him very pleasant and felt that they would get on well together. However, it was not long before she was writing to her mother complaining of his company exerting a terrible strain on all who happened to be with him, whether it was Marda and herself, or his son, Max, and daughter-in-law, Edna. Gwen found Max charming and cultivated. He had suffered a 'down and out' period in his life, from which he had been rescued by his marriage to Edna, and by his father building him the substantial house in the Transvaal, where now the father, Marda, and Gwen were accommodated as guests. Gwen wrote home:

> 'The old man calls me Sister Gwen, but is a great strain on all...as Edna says
> - he built this house for them but wants their souls in exchange!...These
> dominating selfish males are led by the nose by any female who would flatter
> them sufficiently.'[41]

On the other hand, Gwen found Myles and Marguerite Bourke 'adorable'. These were Marda's good friends who lived in the Cape. They accompanied Gwen and Marda on both their safari trips into the Game Reserves, the first in the Transvaal, and the second in the Cape. This experience with the Bourkes was Gwen's most treasured memory of her first visit to South Africa. It was largely because of the warm friendship forged with the Bourkes that Gwen would make that crucial decision, in a few years time, to abandon the London stage and return to South Africa.

In writing to her mother, while in South Africa, Gwen would frequently say how she wished her mother could be with her enjoying these new experiences. She went further and many times promised that when she next visited the country her mother would be with her. She makes her descriptions as graphic as she can so that her mother will live through in her imagination the many new sensations that Gwen herself is undergoing. As she travels by train to Johannesburg Gwen tries to recreate for her mother, as though she is sitting in the same railway compartment looking out of the same window, the shape and colour of the changing countryside:

'the red earth getting redder, against a blue sky and a blazing sun, which has almost a blinding effect...The train corkscrews its way to the top of the Hexe River Mountain...and then passes through the Great Karoo, a brown, burnt, trackless wilderness, stretching as far as the eye can see, without anything to break the line except now and again a little hillock or "kopje" and a few stunted trees. We never saw a farm, or a man, or an animal.'[42]

Behind the need Gwen felt for conveying to her mother the excitement and wonder of this new world, might well have lain the intuition that her mother had not long to live.

When Gwen and Marda were taken 275 miles north of Pretoria to the edge of the Game Reserve, and then on safari, her descriptions of their journeys, their living conditions and their adventures are at their liveliest. The relief of not having Sir Willem with them, demanding constant attention, and the welcome companionship of the Bourkes, heightened Gwen's enjoyment, and her excitement and wide-eyed wonder spill over into her writing. She is clearly astonished at the variety and large number of animals she sees for the first time: the herds of antelopes and zebras, the families of giraffe, the troops of baboons, and then the lions.

'Well, I can't say that when we came upon a bunch of six lions in the road, and they moved off and sat in the grass about five yards from the car and watched us with great unwinking topaz eyes, that it wasn't a thrill because it certainly was, and I for one was very conscious that I was in the presence of royalty! But they are quite unperturbed and even bored at the sight of cars, which they do not associate with human beings, and so one does not even put the windows of the car up. Another time we came upon three lionesses at a kill. Two were enjoying lying down devouring a buck, and the third stood up facing us, her nose rather pink from the effects of her undercooked break-fast.'[43]

The trip to South Africa came to an end with a ten-day safari with the Bourkes in a Game Reserve near the Cape. It was to be another entirely new adventure for Gwen.

'Myles has left to-day with a lorry load of tents, beds, provisions and guns, for we are to shoot our own food 150 miles away from the nearest town! It should be a marvellous experience and one we should never have had but for the Bourkes who have been angelic to me.'[44]

She then tells her mother of the arrangements for the return journey. They were due to leave from Cape Town on 15th August, arriving in England on 6th September. They had at first planned to sail on a German ship, but an Italian line offered them each, as celebrity passengers, a double cabin with bathroom, for the price of a single fare. Gwen turns her thoughts once more towards Europe. She reports that a South African clairvoyant has pronounced that there will never be another war between Germany and England. This does not prevent her asking anxiously in one of her last letters to her mother whether there has been any improvement in the political atmosphere in Europe. When she landed in England she visited her mother in her home at Beaconsfield and then made her way to the refuge of Tagley Cottage, and from there moved back to her London home at Holly Place, Hampstead. There she received a message from Marjorie that her mother was too ill to see anyone, even Gwen. A specialist had been called in as well as Robert King, the Christian Science practitioner, in whom Annie had placed much faith.

The excitement of the South African adventure was giving way to more sombre considerations.

Annie's Death

In Annie's letters to Gwen, written at the end of 1934 and the beginning of 1935, there enters a note of urgency. She encourages Gwen to say the Lord's Prayer daily, believing that 'it contains everything that we can want. Our "trespasses" are just our ignorances and mistakes, and "bread" our motor cars and clothing...Say it as you are making-up or finishing your hair and dressing, the last thing before you go on. The old mystics say that where the hands are busy the heart can be turned to God.'[45] When she wishes Gwen a happy new year for 1935, she presses her to go on and achieve even greater things saying, 'You are still climbing up to your meridian and have triumphs still ahead of you. May all your dreams come true, and yours be a lasting name in the "role of honour" of your profession.'[46] She mentions the success of *The Barretts of Wimpole Street*, which was then enjoying its revival at the Playhouse Theatre, but she regrets that Sir Cedric Hardwicke 'still has the honours as Mr Moulton Barrett'. Despite the splendid reviews given to Gwen for her performance as Elizabeth Barrett, Annie would have preferred Gwen to be the sole attention of the reviewers' accolades. She reports that her bank manager had seen Gwen in all her roles, and thought her best as Prue Sarn in *Precious Bane*. She advocates that it should be put on again, but that Colin Keith Johnstone should replace Robert Donat. Her great ambition for Gwen to be the queen of her profession might have been well-received by her daughter when she was on the crest of a success, but might have had a depressing effect when Gwen found herself in poor parts in inferior plays as a stark endeavour to reduce her bank overdraft. As the months progressed, however, Annie became engrossed with worry about her other daughter, Marjorie, and by the beginning of 1936 she launched into a series of letters to Gwen, seeking to protect her estate, in the event of her death, from Marjorie's fecklessness.

During 1935 and 1936 Marjorie's marriage to Malcolm Norbury was reaching breaking point. They had two children, Doreen (Nan) and Heather. The two girls, particularly Heather, did not get on with their mother. Heather found herself staying with her grandmother Norbury or, after the separation, with her father, until she was sent to the School of Ballet then under the direction of Ninette de Valois. The elder daughter, Nan, was destined for drama school. Malcolm and Marjorie lived in a handsome house, Mellor Hall in Debyshire. Marjorie was weary of the marriage and determined to break away from Mellor, Malcolm and the children. Her intention was to make her own way as a singer, like her father, and like her father give concerts in London, in America, and on the continent. Her first step was to find lodgings in London and to launch herself into the concert world from there. In these endeavours she was greatly encouraged by Constance MacColl, like Marda a friend of Dutch descent. Constance was planning concerts for Marjorie in New York. The two women lived together, rather extravagantly, expecting Malcolm to meet their expenses.

For a long time Marjorie had been planning to reissue her father's book *Singing For the Future*. The book was not published until 1938, when it appeared with a supportive introduction by Ernest Newman, the distinguished music critic, who had not thought highly of the book when it was first published in 1905. By the middle of 1935 she sent a copy of her father's book to a friend for comment. She intended to write an account of her father's life, which in the 1938 edition extended to sixty-five pages. Her hope was to re-establish her father's place in the esteem of the music-loving world, both as a singer and as an author, with innovative ideas about the teaching of singing, and also, by this publication, to advance her own publicity. It was not an enterprise that she would willingly have divulged to her mother because, in a way, it was a veiled criticism of her mother's inadequacy in dealing with and nurturing the genius to whom she was married. In her account of her father's life, published two years after her mother's death, she touched on her parents' relationship:

'...a shadow of misunderstanding dimmed their happiness from the first - which grew imperceptibly with the years. She had been brought up in a restricted environment and was by nature unemotional. Ffrangcon had felt the Spirit that bloweth where it listeth; his reserves were not withholdings, but unexhausted stores, and his emotions as necessary to him as his ideals. Nan, too, found his serious absorption in his work perplexing and his ambitions dangerous; but for Ffrangcon his art was his goal - he must attain it, whatever the cost.'[47]

Annie, although she did not live to read these words in print, had a fair enough measure of Marjorie to sense her criticism of the way she had treated Ffrangcon. Part of her reply would have been that she had three children to raise when their father was mostly absent from home and often, when at home, the worse for liquor. She would have had sufficient perception to read into Marjorie's advocacy of her father's pursuit of his artistic goal 'whatever the cost', Marjorie's own stance. Marjorie believed that she was greatly gifted as a singer, and that it behoved her to use this gift even if it meant a divorce from her husband, and abandoning to others the responsibility for her children. Marjorie, with Gwen, was named as an executor of her mother's estate in the event of her mother's death. Whereas Annie could trust Gwen entirely with all her money matters, she became very apprehensive about Marjorie's erratic, extravagant, and irresponsible ways. She made arrangements with her bank manager and with her solicitors that Marjorie should have restricted access, but to Gwen she allowed access to the key of her strong-box at the bank. She was anxious that most of her investments should be placed with her solicitors for safe-keeping. Marjorie was urging her to change her fuddy-duddy solicitors for a younger and more up-to-date firm. Annie would have none of it.

Annie died in October 1936. During her last illness and when she was taken into hospital, Gwen was rehearsing for *Charles the King* by Maurice Colbourne. The play was at the Lyric Theatre, and Gwen's role was that of Queen Henrietta-Maria. Her magnificent costumes were based on original Van Dyck portraits of the Queen. Despite the pressure of rehearsals Gwen was with her mother when she died; Marjorie was on a concert tour, which began in Holland at the Hague, and would take her to Vienna. On the Sunday, after their mother's funeral which took place the day before, Gwen wrote a long letter to Marjorie telling her of their mother's death, her own difficulties in managing dress rehearsals and a first night in the midst of this major family crisis, and ending with a full account of the funeral service.

'My darling Marjorie,
    At last this long long week is ended, and I sit here in the quiet of the cottage to try and tell you a little of our dear. There is no need to recall what at the time I was fighting to know as untrue, so I will not speak of it; I only want to tell you that I was with her when she went to freedom; I had been at the hospital all afternoon with Auntie Rosa, I was sent for as I left rehearsal at 1.45 - I stayed till 6 and then had a dress rehearsal lasting till 11.30. I was bewildered with tiredness, but felt I could *not* go home and leave her, and yet I knew I had my work next day and that without sleep I should collapse; Joyce Kennedy was an angel to me that night and confirmed what I knew to be true, that I *must* go...Marda and Lena [Caroline Ramsden] took me to the studio and gave me food. (I'd had nothing all day) and when I was a little refreshed, drove to the hospital, where we arrived about 12.30. I was prepared to sit up all night and Marda wanted to stay with me but I sent her away with Lena, as the night sister said it was all right and I could have a room and sleep. The kindness and true love of all the people at that time is something I can never forget - the sister tucked me into bed, I didn't undress, and gave me a hot bottle, promising to call me if there was a change - I had hardly turned out the light when the nurse came running for me - I ran down the passage into the dimly lit room to face the moment I had so greatly feared - and so needlessly - She wasn't there any more, only a little fluttering breath; I stood at the foot of her bed, the nurses bending over her. I did not look at her, but I found myself standing with my arms upstretched in a kind of exaltation, I was unconscious of myself. I found myself saying all the lovely true things to lift her up - up - and Geoff was there I *know* it; "Freedom" was the word I said over and over, Life, Love and never once did I look down - and the little fluttering breath was still - and there was silence and a surge of *life* in the room -

And then Auntie Rosa came hurrying, the dear, and for a moment fell upon her and took her in her arms and sobbed and I lifted her up and held her and in a moment she too was caught and sustained as I was - I touched mother's hand just once but I didn't look at her because I knew that she was free and not there - Then I took Auntie away and put her in my bed for a moment, as she had been awakened and came running and was rather inclined to have a heart attack, but the sister gave her brandy and soon she was calm - Then I took her to her own room and saw her safe in bed and left her knowing she was all right. I phoned for Marda and she and Lena came back for me and I went home - I wasn't in the hospital more than about fifteen minutes before the end, it was as if she had waited until I could come - I had no sense of grief or loss or of anything but her freedom and happiness -Next day we went down to Jordans [Beaconsfield], and I had not realized quite what that would mean - and Marda and I had our sorrowful hour - for she too loves mother very dearly. But we helped each other and did what we had to do, and came back to arrange details...The question of where she was to rest was not settled as nothing was said in the will, but Auntie Rosa was *very* against her being in East Finchley as I was myself. There was never any feeling for that place - We thought of Jordans but it would have meant Chalfont St Giles and then I said in a sort of tentative way "Of course where I would love best of all is here in the little churchyard at the end of Holly Place but I don't suppose for a moment it's possible" – "Oh" said the man from Harrods "I can easily find out" - went away and came back in half an hour with the news that it would be very possible, only needed the consent of the vicar, which we got that evening. From that moment everything fell into place with the most exquisite harmony. The vicar came to see me the next morning...we arranged the service, a simple spoken one...we chose the 91st Psalm (He that dwelleth in the secret place of the Most High...) and the 21st Revelation (And I saw a new heaven and a new earth...), and he said that she could be brought to lie in the church on Thursday evening... On Thursday evening they welcomed her in, Auntie Rosa and Joan were there, and at midnight Marda, Edith and I came from our respective theatres. They had kept the church open for us, the verger was in attendance and the vicar was kneeling, praying as we stole in. Marjorie I would have given anything for you to have shared the beauty of that moment...There was such peace, such beauty, just as she would have loved. On Friday I had my first night and was marvellously helped and sustained and knew that I would be so on Saturday...I felt that we would have a joyful festival to send her on her way and so we did. Lovely, lovely flowers had arrived, masses of them with lovely messages. Ethel dealt with them all, copied the messages and names and with such loving service. Marda had arranged what I am afraid I should not have thought of, food for everyone afterwards - so that it was as if mother had been there giving her sweet hospitality as she always did...At about twenty to twelve we walked down to the church, all carrying little bunches of flowers in our hands - Auntie Rosa with me - no tears - We entered the church which was beautifully decorated with flowers, with tall candles burning on the altar and a shaft of sunlight streaming in, and sat while Reggie played the chorales from the Matthew Passion, weaving them in a lovely string with "The King of Love my Shepherd is" and "I will go back to the Country of the Young", and finishing with the Easter Hymn. Then the silver clock chimed twelve again and the little angelus bell overhead struck - as the sound died away the vicar came down to us and lovingly spoke simply and from the heart all the things I could have wished. Among the verses he chose was "Eternal God is thy refuge and underneath are the everlasting arms." We read the 91st Psalm in alternating verses and we *all* read. There was no faltering voice, no sound of sobbing - and the service, very short, finished with the old prayer "Go forth upon thy journey Christian Soul", the prayer that father had so often sung. I had not chosen it, but could I have chosen anything more fit? Then gently and quietly they took off the velvet and replaced our wreaths, yours and mine which had lain on the coffin all night as you wished, and we followed down the aisle with the organ playing "Softly and gently dearly ransomed soul I hold thee" with heads upraised, out into the little churchyard...with flowers in our hands...Into the quiet little garden gay with flowers, up into the corner where she was to lie. The grave was buried right up with autumn leaves starred with blue scabious and shot through with shafts of mimosa, no earth at all, just flowers, and into that gentle bed they lowered the coffin. Even at that moment as I stood at the head of the grave I had no sense of anything but peace and beauty, and that beauty and truth were so strong that there were no tears from Auntie, for I said to her "Look *up*" and she did. Then we threw our flowers gently down to rest and with loving blessings left the place. I spoke to all the Jordans friends, and old Mrs Keed and many old friends and then we walked home. I took all the family, aunts and cousins and all Theresa's folk and Mabel and Peggy and Edith, and we all had some food and there was no sorrow but only *love*, such love - I think there has never been such a wonderful funeral in that little church before. When you told me about Laura's I could not understand how such a thing could be - but now I know - I wished so much for you to have shared that beauty -

Goodnight my dearest,
Your loving
Gwen'[48]

Chapter Four: Afternoon
(1936-1948)

Reflection and Forecast

Gwen had felt that her whole family had been involved in her mother's death and funeral. Geoffrey's spirit was at his mother's bedside as she took her last breath; her father seemed present at the funeral when the vicar spoke the words from *The Dream of Gerontius*, 'Go forth upon thy journey, Christian soul!'; and with Marjorie she had conjured up, however unconsciously, the evocation of the dead members of their family, so that the two remaining living members might reorientate their lives, and live with a renewed sense of mission. Father, mother, and Geoffrey had all believed, in very different ways, that their lives had a mission. Annie had certainly inculcated that belief in Gwen, for her to see her work as an actress not merely as the accomplishment of a personal ambition and the achievement of fame, but as a channel for the propagation of beauty, truth and spiritual goodness. Such aims, however high-flown and fanciful they may now seem, were, for so very many of those who knew her well or saw her perform, incredibly fulfilled, as her correspondence testifies. Marjorie's artistic and spiritual ambitions were along the same lines as Gwen's, but she never convinced her mother that she had the talent or the temperament to achieve those ends. Gwen felt it her task during her mother's last years to reconcile her to Marjorie and, once her mother was dead, to give Marjorie all the love, encouragement, and monetary help she could to advance her career as a concert artiste.

At the beginning of 1936, as has already been noted, Annie had remarked on Gwen's restlessness and the appearance of a crisis in her career. This had been brought about by a combination of events: the state of her personal relationships; the hiccup in her professional ambitions; and the darkening European political climate. Gwen had, however, achieved three resounding successes on the London stage before the outbreak of war: as Olga in *The Three Sisters* (January 1938); as Mrs Manningham in *Gaslight* (December 1938); and as Gwendolen Fairfax in *The Importance of Being Earnest* (August 1939). On the other hand she was beginning to see herself as a second choice. For instance, she had taken over the part of Florence Nightingale from Edith Evans in *The Lady with a Lamp*, and Flora Robson's part of Liesa in *Close Quarters*. Gielgud had chosen Peggy Ashcroft in preference to her as Juliet in 1932 and again in 1935, and she was to follow Peggy Ashcroft in the part of Beatrice in *Much Ado About Nothing* towards the end of the 1950 Stratford-upon-Avon season. From 1936 she was beginning to feel that her meridian hour had past. Yet there was such a spirit and such abounding talent welling up inside her that she knew that as an artist she still had much to achieve.

The outbreak of the war in September 1939 was a great challenge for such artists as Gwen, intensely patriotic, and dedicated both to her country and her art. The wartime lives of her fellow actors and actresses show an extraordinary redoubling of effort. They willingly undertook exhausting tours for the troops abroad, under the auspices of ENSA, or like Sybil Thorndike and her husband, Lewis Casson, deliberately chose to visit the coal-mining areas in Wales and the north-east of England where no professional theatre existed. There they would present, in whatever local halls could be made available, such classics as *Macbeth* and Euripides' *Medea*. It is this period that gives rise to some of the most interesting letters to Gwen from, for example, John Gielgud, Edith Evans, Sybil Thorndike, and Emlyn Williams. During the war, Noel Coward and Laurence Olivier, Gwen's friends and correspondents, produced such films, respectively, as *In Which We Serve* (1942) and *Henry V* (1943/4). Just after the war, 1945/6, there was the memorable Olivier/Richardson season at the New Theatre which included the two parts of *Henry IV*. The redolence of Englishness, pitched between the Boar's Head tavern and the Cotswold countryside, was richly savoured; and the divided country seemingly healed at the end of the second part by the accession of the young hero-prince.

Why then, soon after the beginning of the war, should such a patriot as Gwen Ffrangcon-Davies decide to go to South Africa, and spend most of the war years there? The answer, which is complex, is not found elucidated in the mass of letters of this period. The correspondence does show that, far from being reproved for leaving England at this time, she is urged on to do so by such friends as Edith Evans and Sybil Thorndike, and positively praised and encouraged in the work that she undertook in South Africa. Encouraging letters from Myles and Marguerite Bourke strongly persuaded Gwen to return to South Africa in order to lead a movement, with Marda Vanne, for the establishment of a recognised theatre in that country. During her 1936 visit, Gwen had been greatly moved by the warmth of the Bourkes' friendship. In addition they had been particularly supportive in their writing at the time of her mother's death. She was quick to realise that Myles was not only very active in the theatre world, but enormously influential within it as well.

At the beginning of the war, in 1939 and 1940, the stringent blackout regulations and the transport difficulties combined to threaten the closure of many theatres. The employment of actors and actresses was put at hazard. Strangely enough, it was the subsequent bombing of London that brought out the fiercely defiant mood of Londoners, including, significantly, the theatre-going public. Gwen left London with Marda in March 1940. They travelled overland to Venice, and then by ship, through the Suez Canal, to South Africa. They were virtually out of western Europe before the German onslaught on it began. Gwen's friendship with Marda was an important factor in her decision to leave England for South Africa. Marda, born in South Africa with a Dutch family background, and with strong Boer sympathies, felt not a tittle of the patriotism that welled up in Gwen. In her diaries and journals she even expressed the hope that England would be beaten in the war, a feeling not at all uncommon among the Boers. The two women were seriously at odds politically, but their mutual feelings were so strong that such major differences were overcome. At this stage in their relationship Gwen no longer wished to have their love for each other expressed physically. This was not so with Marda, but a modus vivendi was reached which kept their deep affection for each other in tact, if not on an even keel, until Marda's death. In going to South Africa they shared a sense of mission. If crusaders for culture, for the theatre, for the refinement of the spirit of man, were needed in England during the war, they were no less needed in South Africa.

Gwen was forty-five years old when her mother died. She could look back on those years, which included the family tragedies of the death in war of her younger brother, Geoffrey, and the mental sickness and death of her father. She could also recall the unremitting support given her by her mother, first in encouraging her to go into the acting profession in spite of her aunts' and uncles' sighs of disapproval, and second in following her career so enthusiastically, even in its unpromising beginning, with wise counsel mixed with spiritual exhortation. Neither counsel nor exhortation was lost on Gwen. She strove to perfect her art for reasons beyond personal gratification. When she went to South Africa in 1940 it was clearly with a sense of mission. She was nearing fifty. Times of war tend to concentrate man's energy: the singular characteristic of great actors and actresses is their super-abundance of energy. Gwen's war-years in South Africa proved astonishingly productive. Her father had died at the age of sixty-two; her mother had reached her eighties. In 1940, as she sailed south towards so different a life from what she had previously experienced, she could scarcely have known that all that energy which was bottled up within her had over fifty more years in which to expend itself.

Family Affairs

After her mother's death Gwen's primary family concern was for her sister. The last few years of Annie's life had been haunted by her younger daughter's marriage difficulties, and the damaging effect this was having on her relationship with her children. Marjorie's soaring ambition was based on her wish to emulate the concert achievements of her father. From Annie's point of view there were many drawbacks to such an ambition. Marjorie, since her teenage years, had been plump. Her brother, Geoffrey, had jokingly called her 'Bargie'. Annie, seeing her on the concert platform, had despaired of her appearance. She thought a friend of Marjorie was trying to be of some help, and she wrote to Gwen in South Africa about this problem:

'I think Constance [MacColl] has helped Marjorie in many ways, she is much more "a woman of the world", and I rejoiced to see that Marjorie has at last had her hair tinted a very pretty colour just as it was at 25; she looks ten years younger for it. But of course her figure is *all wrong*, no dress could possibly look anything but a sack on her! However, I have persuaded her to go to Mrs Henderson Bland to be fitted for a "Beauty Form Corset" for which I will pay!'[1]

Many of Annie's subsequent letters included passages about the preparation of this corset, and the apparent friendship that developed between Marjorie and Mrs Henderson Bland. An even more intractable problem than Marjorie's figure was, for Annie, her choice of repertoire. Annie seemed to be of a mind with Robert King, her Christian Scientist practitioner, who also read her horoscope. King, as already mentioned, had made pronouncements about Gwen's future. He did the same for Marjorie, as Annie reported to Gwen:

'He will not budge from the position as regards Marjorie and the next two years. The tragedy being that if she would *learn* she might have one of the most beautiful of living voices. He declares she can't sing Wolf or anything of that genre, even *Gerontius* is quite out of her depth...Ballads are her only wear! He also said that he wished she could *now* have a lesson from her father who would scarify the flesh off her bones for her cocksureness!'[2]

Such criticism would have infuriated Marjorie, who took pains to extend her repertoire into classical fields. She thought of herself as a foremost exponent of Mahler's songs, and with a strange pride believed that she was bringing her repertoire of Mahler to Vienna as a musical missionary. However, once in Vienna, she decided to change her repertoire. She wrote to Gwen before her concert there on 3rd November 1936:

'I have done a thing that I feel is a demonstration of freedom. I have changed my programmes and made them considerably lighter. I have now established the fact that I am a *serious* artist and I don't have to go over that ground again, and I can now give way to something lighter. In my first Vienna programme I have cut out the Brahms group, and put in some Hebridean folk songs as well as Irish ones. They really love the English ones and I feel it is quite a step towards freedom.'[3]

In October Marjorie wrote to Gwen of the warm reception given by the audiences to her concerts in Holland, but the press reports were not favourable.

'We hear from all sides that the reputation of the Dutch press is very bad, and that their enmity may do more good than harm. What people usually do is to entertain them and to bribe them and without these steps they don't function. Another person told us that they are determined to boycott English artists and another paper said with such an accent and programme I certainly was *not* English!'[4]

Gwen's response to Marjorie's letters about her concert preparation and programme was invariably supportive and, unlike her mother's, entirely uncritical. Yet Gwen, such a shrewd judge of character, must surely have wondered at times at the naivety that Marjorie showed when being praised.

In Vienna Marjorie was met by her agent and a friend, Professor Erich Meller. As she settled down to prepare for her concerts, she wrote of Meller and his assessment of her musicianship:

'The perfect love of music which he has, and which is expressed in the appreciation of my work makes it so much easier. Working, as he says, year in and year out at the opera he has plenty of chance to see and hear and he says he has never met any one with a finer understanding of music than mine. After rehearsing some of my Mahler, the great songs beloved by him for years, he just said simply "Better than that they could not be sung".'[5]

Gwen, who had sung Wolf and Mahler herself as a concert artist, and who had achieved such adulation for her acting and singing in *The Immortal Hour*, was wholly reticent about Marjorie's singing abilities and the composition of her programmes. Very many of Marjorie's letters deal with her concerts, and the audiences' and the critics' response. Gwen replies giving encouragement wherever she can. She will bemoan the unpleasant criticism, rejoice at whatever praise is given, but offer not one word of advice. Perhaps she realised how fruitless it would have been. She was a generous-hearted woman. This was apparent in the understanding manner in which she helped to foster her sister's singing ambitions. It was also shown, after her mother's death and funeral, in the way she wished Marjorie, to share in those experiences. It was shown, too, in her dealings with Marjorie over their mother's will.

Marjorie in *Oithona*

Apart from a number of bequests Marjorie and Gwen shared between them their mother's estate. Marjorie, in her letters to Gwen at this time, expressed the wish to have some paintings and some items of furniture. She was in no way pressing and realised that Gwen, who bore the main worry of settling the estate, had to arrange storage following the sale of Conway Cottage, Annie's home in Beaconsfield. Marjorie was entirely in accord with Gwen's suggestions about sharing among the family many of their mother's clothes. For instance 'Auntie Nellie should have her lovely nightgowns as she certainly is the poorest'.[6] She also asked Gwen to send her the cards of those who had sent flowers for the funeral. She did express surprise that the Rayner Estate, a separate Trust, should pass to Aunt Rosa and the Rayner children. In the event, part of the Rayner estate passed to Gwen and Marjorie, and the latter borrowed money on account from her share of the Trust. When, therefore, Marjorie wrote to the solicitor claiming payment of her share of the sale price of Conway Cottage, therefore Gwen replied:

'Dearest Marjorie,
Mr. Madgett phoned me this morning to say he had heard from you and that you wanted him to send you your half of the money from Conway Cottage. He explained that he cannot do that until he knows what arrangement you are making about paying off the money you have raised on the Trust. It appears that the mortgagees have the first claim upon any money realised from the Trust, unless you have made some arrangement with Day Whatley & Co to continue to pay the interest and then of course they will want some security....'[7]

Neither of the sisters was an expert money-manager. Gwen was constantly overdrawn at her bank, and there were times when her bank manager had to speak severely to her on this issue, but Gwen's earning power, although sporadic, was

94

considerable. In the 1930s, apart from her stage work, she made a few films and was in constant demand as a broadcaster. Marjorie, on the other hand, categorised by her mother as 'extravagant', was a much worse manager than Gwen, and without the potential income. This became one of the difficulties within her marriage, and Malcolm, her husband, was reluctant to pay for her various residences once she had left the family home, Mellor Hall in Derbyshire. The divorce became a protracted, bitterly-fought battle. Settlement was finally achieved in the last year of the war, and soon afterwards Malcolm married again. The whole affair took its toll on the happiness of the children, Doreen and Heather. Marjorie's decision, before her mother's death in October 1936, to go abroad for a considerable time in order to give concerts in Holland and Austria while leaving her teenage children in England, created additional problems for the family.

Plans had been made for Marjorie's departure for the continent well before her mother's death. Marjorie's friend, Constance MacColl, was to accompany her. Annie in her correspondence with Gwen, had expressed increasing concern at the growing influence Constance was exerting on Marjorie. She felt that Constance had been widening the rift between Malcolm and Marjorie, all the time urging Marjorie to strike out for her personal freedom and artistic ambition while leaving her family responsibilities behind. Gwen, on the other hand, had written to Marjorie saying what a tower of strength Constance must be to her, with which Marjorie was only too pleased to agree. For the two daughters, Doreen and Heather, to be shuttled between their schools, their Norbury grandparents' home in Manchester, and their father's much smaller house acquired after selling Mellor Hall, was scarcely conducive to their health or happiness.

Before Marjorie left for the continent Doreen, when not away at school, had spent most of her time with her grandparents or with her mother. Heather, on the other hand, had developed an antipathy to her mother, and she stayed with her father. She had been trained in a ballet school in Manchester and then was accepted at the prestigious ballet school in London, directed by Ninette de Valois. Because she was in London while her mother was abroad, Gwen took it upon herself to keep a close eye on her. A particular problem, into which Gwen was inevitably drawn, arose at the ballet school. In January 1937 she wrote to Marjorie about it.

> 'I saw Miss de Valois today, and had a nice talk about Heather. She says that Heather has lots of talent and is a sweet child. They are watching her carefully this term to see if she has the aptitude necessary for a ballet dancer. If she doesn't appear to them to promise sufficiently they will tell us, and she can then turn to some other form of dancing, but Miss de Valois says that she has been excellently taught and was surprised to hear that she had had such a good training in Manchester! She says the serious thing wrong with Heather is that she is *far* too fat! She must get off nearly a stone she says if she is to be any good as a dancer. She advised me to take her to a doctor to give her a diet as she says it is not safe for young girls to diet except under medical advice. But she must get thinner she says....'[8]

Gwen arranges a meeting with the doctor; she encourages Heather's landlady to give Heather sandwiches made with Ryvita 'which will nourish and not fatten'. She also follows Miss de Valois' advice in enrolling Heather for a class in Spanish dancing, and one in mime and character. However, the hoped-for reduction in Heather's weight did not take place. It was time for Aunt Gwen to have a heart-to-heart talk with her niece. She reported to Marjorie on 20th February 1936:

'I had a talk with Heather on Thursday; I am a bit puzzled about what is right for that young woman. Obviously she *cannot* diet to reduce herself and keep well - and if Miss de Valois feels that her physique is too heavy for a ballet dancer then she'd better be something else. I talked to the child very frankly and asked if she really wanted passionately to dance, and she confessed she did not, and seems much more interested in the idea of sports and games. Mrs Shipner says she has a great talent for organising...I think a year abroad...as an au pair in a family in Vienna or in Switzerland to give her languages...but I doubt whether the artistic life is one to which she really feels an urge - and unless she is *mad* to dance for heaven's sake keep her off the stage. It is far too overcrowded as it is!'[9]

Heather did not join her mother in Vienna, nor work as an au pair in Switzerland. During the war she drove an ambulance, and soon after the war she married Colin MacDiarmid. The wedding, at which the bridegroom wore a kilt, was reported to Gwen when she was in South Africa. Marjorie gave her sister a description of her helping Heather over the preliminary stages of the preparation,[10] but she does not appear to have been present at the wedding itself. In 1948 Heather gave birth to her first daughter, Ann, and in 1951 to her second, Margaret.

At the beginning of the war Marjorie moved back to England and made her home at Lower House Farm, Finchingfield, Essex. Doreen came to live with her and from there wrote a very descriptive letter to her aunt in South Africa. Her letter is dated 30th May 1940. She delights in the beautiful Finchingfield countryside and declares what a sight their cottage looked when the white and pink apple blossom was out. All the plants that Gwen had given them 'in the autumn have taken most beautifully and they are going to make a grand show.' Although as yet untouched, Finchingfield is sensing that the war is creeping nearer since the fall of Holland. Doreen has been riding on a friend's horse: 'Bachelor' is his name. 'It was the first time he was out, since he was badly hurt in a hunting accident several weeks ago. He seemed very fit and we had a lovely time.' She then describes a music festival held at Saffron Walden:

'Mummy sang beautifully and had a grand reception. The show was actually held in the Town Hall and Mum nearly blew the roof off. The Mayor and Mayoress were there in gold chains and Mummy had a long talk with them.
Mummy is also singing at Stambourne and the Reverend Horn looks across the chancel at her so adoringly that it makes her feel embarrassed, and of course it does not make me take the service so seriously as I should. Last Sunday she sang "Lead kindly Light"...and this week she sang "Nearer my God to Thee" and "There is a green hill far away"...I am continuing this letter after having been to London...with Mummy...We saw *Lear* and both thought it a lovely production. For myself I thought that Lear as portrayed by

Mr Gielgud was the nearest to the original Lear a modern actor could achieve...Some of the supporting parts were not good but Robert Harris as Edgar was very natural and took it well into his stride.'[11]

Doreen who, like her aunt, thought she might make a life for herself as an actress, trained at the Old Vic Theatre School, and secured a number of small parts during a Stratford-upon-Avon season. When Gwen was in South Africa she invited Doreen to join her touring company, and her niece thought very carefully about the offer, but she did not take it up.

During the years 1935-1937 Marjorie was planning and writing the book about her father. It was published in 1938. From now on, as author, singer, and for all other purposes, Marjorie reverted to her maiden name, Ffrangcon-Davies. Annie would not have greeted her book with any great enthusiasm, because of the slighting references to herself. There is no evidence of Gwen's reaction to the work, although it would be consistent with the rest of her treatment of her sister for her to have applauded Marjorie for her achievement, without alluding to the references to their mother. As the war was nearing its close in 1945 Marjorie was once more planning to take her talents abroad. She intended to visit Vienna once again and then move on to Russia. She busied herself with learning Russian songs for her new repertoire. Her father had included many Russian songs in his programmes. She was going to follow suit. She managed to engage the interest of the Foreign Secretary, Ernest Bevin, in her application to travel to Vienna. Bevin, apparently, was well acquainted with her work. Her permit to travel came through, and very soon after the war in the West had ended Marjorie was on her way to Austria. Gwen was in South Africa, where she was to stay for another two and a half years, intensely busy with her travelling theatre company. Now she was to be busy in an additional way: sending innumerable parcels, some small and some very large, to Marjorie in Vienna, in an attempt to keep her sister clothed, fed, and warm.

On the London Stage (1937-1939)

Emlyn Williams as playwright, actor, and friend was to become influential in Gwen's life during the late 1930s and her time in South Africa. They maintained a regular correspondence, which flourished particularly when she was planning to produce one of his plays. In 1933 Emlyn Williams presented an adaptation from the French of *The Late Christopher Bean* which, with Edith Evans playing the part of Gwenny, ran for over a year. His *Night Must Fall* in 1935 also proved a success. In 1937 John Gielgud directed and took part in *He Was Born Gay*. He played the part of Mason; Gwen played Mrs Mason. It proved a failure. It was Gielgud's second failure with a play by Emlyn Williams. The first, in 1934, was *Spring 1600*.

It was in the spring and summer of 1937 that Gielgud was planning a season of repertory plays to be performed at the Queen's Theatre. As one of his very dearest friends he had spoken a great deal to Gwen of this project, fully intending to enlist her as one of his star-studded ensemble. Following the disappointment of *He Was Born Gay*, Gwen was to receive an even greater setback. Gielgud changed his mind about her inclusion in the company and wrote from Finchingfield trying to explain his decision:

'Dearest Gwen

You will have guessed by my silence that something was afoot, but can't go on making plans without telling you. I'm afraid you'll think me a bad friend after all your kindness and sweetness in the past, and particularly over the last play when you gave not only your lovely work and continual enthusiasm but infinite encouragement and advice and help to cheer me along - and believe me I did truly and sincerely appreciate it. But you'll hardly think so when I tell you that I'm going to do the repertory season of which we talked so much - especially on that picnic after Stratford - and that I'm having Peggy for leading lady. We hope to do *Richard, School for Scandal, Three Sisters,* and *The Merchant* - with almost the same company right through, and not with Brownie.

Originally as you know I was keen to do *Macbeth,* and I have had to give that up because Larry wanted it for the Vic - also as you know I had planned to do other plays, with you, Angela, and Peggy to share the leads - but the budget seemed to forbid more than one woman star. Even then, I hoped to offer you Portia if you were free when we do it, but to my surprise, Peggy is very anxious to play it again. I told her that I didn't like her performance in it when we did it together before, and she knows that, but was very unhappy at the time, and feels she didn't do herself justice, and as we are both being so frank about it, and if she was to be in the other three plays, I thought it best to agree and not to break the plan of having her throughout as leading lady. *The Merchant* anyhow will not be done till February, and so I could not have been sure of getting you, even had you been willing. Dear Gwen, I feel so badly about it all, and so does Peggy - who is not a fool, and knows how much I love to act with you - and has not forgotten Juliet. Please don't hate us both too much or feel you have been passed over - and forgive my stupid tongue that talks away so thoughtlessly without knowing for a moment whether I can perform the promises I make…don't think me smug in writing, imagining that a tactful letter of conventional charmingness can make up for a piece of bad faith. It really rather appals me when I find that a successful (sometimes) career gives one the responsibility of hurting people one is fond of - I can only try to be frank and trust to your unique quality of sympathy and philosophy to understand.

Ever most affectionately
John'[12]

Gwen replied with some spirit. She had not forgotten being passed over for the part of Juliet, when Gilegud, having planned such a production with her, chose Peggy Ashcroft instead. Gielgud found himself even more on the defensive, and in the middle of his repertory season at the Queen's Theatre, sought to recruit Gwen for the part of Olga in *The Three Sisters.*

'November 2nd (1937)
Dear Gwen,

Your letter is hard to answer - indeed perhaps you will think I ought not to have answered it at all - but I too feel hurt that you should think me as insensitive as you do. I am often tactless, I know, but in the theatre, where insincerity is so often rife, I cannot see that frankness is more painful to others than elaborate subterfuge.

I feared you might be hurt at my suggestion - though I hoped you would not be - I suppose I was deceived by your extraordinarily generous behaviour when you wrote to me before the season began - But I was most anxious to try and persuade you to play Olga, which is a beautiful part - and I am not particularly interested in doing *The Three Sisters* at all unless the play is done by the very finest actresses possible. On the other hand I didn't want St Denis to hint at the idea in a roundabout way, so that you would imagine I was ashamed to offer you the part myself on the best terms I was unfortunately able to offer you - (though I know the money side has nothing to do with your refusal, I was none the less embarrassed by it). I know now that I should not have suggested the idea to you at all, but I was not prepared to lose you for the sake of a possible refusal - here you will say I was inconsiderate - but - apart from our friendship and your feelings about the season, I cannot see that the offer was any insult to your professional prestige - and in trying to cast my play with the finest talent I know of I merely try to do the best I can for a play which I have chosen in order to make a perfect thing of its performance.

If I often appear conceited or inconsiderate I do not mean to - that as you say is no excuse - you must of course consider your own career absolutely from your own point of view - I am sorry indeed to have hurt your feelings, and I regret infinitely that you cannot be persuaded to appear in the play. I value your friendship as greatly as ever, and wish you success and happiness always

John'[13]

The two friends were at loggerheads - but not for long. Michel St Denis was to be the director of *The Three Sisters*. He was greatly gifted, especially in the production of such 'mood' plays as those of Chekhov. Perhaps it was with his gentle persuasion that Gwen did eventually agree to join the cast which, as Gielgud had indicated, contained the cream of the acting profession: Carol Goodner (Masha), Peggy Ashcroft (Irina), Frederick Lloyd (Tchebutykin), Michael Redgrave (Tusenbach), Glen Byam Shaw (Solyony), Marie Wright (Anfisa), George Howe (Ferapont), John Gielgud (Vershinin), George Devine (Ptozorov), Leon Quatermaine (Kuligin), Angela Baddeley (Natalya), Alec Guinness (Fedotik). The production was an unqualified success, with the leading critics united in their praise of a rare triumph of artistic perfection. No adverse comment was made about Constance Garnett's rather stilted translation. In 1938 there was no competitor in the field. The honours go to the masterly orchestration of the piece by Michel St Denis, and to the intricacy and sensitivity of the ensemble playing. Extracts from the critics' comments read as follows:

'It provides...one of the richest experiences which the London stage has ever offered, or is likely to offer. It fulfils the highest function of the theatre...For this is a masterpiece as a dramatic conception, and in the manner of presentation and acting: nothing that I have seen in the theatre for many years

The Three Sisters by Chekhov, with Gwen as Olga, Peggy Ashcroft as Irina and Carol Goodner as Masha, 1938

As Gwendolen Fairfax in *The Importance of being Earnest*, with John Gielgud as John Worthing, 1939

has so profoundly moved me, and so burned itself into my memory.'
A. E. Wilson, *The Star*, February 3rd 1938
'The production of Chehov's *The Three Sisters*, by Michel Saint-Denis, with which John Gielgud continued his season at the Queen's last night, is one of those theatrical events which I shall remember all my life, and whose beauties I shall exaggerate for the benefit of incredulous grand-children...It was more like an orchestration than a production...The cast glittered with names - Gwen Ffrangcon-Davies, Carol Goodner, Angela Baddely...but what I want to put on record is the deep content with which their collective efforts filled me.' W. A. Darlington, *Daily Telegraph and Morning Post*, Saturday January 29th 1938
'...Not to be niggardly, we shall never see this production of *The Three Sisters* surpassed; and we owe homage to the genius of Michel St Denis that has given it to us...M. St-Denis...by sheer accomplishment of technical craft, has created the life of a town behind the scenes, a bustling life that reaches us in audible murmurs through the walls, in the sounds of door-bells and sleighs and military orders and the shouts of carnival roysterers - a fretful undercurrent that perfectly matches the discontentments and sudden gaieties of the lives inside the house...[St-Denis] is fortunate in having to his hand Mr. John Gielgud's company, a constellation of actors and actresses, without thought of personal vanity. They seem to have embraced their characters finally and naturally; they grow in them as flowers bedded in good earth.' Lionel Hale, *The News Chronicle*, Friday January 28th 1938

The perfection in the presentation of this play, which Gielgud had hoped for, had apparently been achieved. All the drama critics had been deeply impressed by the integrity of the ensemble playing. Ivor Brown, writing for *The Observer*, remarked 'how all the players seemed on this occasion to be above their usual best...as an all-star cast in a no-star play'. Notice was taken, too, of how the peculiar mannerisms, so often associated with star players, in this production seemed largely eliminated. A number of critics expressed surprise at seeing Gielgud bearded and monocled, and Michael Redgrave hiding his handsome figure in the pose of the indecisive, ineffectual Baron. Gwen was to gain greatly, through Michel St Denis' personal insight into Chekhovian drama, and she was later to speak publicly of this indebtedness. In the years ahead she was to perform in two more of Chekhov's plays with equal distinction. With the 1938 production of *The Three Sisters* at the Queen's, director and actors had accomplished what all must have dreamed of. To have achieved that standard once in a life time might have been sufficient to hope for, but yet another masterpiece of direction and performance was acclaimed in 1939, although for a very different sort of a play, *The Importance of Being Earnest*. For Gwen Ffrangcon-Davies, however, between those two remarkable peaks, there was another role to tackle: that of Mrs Manningham in Patrick Hamilton's *Gaslight*.

Gaslight is a thriller, bordering on the melodramatic. It was staged at the Apollo in January 1939. It is the story of a homicidal husband contriving, through raising and lowering the gaslight and other ghost-like devices, to drive his wife to the point of insanity. In this eerie Victorian house he had killed his first wife twenty years ago and is still searching for the jewels that were the motive for that murder. The cast is small: two maids, Mr and Mrs Manningham, and the ageing detective. Manningham was played by Denis Arundel, Milton Rosmer played the detective, and Gwen Mrs Manningham. The play has some elementary flaws, but the audiences were rapt by the passionate intensity of the acting, which was of so high a standard as never to tip over into melodrama. James Agate reported:

> '...And as for the wife, a suffering and tortured soul, she is indeed a part after Gwen Ffrangcon-Davies's own heart. This intelligent actress never over-stresses her effects. Fluttering and panting like a caged bird, expressing a wilderness of woe in the trembling of her sensitive hands, or a raising of a finger to that tremulous mouth, she sweetens and at the same time intensifies the horror of her predicament, and then astonishes us all by the tirade of revenge which she delivers to her would-be murderer before the curtain finally falls. It is a noble performance.' *Country Life,* February 11th 1939

The manner in which Gwen was able to enthral an audience by her performance in this play was also recognised by Alan Bott:

> '...the excitements and nerve-strains are ably devised; and Miss Ffrangcon-Davies works wonders with dramatic jitters. Through sobs and moans, glazed mien and somnabulistic walk, bouts of courage that are more pathetic than the hysterics, she holds interest at hair-trigger tension. She achieves the effects of melodrama without using any of its properties, and all but curdles the blood when, after Manningham's arrest, she gloats over the scoundrel at whose mercy she has meekly lived.' *The Tatler,* February 22nd 1939

Whilst still performing in *Gaslight* Gwen was rehearsing and then acting in eight matinée presentations of *The Importance of Being Earnest* by Oscar Wilde. John Gielgud directed and played John Worthing. Once again he had gathered together a constellation of stars: Jack Hawkins (Algernon), Edith Evans (Lady Bracknell), Gwen Ffrangcon-Davies (The Hon. Gwendolen Fairfax), Peggy Ashcroft (Cecily Cardew), Margaret Rutherford (Miss Prism), George Howe (Canon Chasuble D.D.). The matinées served as a trailer for the August presentation of the play at the Globe. The play is the supreme example of dramatic craftsmanship in the field of comedy. It became a classic in its own day, and the Gielgud production of 1939 amply confirmed that judgement. Edith Evans' appearance and performance were inevitably commented on:

> 'This Lady Bracknell goes through the play like a sloop under full sail. There is no other actress than Miss Evans who can somehow introduce a French rolled R into her horrified exclamation, "Hand-bag?" There are vowels in Miss Evans' throat past the prayers of phoneticians. She has to ride over the laughter of her audience to make herself heard. When she speaks, a comma is a cataclysm.' Lionel Hale, *News Chronicle,* August 1939

The judicious drama critics also noticed that, playing the part of her daughter, Gwen was not only made up to have a physical likeness to Lady Bracknell, but also developed some vocal similarities as well:

'There is Miss Ffrangcon-Davies' gift of reproducing some of Miss Evans' most formidable voice notes, so that when Gwendolen says, for instance, "I have the gravest doubts, but I intend to crush them," you hear with appalling clarity, that she is her mother's daughter.' J. G. B., *Evening News,* August 1939

James Agate saw a production of the play at the Golders Green Hippodrome on the afternoon of Thursday, September 14th. By this time the country was at war with Germany. He made the point that the choice of the play at such a time 'had an insistent and particular message for us - nothing less than the importance in serious times of being trivial.' Agate, too, drew attention to the likeness of Gwendolen Fairfax to her mother, Lady Bracknell:

'Miss Frangcon-Davies brings to Gwendolen a certainty of attack that compels admiration. One of the wittiest strokes that any actress of high comedy can ever have brought off is to make us see again the mother in the daughter; we hold our breath as Miss Ffrangcon-Davies rises to the audacity of imitating that swell of tone and bosom. In short the performance is perfection.'

Fifty years later, when speaking about this production, Gwen revealed that Edith Evans was none too pleased at the time with her clever cultivation of such details of family likeness.

The outbreak of war brought with it, within the very first days, incessant air-raid warnings in London and the home counties, followed by as many 'All-Clears'. It was an unsettling time for all. Theatre business was decimated; closures followed. For Gwen it meant making a reappraisal of the direction of her life and profession. She resolved to go with Marda to South Africa. A new chapter in her life began to unfold.

South Africa 1940-1941

Since the outbreak of war Marda had been urging Gwen to travel with her to South Africa to start another life, devoting their professional talents to the revitalisation of the theatre there. During the autumn and early winter of 1939 Gwen was touring England with the production of *The Importance of Being Earnest.* Marda, from their joint homes at 8 Holly Place, Hampstead and Tagley Cottage, wrote a stream of letters which reached Gwen almost daily. She had refused a series of offers of parts in plays planned for the provinces. On December 4 she wrote to Gwen saying that she had already sent off to her a letter from Bargie (Marguerite Bourke) outlining their possible role in South Africa. The covering note underlines Marda's desperation:

'For my Life's sake, and yours, read this letter carefully, word for word, line for line; and for God's sake - I really *mean* God's sake, i.e. creation of something in his *service* - SEE that this is the way we must go. Here - in this letter, is the sign we have been waiting for. Here is the opportunity *offered* for us to make a National Theatre in South Africa. Here also is a livelihood for us...and here is friendship such as makes one reverent and humble.'[14]

In her letter of December 4 Marda wrote that when in South Africa she herself would perform in the plays for which, in England, she had been so warmly applauded, such as *The King of Nowhere*, in which she had starred with Laurence Olivier, and *Many Waters*. She tempted Gwen with the fulfilment of the wish nearest her heart:

'You shall play Juliet again my Darling! John was no less raw when you made your big success with him than some S. African Romeo would be!'[15]

Gwen was sufficiently balanced in her judgement not to be beguiled by such an enticement; but she was swayed by the Bourkes' friendship and promise of support, and she began to look on the project, not just as a yielding to Marda's incessant pressure, but more as a mission to be fulfilled. She read Marguerite (Bargie) Bourke's letter with great care. It emphasised the friendly welcome that South Africa would extend to Gwen and Marda, and outlined Myles's plans for establishing a national theatre in Pretoria. Gwen and Marda would be offered posts as directors for a modest fee. Discussions were in hand at government level, although the outbreak of war had temporarily halted developments for the building of a new theatre, rehearsal rooms, library and restaurant. Bargie added 'S. Africa is rolling in money and we, the S. Africans, are profiting horribly through the war'.

Marda was desperate to leave England with Gwen for South Africa, yet she knew that if she persuaded Gwen to make such a move against her better judgement she would put their happiness at risk. She wrote to two of her best friends for counsel: Margaret Webster and Gordon Daviot. Each replied with long and intricately argued letters. The middle two paragraphs of Margaret Webster's letter underlined the problems of decision-making:

'Naturally Gwennie told me a lot about you and your joint troubles and problems - at which you had already hinted in your last couple of letters. The older I get the charier I am of offering comment on other people's lives, since at the best one can understand only a small proportion of the human heart. I think I can guess at something of what you must be undergoing at this time, dear Marda. But I don't believe anyone in the world, including your two selves, could confidently predict what the final solution might be, or what is best for either of you, or if your twin "bests" will coincide or not.

Only this much I do believe: both for your own sake, and above all if you really love HER, and want what is best for her even at your own expense (and that after all, is the true genuine test of loving anyone), you must above all, not try to rush her or yourself into crystallising a premature decision – "it shall be this way", or "we will decide to live thus or so". Of course there is and must be, a tremendous pull together and, for both of you, a great loneliness and loss of each other's absence, remembering all your happy years. But there are also strong divergent things - your ultimate roots in Africa, hers in England, the diverse elements of challenge, frustration, opportunity or dissatisfaction, for both of you, in your *work* in either one country or the other; and the ultimate relative importance to both of you of your work as against your personal life. Lastly, there seems to be, again for both of you, recent memories of bitterness and stress. (Don't get me wrong - Gwen has never once spoken to me of you with bitterness, but only with love, bewilderment, regret - but finally, always with deep and real love for you and anxiety for what is ULTIMATELY best for you.)'[16]

Gordon Daviot in her letter dated 7th January 1940, is much starker in her caveat about Marda taking Gwen to South Africa at a time of war:

'Since you say Gwen's career is to be the yardstick, let us consider Gwen, and what she has at the moment (not what she hasn't). She has an assured position (no, I didn't say income, I said position; a hundred people know Gwen's name for everyone who knows Peggy Ashcroft's) in the English theatre; and the interest and backing of Binkie if and when a 'Gwen' play came along; a London home and a country cottage, both of which are perfect settings for her, and therefore of professional value; the prospect of a European tour, as continental preliminary to acting in German in the new Federated States of Europe (let us not be *too* serious about this business!).

Now an actress, even more than a doctor or a dentist, lives on "goodwill". If this were peace time, I think Gwen could go to South Africa for even as long as three years, and come back to find her position with the public undamaged. She would just be 'Gwen Ffrangcon-Davies, back from a world tour'. If she goes in war time she joins the company of "those who went" willy-nilly. They won't care where or why she went; they will only know that she wasn't visible while they were at war; and in the new world after the peace they will have no use for her. (I can't speak for the theatre people, but I should think their unspoken attitude would be: "Oh, no! *We* had the thin times, we have the parts! Why didn't you stay in South Africa?")'[17]

In March 1940 Gwen and Marda, with a considerable amount of luggage, began their journey to South Africa. They crossed the Channel to France, and reached Paris by train. There they stayed two nights with friends before moving on, by train, through the Simplon Pass, to Venice. In Paris Gwen had been surprised to see so little of the war-preparedness that she had been accustomed to in London. Where were the sandbags? How inadequate were the blackout arrangements at night! But, oh joy! In Paris there was no shortage of butter or sugar! She wrote constantly to friends of her overseas experiences. For this period in particular, her most regular correspondent was Margaret Drew, a close friend of Gwen and the Gielgud family, highly intelligent, and, of course, a devotee of the theatre. Unfortunately during these war years Margaret Drew suffered greatly from ill-health, but she resolved bravely to give Gwen as close and as clear a picture of London suffering from the bombing, and of its continuing cultural life as she possibly could. She supplied Gwen with news of her friends, John Gielgud, Edith Evans, Sybil Thorndike and Lewis Casson, Laurence Olivier and Vivien Leigh, and she reported at length whenever she was able to see plays in the West End. Gwen in turn passed on to her news from South Africa. At the same time Edith Evans maintained, as always, an affectionate correspondence with Gwen, giving her version of life outside London (Salisbury), until she returned to the capital towards the end of the war. In 1947 she was to join Gwen in South Africa for an extended holiday.

Margaret Drew received a letter from Gwen dated 14 March 1940 which described their journey, including their stay in Paris, and their arrival in Venice, when fifteen pieces of luggage were unloaded from the train onto a gondola and they made their way down the grand canal to their hotel, the Danieli. They were eager for news of England, but could only obtain a three-day old copy of *The Times*. An overriding impression that both Gwen and Marda had of the Italians was that they were very anti-German.[18] Their journey took them to Mombasa and on to Durban where they landed. They sailed in an Italian ship and reported how impressed they were by the pro-ally stance of the ship's officers. Having for most of their sea journey passed through neutral territory, once in South Africa they felt immediately that they had again entered a war zone. They quickly travelled on to Pretoria, where they met the Bourkes and made plans for their first production, which was to be *I Have Been Here Before* by J. B. Priestley. Auditions were to be held the following week.[19]

When the Bourkes took Gwen and Marda to inspect the stage of the Lecture Hall, where their first production was to take place, their hearts sank. Gwen compared it to the confined conditions at the Gate Theatre, but she thought that what Norman Marshall had been able to achieve at the Gate, they should try to emulate at the Lecture Hall in Pretoria. They set about their work with some urgency. They were given by the Bourkes a 'Hansel and Gretel' cottage on the estate. Each had their own rooms and there was a small garden with magnificent views over the surrounding countryside. The cottage also had a large store room which served to accommodate some of the theatre material which arrived from England in seven packing cases. Gwen, who had not worked as a director of plays before, had the foresight to anticipate in South Africa a dearth of some of the basic requirements for good production. Her long apprenticeship at Glastonbury, on tour through most of the provincial towns of England, and her experience of the Birmingham Repertory days, had equipped her well for her present task. The contents of those seven packing cases were to prove invaluable. She wrote to Margaret Drew of conditions in Pretoria: their cottage, their plans to open with the Priestley play in June, and their ambition, as there was no professional theatre in South Africa, to form their own company in the fullness of time.[20] In exchange for Margaret Drew's letters about Gielgud's *King Lear* and *The Tempest* at the Old Vic, Gwen was responding with news of having met representatives of the Afrikaans Volkstheater. Her first impression was one of friendliness, but their anti-government attitude made her cautious.[21] She now learned that Italy had entered the war on the German side. She will have reflected ruefully on those vehement pro-ally protestations she had heard from the Danieli waiters and the ship's officers.

I Have Been Here Before ran for six nights, 24-29 June 1940. Margaret Drew and Edith Evans sent cables for the first night. All the dignitaries in Pretoria and their wives turned out, including the Governor-General and the High Commissioner, Sir Edward Harding. A profit was made on a production that cost £200. Gwen described a typical production problem that beset her. There were no dimmers to be found in the Lecture Hall. She persuaded the electrician from the nearby municipal hall to help. He brought over two dimmers, fixed them up and made another from a soap-box. The variety of gelatines that was required was to be taken from one of those packing cases that Gwen had brought from England.[22] Their next venture was to stage *To See Ourselves* by E. M. Delafield. Marda was to take the part she had already performed in the London production. Their company, still largely amateur, was becoming aware of the greater possibilities of extending their repertoire, of touring, and of working independently of the Afrikaans Volkstheater, a group or 'firm' as Gwen calls them that was having a stifling effect on her company's ambitions. However, the time had not yet come for them to launch their own company, and their next production was still under the auspices of the Afrikaans Volkstheater. It was Shaw's *Major Barbara*. The director was an accomplished South African, Léontine Sagan, who also took the part of Lady Britomart. Gwen, who had played so many Shavian roles, came to the part of Major Barbara for the first time. For South African theatre the event was looked on as epoch-making.

'It is with the greatest pleasure that I record the reappearance of the theatre proper in South Africa. After a dismal period of several years during which melodrama companies sought to revive public interest with the lowest of plays and various quasi-amateurs presented shoddy productions, the true theatre has at last appeared. Its renaissance began on October 4, 1940, when African Theatres presented Gwen Ffrangcon-Davies in *Major Barbara* produced by Léontine Sagan at the Standard Theatre, Johannesburg.

I do not propose to review the play - to pay totally redundant tribute to the superb artistry of Miss Ffrangcon-Davies or to praise the polished production of Miss Sagan, the remarkably high standard of the acting of the male members of the cast or the sound work of the supporting players; but I do propose to mention the exceptional pleasure which effortless acting and faultless production revived in those who had almost forgotten that South Africa theatre was capable of inspiring it.'[23] Thelma Gutsche, *Forum,* October 1940

The central part of Thelma Gutsche's article deals with the diet of films that the South African public has been served with, namely what she terms the rude stimulation of the cinema at the expense of the amateur stage. Gwen also had taken this line in her correspondence, laying the blame directly on the Afrikaans Volkstheater, which deliberately chose well-known films at a time when a stage presentation of any quality might be offered. The undermining of quality, restricted vision, and financial meanness were some of the criticisms raised against the Volkstheater which made Gwen resolved to break away from their clutches at the earliest opportunity.

'*Major Barbara* which I did with African Theatres and Sagan was a riot - acclaimed as the finest thing S. A. had seen for years - It was no great shakes by our standards...African Theatres are a loathsome firm - just on a par with some of our worst touring managers - no standards or taste and afraid to spend any money – To their amazement Shaw and self combined to make a

Gwen as Major Barbara in South Africa, 1940

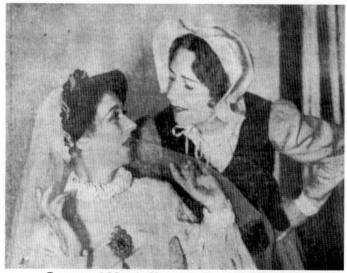

Gwen and Marda Vanne in *Twelfth Night* 1941

gross receipt of over £2000 - since when they would put on anything I wanted - But I would never work again with them on their terms, or be associated with such a shoddy production. So it looks as though we'll have to start on our own after Xmas - Greatly daring we put on *Twelfth Night* for our last show of the season. It *was* a gamble, with a cast who had none of them ever spoken a word of Shakespeare to an audience who were very anti...Also we put into practice our idea of bringing the English and Afrikaans sections together, and Viola and Olivia were Afrikaans actresses who had never played in English before!! You can imagine the work - 9 weeks rehearsals every night and private coaching in the day - We had a charming set inspired by the Granville Barker...The costumes were designed by me, again mostly copies of Motley ones or at any rate inspired by them - We got lovely stuffs, odd remnants at bargain prices - and really they would be a credit to any theatre - one of the big shops made them for us for nothing - an excellent English girl in charge who cuts and fits very well indeed, but who had no knowledge of period clothes - here my practical experience of Glastonbury and Birmingham days stood me in good stead, because I could show her exactly how to cut and fit and pad and stiffen...All the jewellery I made myself, having brought out boxes of treasure from London and what a good thing we did, as there was not an artificial pearl to be had in S.A!! All the braids I got as throw outs from a furniture shop at a 1d or 2d a yard - miles of it! I made all the boots from felt mounted on to tennis shoes, we made sword belts and hilts on to modern fencing foils and sheaths, in fact our inventiveness never stopped and the result was we had 23 most beautiful costumes with hats, shoes, boots, swords, and all accessories for £54!!!'[24]

Gwen's great success as Major Barbara would have guaranteed a full house for *Twelfth Night.* Yet, even without her playing in the original cast, there was an enthusiastic audience response. Cecil Williams who had played the part of Adolphus Cussins in *Major Barbara,* played Duke Orsino in *Twelfth Night*; Marda played Maria. Gwen paid special attention to the actress playing Olivia.

'Olivia is small and exquisite and wears her clothes beautifully. We have produced her in the way John (Gielgud) always wanted me to play - like a tiny Spanish Infanta rather precious and sure of herself until she falls for Caesario, and then a touching(?) child so real in her passion and Viola too. They neither of them know enough to have tricks and be phoney though both have been on the professional stage for some years. They are *actresses* and have entered a new world of magic and delight.'[25]

Gwen's enthusiasm for the actress playing Olivia waned somewhat when the company was due to present *Twelfth Night* to the troops at the Garrison Theatre.

'I had to play Olivia at the last moment, as Miss Grunewald, one of our Afrikaaners, waited until two days before the show and then told us she couldn't bring herself to play to soldiers as they had insulted and outraged "her people" (there had been riots in Jo'burg between the military and Afrikaaners).'[26]

It says much for Gwen that Berdine Grunewald and she remained staunch friends for the rest of their lives.

With extraordinary boldness Gwen and Marda began to plan their own professional touring company, with all its attendant administrative, financial and artistic hazards.

By the autumn of 1941 they had formed their own company and published their programme. The company played in Pretoria, Johannesburg, Maritzburg, Durban, and then moved on to the Cape. Their programme comprised *Twelfth Night*, with a much changed cast from the original production, and James Barrie's *Quality Street*. Gwen and Marda performed in both plays for most of the tour. The country's press acknowledged the great benefit that the company's performances had brought to all the communities where the plays had been staged. The houses were packed in the evenings, and in addition the schools came to the matinée performances of *Twelfth Night*, and on many occasions the company visited the schools. The work of the company was met on nearly every occasion with great enthusiasm.

The *Cape Argus* September 10, 1941, published an article giving an account of an interview with Gwen, in which she outlined her hopes for the future of the theatre in South Africa:

'Miss Ffrangcon-Davies is enthusiastic about the response in South Africa to what might be called their revival of the theatre and she said this morning that the success of the tour so far encourages them to hope for the establishment of a permanent theatre in the Union, the formation of a permanent company, or two permanent companies, which would tour the country more or less continuously.

Such a company, or companies, would have to be on a professional basis for, as she pointed out, "no art can produce anything of importance unless one devotes all one's time to it. Art is no spare time job."

A large proportion of the present company are Afrikaans speaking players and Miss Ffrangcon-Davies hopes, in the near future, to be able to put on Afrikaans plays as well as English ones. She feels that such work can do much to consolidate the two races in this country.

She has been, she says, particularly delighted with the response from children and young people to Shakespeare. "They make the most wonderful audience," she went on, "their response is just what you would find at the Old Vic. And these are the future South African audiences. They are discovering that Shakespeare is not dull as they thought, but exciting and amusing - and contemporary." '[27]

Gwen's and Marda's work was referred to in the press as 'a mission'. This, of course, was the way they thought about it themselves. It was showing every sign of succeeding at both cultural and political levels. Support was being promised by the South African government and also by the British Council.

At this moment Gwen received an urgent request from John Gielgud in England: he was planning to produce *Macbeth*; an extended tour in the provinces was planned before bringing the play to London; would Gwen return to play Lady

Macbeth? She accepted Gielgud's offer and made plans to return to England. However, before she left South Africa she received a letter from the Provincial Secretary of the Administration Office of the Transvaal:

'Now that you are on the point of leaving us, I have been asked by His Honour the Administrator, General Pienaar, to convey to you his appreciation of the splendid work you, in cooperation with Miss Marda Vanne, have done in the field of dramatic art in the public schools of the Transvaal. As I have had occasion to say to you, you have not only re-awakened the interest of our people in legitimate stage and drama, but you have proved how greatly South Africa felt the need of that art.

However much the adult population appreciated your public performances, the work you did amongst our schools, both in those institutions themselves and through the medium of your presentations in the theatres, has been of incalculable value.

General Pienaar, as you know, takes great interest in the development of dramatic art in the Transvaal. He has set his heart upon the establishment of a national theatre in South Africa. He feels that you and Miss Vanne, more than anybody else, have given a new impetus to this movement, and that a great deal may be done here through the medium of a national theatre to knit together the two races in South Africa.

General Pienaar joins me in congratulating you upon being chosen to play the lead with John Gielgud in *Macbeth*, but we hope that when your season in England is over, we may again have at our disposal the benefit not only of your talents, but your enthusiasm for your art. In short, we are not saying "goodbye" but "au revoir".

Once more, our grateful thanks for the great work you did for dramatic art during your all too short stay in South Africa.'[28]

The letter was dated 7th November 1941. When Gwen left for England shortly afterwards she felt, at least figuratively, a fair wind filling her sails.

Lady Macbeth

When Gwen sailed from South Africa she left Marda with the responsibility of keeping their touring company in being until her return. There was a new programme to plan, fresh plays to choose, new venues to explore and, above all, the need to maintain the loyalty and sense of mission among the actors and actresses who, by the very nature of their work, felt under constant stress; moreover, their tireless efforts reaped very little monetary return. The letters from Marda to Gwen for the next year detailed all these problems but, more than anything else, they showed Marda's emotional need of Gwen as a steadying influence. She lacked Gwen's leadership qualities and sound judgement. From the time that Gwen had landed in a much-bombed Britain to the time she left again for South Africa, after a year's most strenuous work, she was constantly harassed by Marda's personal and professional problems. She responded with patient and wise counsel, but this was called for at a time when her own personal life was again in turmoil, and when her professional performances had to face the most trenchant criticism.

Gwen had left South Africa trying to explain to Marda that she must be allowed her freedom to act as she thought best. Parting for both had been a deep wrench. Although Gwen knew instinctively that she had to respond positively to John Gielgud's offer for her to play Lady Macbeth, she also realised that in playing this part again she would do so, under Gielgud's guidance, in her own imaginative way. That way was not acceptable to the critics and they, almost without exception, condemned it. Her reputation and her whole career seemed to hang in the balance.

Why had Gielgud chosen *Macbeth* as the play in which he and his dedicated cast would invest nearly a year of their lives at such a critical time, 1941-42? He had played Macbeth before, at the Old Vic in 1930, and then had recognised his limitation in the part. 'I knew I would not be able to play the warrior, but I found a romantic and visionary quality in the character,' he had written.[29] Now he seemed compulsively drawn once again to the poetry and the passion of the play. In choosing Gwen as Lady Macbeth, he was well aware of the criticism which Agate had levelled against her performance of the part in Oxford, 1930. He fully realised that some of the critics would say that both the main characters had been miscast. His aim, however, was larger than personal ambition.

As with the 1938 production of *The Three Sisters* he wanted to create a work of art of outstanding beauty and truth. This time it would be based on the work of an Englishman, not a Russian. It would have its settings and costumes designed by one of the most brilliant artists and sculptors in the country, the young Michael Ayrton, and the music was to be composed by William Walton. Gwen, writing to her sister Marjorie, recounted that after a performance of the play in Glasgow in February 1942, Gielgud in his curtain speech had said that 'he wanted the theatre to have at any rate one worthy production of Shakespeare in these dark times - and the house rose to him.'[30] It was not, of course, just in Glasgow that the house responded in this way. Throughout the extensive tour the provincial towns responded in a similar manner. When the players reached Coventry, they had to stay in a hotel in Warwick, because all the Coventry hotels had been flattened by the bombing, but the audiences in Coventry were larger than anywhere else on their tour. Gwen asked in amazement: 'Where do they all come from?'[31] Gielgud succeeded in putting before the English - and Scottish - people, a work of great beauty by an English playwright, when the survival of England itself as a free country was in the utmost peril.

Hugh (Binkie) Beaumont had planned for the production with John Gielgud. Their intention was to open in Manchester in January 1942 without inviting the London drama critics, and then to move on to Glasgow and Edinburgh. The weather over this January/February period was extremely cold, with heavy snowfalls. Before the opening, rehearsals were held until 5 a.m. each day[32] and, after the opening, rehearsals continued for the many months ahead, until the play reached London, and was presented at the Piccadilly Theatre in July. Improvements were continuously being made, characterisations sharpened, and subtleties and nuances added. There were also grimmer reasons for some rehearsals. In theatrical circles *Macbeth* is thought to have a curse on it. In this production, one of the witches, Beatrix Fielden-Kay died within the first week; on tour Marcus Barron, who played Duncan, also died, and Milton Rosmer, playing Banquo, fell ill.[33] In Glasgow, Gwen bumped into a lamp-post at night in the blackout and had to go on

Lady Macbeth, 1942, with John Gieldgud as Macbeth

113

stage for about five nights with a bruised and swollen black eye. Following the first night, the account appearing in the *Manchester Guardian* was less than enthusiastic. Gwen felt the brunt of the criticism more than John Gielgud, but the *Sunday Times* report on February 8th written by James Agate, after seeing a performance in Glasgow, was particularly damning, especially of Gwen's interpretation of her role. His criticism, like that of her performance twelve years ago in the Oxford production, hinged on her slight frame. When Gielgud read this account, he suggested to Gwen that she should write to Margaret Drew, and ask her to respond to Agate, referring to Mrs Siddons' comments about the part, taken from one of William Poel's books, which both knew was in Margaret's possession.[34] Margaret Drew's letter to the editor of *The Times*, dated 13th February 1942, appeared the following week. Her refutation of Agate's case against Gwen's Lady Macbeth, based on her inadequate stature, contained the following telling passages:

> Sir,
> I was not a little astonished when reading Mr. Agate's interesting article in your issue of Feb. 8th that in his reference to the casting of Miss Ffrangcon-Davies for the part of Lady Macbeth in Mr. Gielgud's production of *Macbeth*, now touring the provinces, he asks: "Has anybody, reading *Macbeth*, ever conjured up a small, slight figure?" One reader, at least has; a lady whose name will be identified with the part perhaps for all time. I refer to Mrs. Siddons, who wrote of Lady Macbeth as "a character which I believe is generally allowed to be the most captivating to the other sex, fair, feminine, nay, perhaps even fragilè".
> Dr. Bucknill...held a similar view... "probably she was small, for it is the smaller sort of woman whose emotional fire is the most fierce, and she herself bears unconscious testimony to the fact that her hand was little."[She then cited Professor Dowden's reference to Lady Macbeth as "probably having a delicate frame filled with high-strung nervous energy."] May I conclude by quoting from that great Shakespearean scholar Mr Granville Barker? "There is certainly no textual evidence that Lady Macbeth was physically fragile...but the dramatic gain in making her so is hardly disputable. The effect of the undaunted spirit is doubled if we marvel that so frail a body can contain it".[35]

Gwen was fully aware of some of her own inadequacies in the role when the play opened in Manchester, but in her letters to Margaret Drew and her sister, Marjorie, she described how, with constant rehearsal, she was able to refine her performance. Tyrone Guthrie and Alec Guinness went to see the play at Manchester; Sybil Thorndike and Lewis Casson went to a performance in Newcastle; Gordon Daviot spent two weeks in Edinburgh during the play's run there. During that time she and Gwen visited the merchant's house in Leith where Mary Queen of Scots had taken shelter in 1561 on her return from France. Gordon Daviot's *Queen of Scots*, had been dedicated to Gwen. Her performance in that play in 1934 had been acclaimed by the critics, but the play itself disparaged. Now, however, it was not Shakespeare's play that was being disparaged, but her interpretion of Lady Macbeth. Her friends, knowing that she was under a fearsome attack from the drama critics, gave her what support they could. Above all, John

Gielgud continued throughout the run to express his great pleasure at the accomplishment of her interpretation of the role of Lady Macbeth. On the day that Agate's review of the play was published John Gielgud wrote to her, on a small card in his tiniest writing:

'Darling Gwen –
    I know the light of battle is in your eye to-day, and you have only to step onto the stage and let 'em have it. I have not been the half I should have liked to be - but I can assure you that your performance is of real beauty and that you are going to have a big triumph -
    You said once you did not disdain cheap jewellery - so here is a little bit - do change it if you don't like it -
        Much love, my dear, and a thousand thanks
            And good wishes
                                                                John'[36]

Barbara Ayrton Gould, Michael Ayrton's mother, had seen the play at Manchester and again in July at the Piccadilly Theatre. On her second visit she found it 'tremendously improved' and wrote to Gwen:

'I feel I must tell you how much I have again enjoyed your very fine Lady Macbeth.
    I would not have ventured to bother you with a letter...if I had not been so enraged with nearly all the criticisms I have read about your rendering of the part. Dramatic critics seem to me to be incredibly stupid and prejudiced. They seem to have decided that Lady Macbeth was a female Macbeth and that no other reading of the part is possible...Your rendering of the part appears to me not only a fine performance in itself, but to show the woman and her development of character as I believe Shakespeare saw it. So I feel I must tell you that you have given me the first really satisfying Lady Macbeth I have ever seen.'[37]

James Bridie, also repudiating James Agate's criticism, added his support:

'I thought what J. A. wrote about your Lady M. was idiotic and also infuriating. So I slept on it and answered him. I had better answers still, but I thought he had had enough.'[38]

Tyrone Guthrie reflected on Gwen's performance in *A Life in the Theatre*:

'It is often said that we owe to Mrs. Siddons the "tradition" of Lady Macbeth as a beefy, booming contralto. But this hardly squares with the sort of performance which a boy would have given in the original production; nor, to my mind, with the music and balance of the text. Much the best Lady Macbeth I ever saw was the Welsh actress, Gwen Ffrangcon-Davies. She suggested a wild ambitious spirit in a small and fragile person. I read no professional critic's notice which did not say she was miscast.'[39]

Despite the adverse reports from the critics Macbeth attracted large audiences and ran in London until the end of October. Then, with only one week's intermission *The Importance of Being Earnest* was staged once again, but now at the Phoenix. On this occasion, because Edith Evans was not available, Gwen was asked to play Lady Bracknell. She gave her own interpretation of the role, and scrupulously avoided giving an impression of Edith Evans playing Lady Bracknell. The 'handbag' was scarcely emphasised at all.

The time had now come for Gwen to return to South Africa. Awaiting her there was the major task of rescuing her touring company from the morass of mismanagement that had occurred in her absence.

South Africa 1943-1948

During the year that Gwen spent in England her friends in South Africa had followed her career with great interest, reading the reviews of *Macbeth* and *The Importance of Being Earnest*, and listening to her broadcasts. They longed for her to return to take up again the work with her theatre group. Marda had maintained a flow of correspondence, pressing her to this end. She frankly admitted her own inadequacies as leader, manager, organiser, and financial director. In Gwen's absence the company had lost large sums of money, at times played to only a handful of people in out of the way places and, worst of all, were on the point of disintegration because of internal feuding. There must have been moments, in the midst of this disarray, when Marda doubted whether Gwen would ever return. Writing on notepaper headed 'Marda Vanne, Gwen Ffrangcon-Davies: Shakespearean Company', she had not disguised the degree of her mismanagement nor, in her view, the shoddiness of the performances and the bad behaviour of the cast. She must have recalled sharply Gordon Daviot's warning that if she went with Gwen to South Africa, Gwen's return to England as a professional actress would be put at hazard. Now that Gwen had returned to England and starred in plays with her friend, John Gielgud, one of the most prestigious figures in the English theatre, would she ever set foot in South Africa again? John Gielgud had written to Marda from Glasgow in February 1942, expressing his appreciation of Marda's not dissuading Gwen from returning to England to join his company. He explained how both he and Gwen, although not in the tradition of the leading roles in *Macbeth* were, nevertheless, rehearsing constantly to improve their performances, and were greatly enjoying once again their professional and personal association.[40] The unexpected prolongation of the provincial tour, the lateness in the season of the staging of *Macbeth* at the Piccadilly, and then the surprise presentation of *The Importance of Being Earnest*, all added to Marda's dread that Gwen would stay in England. For the sake of her own sanity, however, she had to believe in Gwen's promise to return, and she voiced that faith in a letter dated 9th September 1942:

'...Whether I am personally happy or unhappy, good or bad, disgruntled or on top of the world, it is you my arms go to, you I seek to comfort or be comforted by. There is someone in the world who knows beyond all doubt that you are one of those few people to whom the word GREAT applies. Many people - all those who count, know that you are a great actress. Some people - all who have the privilege of your friendship, know you for a brave and pure-hearted woman; and I, who have worshipped and harassed you through our many years together, know you to be one of God's own, dearly loved, children. What I want to try and tell you tonight, so that you will remember *it always,* especially when the personal Ego has been hurt, is that in all the years I have known you I have watched you living your life to the glory of God. I have never seen you do a mean or cruel thing. I have never seen you fail a fellow human being. If a poor mutt like myself can find inspiration in your lucid and beautiful way of living, remember that others too are affected by it, not only in your work, but in yourself. God our Father which is in heaven, knows His own. And you are one of these.'[41]

Marda was, above all, desperate for Gwen's return for personal reasons. The group of actors, too, yearned for her return as their leader. She alone, they felt, could give them again their sense of direction and mission. There had been a feeling, when Gwen and Marda first started their theatre work in South Africa, that other stars from England would follow. Letters and telegrams with goodwill greetings from John Gielgud and Edith Evans were read to the company and sometimes to the audiences. It was hoped that, once the theatre company had been established, John Gielgud and Edith Evans would join them in their South African theatrical adventure. This hope is frequently articulated by Marda. Although that hope was never fulfilled in the way envisaged, Edith Evans did pay an extended visit to South Africa to see Gwen and Marda in 1947, and John Gielgud in 1953 brought to Bulawayo his production of *Richard II.*

Gwen had told Marda and the company that she would return, and return she did. She regrouped the company, and planned her programme for the autumn of 1943. An early task was to lobby the government for support for her company in the short term, and for the setting up of a national theatre in the long term. Gwen opened her campaign on two fronts: literary and political. She gave a number of lecture-recitals on Shakespeare, and she undertook many broadcasts. These broadcasts comprised talks about the theatre, her performance in radio plays, and recollections of the famous people she had known, such as Thomas Hardy, Bernard Shaw, Walter Sickert, and her own father, David Ffrangcon-Davies. The newspapers throughout South Africa, from Pretoria to the Cape, were eager to receive contributions from her concerning the state of the theatre in South Africa, and the direction in which it might develop. Gwen was only too pleased to respond. She outlined the principles of, what was now called, the Gwen Ffrangcon-Davies and Marda Vanne Company. The Company's aim was to raise standards of public taste and judgement and counter undesirable reactions provoked by the strains of war. It was to help to give to the people a sense of balance, of international understanding, and to create an enlightenment that would make less likely the rise of a Hitler or Mussolini. She referred to the creation in Britain in 1940 of CEMA, the Council for the Encouragement of Music and the Arts. The Council had brought about a renaissance of the arts in Britain, achieved through State support. CEMA's function was to enable the best available art, music, and drama to be taken to the country's much dispersed population. Gwen could speak with personal experience of the need and the effectiveness of such a policy, because the tour of *Macbeth* in 1942 had been supported with CEMA funding. Her argument was, of course, that as deep a hunger for the arts existed in South Africa as in Britain, and the government of the country should seriously consider setting up a similar organisation. She stressed the importance of avoiding the irony of fighting a war to preserve one's culture, but surrendering it to mental sloth. In this context she extolled the work of the British Council, an organisation that helped generously in the years ahead to underpin her work in South Africa.[42]

The programme for the touring company in the autumn of 1943 featured *Flare Path*, *Watch on the Rhine*, and *What Every Woman Knows*. Gwen stressed how difficult it was to keep together a group of amateur actors for an extended tour. Many had given up their regular employment on a temporary basis for the period of the tour. The Company was founded on a non-profit-making basis. Any profit that was made was ploughed back to help finance the next tour. Players were paid a pittance during the tours, and were paid nothing between one tour and another. There was need for the State to help meet the salaries of the cast for those periods when they were not acting. In her vigorous campaign for her cause, Gwen's voice was heard through the press and on the radio throughout South Africa. The response seemed slow, but she succeeded eventually in eliciting financial support from both the South African government and from the British Council. A good deal of her time was spent lobbying local and national government officials. Social gatherings were held following the opening nights of productions, local dignitaries and their wives were regularly photographed with Gwen and Marda, and there were several occasions when they met the President and his wife, General and Mrs Smuts. The first step towards securing State aid lay in receiving the patronage and financial help from South Africa's influential élite. When the 1944 Spring tour came to an end in Cape Town Gwen described how the patrons

'all came on the stage afterwards - It was quite an occasion - We are by way of having a very good snob value public - as our supporters number most of the influential people in SA one way or another. We have been so wonderfully led and protected. And now I don't think any "vested interest" will dare to interfere with us because we have the Press solidly behind us - and the Rhodes Trustee here is John Martin, the chairman of the Corner House...He has handed us over to his aide de camp, a charming man called Richdale, who has constituted himself our financial adviser and is a tower of strength. It is rather like being adopted by the Bank of England! I sometimes feel a slight twinge at being helped by the "bloated capitalist" but until such time as the State is willing to support art, one must take what one can and be thankful.'[43]

In this letter to Marjorie, Gwen also gave an account of a tea party given by the Governor-General of the Cape Province at Government House, at which she first met Mrs Smuts:

'She is the quaintest old soul, dresses like any charwoman and was sporting a particularly dashing line in grey men's socks which came half way up her calf. This with ankle-strap, square-toe shoes, gave her a very unusual look! She never wears a hat and is quite unconcerned as to her appearance. In fact she reminds me of Lil Bayliss. We had a great getting together because her daughter is married to Bancroft Clark - you remember the Clarks at Glastonbury? And so I was able to tell her a lot about him and Roger and Sarah, as she has never been overseas.'[44]

Other plays which the company performed during this period included *Blithe Spirit, Milestones, The Merry Wives of Windsor, The Wind of Heaven,* and *The Taming of the Shrew.* Gwen and Marda directed all of them and acted in each play except *The Taming of the Shrew.* Noel Coward had been glad to give his permission for them to perform *Blithe Spirit,* and had met them in South Africa, in both the Cape and Pretoria, but had returned to England before the first night. This play proved a great box-office success. Replying to news of the success, Noel Coward in his letter to Gwen and Marda, dated 16 October 1944, rejoiced with them. He described how he had returned to a London and found 'the doodlebug offensive still in full swing'. He told them that he 'had done a film-script...based on one of the "To-Night at 8.30" plays - one called *Still Life...*It all took place in a railway station.' And then, knowing that his friends in South Africa were agog to hear what was happening in London's theatre world, he ended his letter with

'The London theatres hit an awful slump during the doodlebug time but now they are all booming again, including *Blithers* which is playing to capacity. I went to the first night of John's repertory at the Haymarket. They opened with *The Circle* in which Yvonne Arnaud is magnificent. On Friday night they did *Hamlet* - interesting and a first rate production. I think Larry's *Richard III* is, without qualification, the greatest acting performance I have ever seen on any stage.

I ate a great deal of garlic the other night and thought lovingly of you both.
Love love love
Noel'[45]

Blithe Spirit formed part of the fourth tour of the Gwen Ffrangcon-Davies and Marda Vanne Company. It had been scheduled for a four week run at the Standard Theatre, Johannesburg, but, because of the great interest shown in the production, the run was extended to six weeks. *Milestones,* a period piece in three eras: 1860, 1885, and 1912 written by Arnold Bennett in collaboration with Edward Knoblock, was also in the repertoire. Gwen was meticulous in paying detailed attention to the period differences in costume, furniture, and décor, and the audiences and the critics were warm in their appreciation of such niceties. A genuine education in taste and discrimination was being inculcated not only by the plays themselves, but also by the way they were presented. 'Miss Ffrangcon-Davies' had proved herself 'an authority on the set of an English ruffle, the cut of a thigh boot, and the shape of a Victorian chair - even the spectacles worn in *Quality Street* were genuine antiques'.[46]

The Merry Wives of Windsor was planned in the autumn of 1944 and opened in Pretoria on 14 April 1945. It was the company's most ambitious production to date. John Dronsfield designed the costumes and set, and his paintings of these were exhibited at the Argus Gallery, Johannesburg, at the time that the play was being staged. It attracted a great deal of attention. The changes of scenery were achieved by the turning of a page of a huge book that acted as a back-cloth. The costumes and colour scheme, suggested by Gwen, were based on a painting by Piero della Francesca. Both Marjorie and Margaret Drew received a series of graphic letters about the problems that beset the company in staging the play. One great comfort, however, was that the wigs had arrived from London in a box carrying Nathans' label. That gave Gwen and Marda a glow of nostalgic satisfaction, especially as the box had reached South Africa in the Diplomatic Bag! Gwen played Mistress Page, Marda Mistress Ford, Wensley Pithy Falstaff, and Rolf Lefebvre Master Ford. Most frustrating was the dearth of men for the parts. Enlistment for war-service was a fundamental reason. Some actors were recruited for limited periods from the armed forces. Gwen was desperate to find men to play the parts of Slender, Shallow, Page, and the Host. Young men of only twenty-one years old eventually filled the parts of Shallow and the Host. Mistress Quickly had a bad attack of sciatica and withdrew within a few days of production. The stage manager fell over and wrenched the ligaments in his leg. Falstaff was unable to attend the dress rehearsal because in playing his part he was given to such excessive sweating that he had lost all the salt from his system and fainted. But come the first night, the play and its presentation worked their magic on the audience, and the company knew that they had a success on their hands. The play toured for four months, at the end of which, when Gwen sat down to take administrative stock, she noted that it had been seen by 62,000 adults and 8,000 schoolchildren.

In the autumn of 1945 a decision was made to produce Emlyn Williams's *The Wind of Heaven*. There was much correspondence between the author and Gwen about staging details, in particular the importance of the background music. Emlyn Williams gave a detailed account of the music used previously, and the points in the play at which it was played. He went further and promised to send the records to South Africa. Once the play had been launched in Pretoria, Gwen sent Emlyn Williams the press cuttings, which greatly impressed him, as did her estimate of Marda's performance of the part of Bet, 'the best and truest thing she has done in her whole career'.[47] The play received its first performance in England only a few months before its South African opening. Its underlying religious theme was not to everyone's taste, but the presentation, with costumes and décor by Gwen, was universally applauded. The play that followed was Turgenev's *A Month in the Country*, designed and directed by Gwen, and she also took the leading role of Natalia. With this elegant, gracious, and subtle production the company's touring season came to an end. In the autumn Gwen flew to England for a short break, not to rest or recuperate, but to plan for the propitious year ahead, when she knew that the royal family would be visiting South Africa.

It was during this visit to England that she first met Sir Terence Nugent, later to become Lord Nugent. He had accompanied the Duke and Duchess of York on their visit to Australia and New Zealand in 1927. At the time that Gwen first met him he was Comptroller to the Lord Chamberlain. He and his wife, Rosalie, were deeply interested in the theatre. Part of his official job, of course, was concerned with the propriety of the plays offered to the public. Gwen, in anticipation of the royal visit to South Africa in the spring of 1947, had in mind a gala theatrical presentation. Nugent advised her on this. He put her in touch with influential acquaintances in South Africa as well as with his senior colleague, Sir Alan Lascelles who, he told Gwen, was another of her particular admirers, having seen

120

The Immortal Hour nine times. Gwen returned to South Africa well-briefed but she did not present her gala performance in Pretoria, because Nugent had pointed out that the King and Queen would be there on Easter Sunday, and a public theatrical performance on that day would almost certainly give offence in some quarters. Nugent and his wife were in South Africa at the time of the royal visit, and renewed their acquaintance with Gwen. She and Marda were invited to meet the royal family on one or two occasions, the most significant of which was an informal dinner for sixteen people. Gwen and Marda sat either side of the King; the Queen sat opposite them. After dinner the Queen and the Princesses were most interested to hear of the company's theatre mission in South Africa and, in exchange, they brought Gwen and Marda quite up to date, in a most informed way, with the latest happenings in the world of the London theatre.[48]

Gwen had invited Edith Evans to join her and Marda for a holiday in South Africa. They had planned for this holiday to begin in early April 1947, but it was delayed for a few weeks because of the death of Edith's father. After the funeral Edith spent a few days in Brussels. She had previously written to Gwen asking for advice about the nature of the wardrobe she should take with her to South Africa. She expressed concern that she should be correctly dressed for those garden parties on the High Commissioner's lawn and for the dinner parties at Government House. On the same day that she returned from Brussels she wrote to Gwen:

'...So many thanks for all the tips about clothes. I can, I think just about make it if one of the dinner dresses will do for the problematical dinner at G.H. However the hat for the cocktail party is a bit of a difficulty, as I ought to have one of those bits of nonsense that are so difficult to pack...What a thrill to dine with the T.Ns [Nugents]. How darling of them to think of it. They must have been very pleased to see you. Tommy Lascelles is a very great Fan of yours. ...The plan for the holiday staggers me...It is terribly good of you to plan such a wonderful trip. It is such an enormous step in my development: this getting around. Though I shall try to get out of the plane a little less like hat stand, than I did this afternoon, having brought back eggs, butter, casseroles, and bottles of champagne etc for the starving English. Not very elegant Miss G. F-D.'[49]

As a young girl Edith Evan's first job was that of a milliner. She was never very deft, as Gwen was, at the making of hats, but she knew how to wear them. Her circle of friends encompassed Nugent and Lascelles, but the nub of her holiday experience was not the social occasions, but the many new sensations encountered on their journey through great tracts of the African continent. She set out with Gwen, Marda and their friends, the Knox-Shaws and Hendersons. They travelled in two cars towards Rhodesia. Gwen, in letters to Marjorie, described their journey:

'We went to the famous ruins of Zimbabwe - Rider Haggard is supposed to have been inspired to write *King Solomon's Mines* by them - They are an African equivalent of Stonehenge, but how or when they were built is a complete mystery.'[50]

'The Victoria Falls were if anything even more wonderful than the first time I saw them and the superb vista from the top of the Matopo Hills where

121

Rhodes grave is - at sunset - with the huge granite boulders turning to purple in the evening light is something I shall always remember. To make the picture quite perfect - there were bloodcurdling shrieks from distant Kloof - where baboons and leopards were engaged in a to-the-death struggle. It completed the weird and Macbeth-like atmosphere...Edith is enjoying her holiday immensely and is, I'm glad to say, delighted with the Knox-Shaws...he is the chief astronomer at the Ratcliffe Observatory in Pretoria, and she is very intelligent...and great fun.'[51]

Edith Evans's friendship with the Knox-Shaws was to be cherished when she returned to England. At the end of the holiday Gwen and Edith spent a restful week together in Cape Town. There they met Francis Brett Young and his wife, who had just bought a small house overlooking the sea.[52] As Edith Evans began her voyage back to England at the beginning of August 1947, Gwen turned her mind once more to the programme for her company for the coming year. The first choice of play was *The Taming of the Shrew*. The production was planned and rehearsals were scheduled to start in the following spring.[53]

Gwen with Edith Evans and Marda Vanne in South Africa, 1947

Gwen produced *The Taming of the Shrew* with Marda's assistance, but for a change neither of them performed in the play. They used a revolve to create continuity of performance, which increased rehearsal time. In addition the costumes needed many adjustments. Gwen found herself working through the night and, as she explained to Margaret Drew, kept herself going on tea and Benzedrine.[54] However, once the play had opened, she categorised it as 'a smash hit'. It proved a money-spinner. And money just now was of great importance. Gwen and Marda, in their work in the theatre, had established style, quality, and artistic accomplishment. They themselves had received for their pay no more than any other member of the professional cast: £10 a week. Any profit was required for an ambitious project. A plan was afoot in Johannesburg to break the monopoly of the

African Theatres Trust, which controlled the large music-hall venues for solely commercial purposes. The municipality had agreed to make a grant of £20,000, and voluntary sources had raised £35,000 for the building of the first small independent theatre in the city, to be run on professional lines for the performance of straight plays.[55] The success of *The Taming of the Shrew* was a material factor in advancing this project.

The Taming of the Shrew opened in April 1948. Gwen's thoughts were then turning to England, and she was making plans to visit again in the late summer and stay for at least a year. She had recently entertained some distinguished friends from England. Ivor Novello had arrived in the autumn of 1947 with his company to perform *Perchance to Dream*. He was an old family friend. He and his partner, Bobby Andrews, spent a couple of weekends in Pretoria, staying with Gwen and Marda. Later they enjoyed a very leisurely Christmas, at Hermanns, Gwen's favourite holiday resort on the Cape coast. In March 1948 Gwen was asked to organise all the arrangements for the short stay that Laurence Olivier, Vivien Leigh, and the Old Vic Company would make in Cape Town on their way to their drama tour of Australia.

'I organised all their engagements re press etc - also made plans for them to be entertained at a heavenly Dutch farm - and all the company - 30 in all - quite an undertaking. But it was a wild success, ending up with a cocktail party at High Commission House for them - to meet a few important editors and Cabinet Ministers.'[56]

Gwen with Ivor Novello in South Africa 1948

Ivor Novello had stayed in South Africa to add his greetings to Laurence Olivier and Vivien Leigh, who were termed by Gwen 'the uncrowned king and queen of stage and screen'. News of the London theatre scene was now reaching Gwen, not just through those letters from Margaret Drew, but from the stars themselves. The pull to return to that scene was, for Gwen, overwhelming. There were other reasons too. She had felt once more the need to assert her claim to personal freedom. In a letter to her sister, dated 28th August 1947, she wrote:

'My personal problem is working out I think - and Edith's visit brought a lot of things to a head - but there is a great change in M. the last few weeks and a sincere desire to do better and I believe that we can work out to a greater sense of freedom and happiness - I am not saying any more because I am awake to what needs to be changed - and changed it will be...every individual has a right to freedom and that I must have ...'[57]

Gwen returned to England and soon afterwards travelled to Vienna to stay with her sister for ten days. When she eventually arrived back in England, uppermost in her mind was whether she would be offered any work. She had her freedom, but what was freedom without work?

Parcels and Letters

Gwen had left England in March 1940, just before the Germans opened their offensive on the western front. From the moment she arrived in South Africa she was greeted by a stream of letters from her sister, nieces, aunts, theatre colleagues, and many other friends, telling her of the seemingly ceaseless air-raids and the devastation caused by the high explosive and incendiary bombs. Even at the end of the war she was made personally aware, by her visit in 1946, of the food shortage and deprivations caused by a stringent rationing system, which continued for many years after peace had been declared. Her absorption in her work to raise the standards of theatrical productions in South Africa allayed some conscience pangs for her defection. The long hours she worked, the extraordinary responsibilities she shouldered, and her refusal to pay heed to her own financial security - she was mostly overdrawn on her accounts in England and South Africa - signalled her inward recognition of the plight of her countrymen. A new urgency and dedication had entered her life.

When she returned to South Africa at the end of 1942 she resolved that she would set by whatever money she earned for her broadcasts to send parcels to her friends and family in England. This resolve she carried through with astonishing thoroughness. Within a few years she had sent well over four hundred parcels. She calculated the need of each recipient and packed her parcels accordingly. The parcels contained clothing, especially stockings, butter, cooking fats, raisins and all sorts of dried fruit, chocolate, tinned meats, tinned milk, tea, coffee, flour, sugar, soap, and cheese. To Marjorie, freezing in Vienna in the winter of 1946/47 she sent a spirit stove and its fuel, a paraffin stove and its fuel, many parcels of warm clothes, and a special seven-pound cheese. Margaret Drew managed to pull round from a series of crippling illnesses through the regular supply of South African chocolate. Terence Nugent expressed to Gwen his and his wife's delight at discovering they had been sent large quantities of dripping. And so the letters of thanks and appreciation came tumbling in: from the aged aunts in Worthing, from Berta Ruck in north Wales, who complained that the raisins had been stolen from her parcel, from Sybil Thorndike, living a frugal life on tour with her husband, Lewis Casson, and from her many theatre friends: Laurence Olivier, Vivien Leigh, John Gielgud, Edith Evans and so on. Her parcels also reached the maids and dressers in London who had worked for her in the past and, towards the end of the war, she sent tinned milk to a friend's daughter who was having difficulty feeding her child in Paris. Gwen's friends in Stambourne were not forgotten. Incendiary bombs had even fallen on that remote village. The folk there, helping to look after Tagley Cottage in the owner's absence, were only too happy to be the regular recipients of food parcels from South Africa.

Her friends knew how deeply Gwen would be missing the London theatre scene, and they took every opportunity to keep her informed. So many of the letters that she received at this time began with thanks for the contents of their parcel followed by an account of plays and players. John Gielgud's letters to Gwen were unusually long, entertaining, humorous, full of anecdotes about their fellow professionals. He kept her up to date about which of their actor friends had been called up and where they had been posted, Glen Byam Shaw, Harry Andrews, George Devine, and exclaimed at how strange he found it that young Alec Guinness should be commanding a mine-sweeper in the Mediterranean. During his far eastern travels with ENSA he told her about their travel programme, the plays they performed, and the various Government Houses they visited. When he toured in the United States and then rested at Noel Coward's property in the West Indies, he gave her a full account of the location and a somewhat critical resumé of the other guests, such as Claudette Colbert and Charles Laughton. Sometimes he wrote more sombrely of colleagues who had lost their lives.

Sybil Thorndike wrote to Gwen regularly throughout her time in South Africa, giving her every encouragement she could in her work there. In a letter dated 9th August 1940 she spent the first three pages of a six-page letter talking about Gwen's work and Gwen's problems, and then she told how her only son, John, who was in the Fleet Air Arm, had been reported missing after the raid on Trondheim in Norway. A month later a telegram came from Geneva to say that Lt. Commander John Casson had been shot down and was a prisoner of war in Germany.

'Yesterday Patricia (his wife) had a letter from him - he didn't crash - he managed to keep control and to go into a fiord and swam till he and his observer were picked up. I can't begin to tell you the relief - and curiously enough it has made me feel more intensely the suffering that so many wives and mothers have now - I never want to have another month like July again.'

She continued her letter with her own plans to take *Macbeth* to the industrial areas of south Wales, and then extolled John Gielgud's work at the Old Vic, *King Lear* and *The Tempest*, with 'how thrilling the acting was'. The letter ended 'God bless you both darling Gwen and Marda - and our love and deep admiration for the work you are doing – it's true service - your loving Sybil (and Lewis)'.[58]

Vivien Leigh in the summer of 1947 had been filming *Caesar and Cleopatra* in the Denham studios. She was pregnant at the time. She fell ill, lost the child and was taken to the University College Hospital, from where she wrote to Gwen on 30th August:

'Darling Gwen,
Do please forgive me for not writing in answer to your lovely long letter long ago, and for not saying how thrilled I was with the beautiful stockings *and* all the goodies. It is most terribly sweet of you and I can't tell you how appre-

ciated they are. I think the pictures of the *Merry Wives* are absolutely lovely...Alas our beloved *Skin of our Teeth* had to be taken off when it was doing so wonderfully, because I have been ordered to rest for six months! - owing to a patch on my right lung...'[59]

She goes on to explain how icy the Denham studios were at the time of their rehearsals, and how this must have contributed to her condition. She ends by urging Gwen to continue to write to her. The lost child is not mentioned. She and her husband had some inkling of how important that child might have been in cementing their marriage. Seven months later Gwen was to greet Laurence Olivier and Vivien Leigh in Cape Town on their way to Australia. Their fragile marriage was scarcely to survive the rigours of that tour.

Edith Evans for a considerable part of her professional life lived in a flat in The Albany. She had a maid called Potter whom she shared from time to time with Gwen. Potter, too, had received a parcel from Gwen, and wrote to thank her:

> '26 Relmerston Rd
> Kilburn
> NW6

Miss Davis, Madam
I received mi parcel quite safe and I do not know how to thank you for the contents which were very acceptable and mi lovely fat I said to Miss Evans I wish Miss Davis was a little nearer so I could send you a jam tart when do you think of coming to England again I often wonder if I shall see you again or think of the happy times we had at Albany I hope you are keeping well and you are having a big success we are having some nice weather not to cold at present but we are all so thankful the war is over and the lights are up again
    Well Miss Davis we shall soon have Xmas here and I hope you will have a happy one
    Once again thanking you for all your kindness to me I remain
>   Yrs Obed
>   Potter'[60]

Gwen was very fond of Potter and would have deeply appreciated this letter, knowing the effort that went in to writing it. Edith Evans also valued Potter, but she probably intoned her name rather as Lady Bracknell had pronounced 'Prism'!

For Gwen the time for sending parcels was over. In November 1941 she had returned to England at the express invitation of John Gielgud, to co-star with him in *Macbeth*. No such invitation had brought her back in 1948. The Shakespearian season at Stratford-upon-Avon particularly attracted her. But would any of the casting directors look her way? Would now that dire prediction of Gordon Daviot come to pass?

'They won't care where or why she went; they will only know that she wasn't visible while they were at war; and in the new world after the peace they will have no use for her...'

Gwen's meridian hour was certainly past; and the afternoon was beginning to lose its warmth.

126

Chapter Five: Early Evening
(1948-1970)

Home-base

When Gwen and Marda bought Tagley Cottage in 1934 they regarded it as an occasional weekend country retreat from their more hectic stage life in London or the rigours of provincial tours. When stage work did not come their way, more time was spent at the cottage. Although not large, the cottage needed regular maintenance. A special 'west wing' was converted for guests. Local labour was recruited for help with cleaning the house, with cooking and with gardening. Also in the early years, a part-time chauffeur was employed to drive and maintain their car. The garden had been laid out with lawns, fruit trees, and a large vegetable patch. Pride of place was given to flowers, roses in particular. Each year there was a systematic replenishing of plants and bulbs. Both Gwen and Marda became keen and industrious gardeners. Gwen was also an accomplished cook, often abetted by Doris, her caretaker-cook and part-time gardener. From time to time other local assistance was called in to help with the garden. Garden produce became the staple part of many of the meals. Weekend parties were held in the cottage: local friends met some of the celebrities who had homes nearby, such as John Gielgud, Dodie Smith, and Diana Wynyard. Christmas time was so regularly celebrated by Gwen at Tagley Cottage with specially invited guests, and in such a detailed repetitive way, always with candles, that it became almost a ritual - a ritual that she maintained to the end of her life.

During the 1939-1945 war years Tagley Cottage had been rented to a variety of tenants, one of whom was the playwright, Terence Rattigan. Another tenant had been Professor J. P. R. Wallis, a South African friend, who had greatly appreciated Gwen's work for the theatre in his country. When in September 1946 he learned that a new production of *Antony and Cleopatra* was planned, for which Edith Evans was due to begin rehearsals in the part of Cleopatra, he wrote a remarkable, closely-reasoned letter to Gwen pointing out how unfortunate such a casting was, and declaring that she alone, of all other actresses, had the accomplishment to fill the role satisfactorily.[1] Wallis was proved right, at least about Edith Evan's suitability for the role. During Gwen's stay in South Africa the cottage was sometimes left empty. She relied on her sister, Marjorie, on Constance MacColl, and on other friends in the neighbourhood to keep her informed about the renting of the cottage and its upkeep. There was a steady stream of parcels from South Africa to her sister and to Constance, but many parcels also reached humbler homes in Stambourne.

When Gwen returned from South Africa in 1948, her theatre work kept her away from Tagley Cottage, apart from brief visits, for the next few years. Her absence, however, did not diminish her yearning for her country home, and when she eventually decided not to invest the rest of her life in trying to develop further the theatre in South Africa, it was the primal pull of Tagley Cottage, as much as her professional ambition, that swayed her judgement. The cottage became a magnet

Tagley Cottage 1986

not only for Gwen, but also for many of her friends. It became identified as a place of rest, recuperation, even spiritual regeneration. Both Marjorie and Edith Evans, each suffering from a minor breakdown, spent weeks at Tagley Cottage looked after by Gwen, until strong enough to take up their busy lives again. In the decision that Gwen had to make in the 1950s about her future life, Tagley Cottage seemed to assume almost mystical importance. A hint of that importance and the magnetism that Tagley exerted is gleaned from one of Marda's journals, written in 1962. Gwen is in England; Marda is in the Cape Town district of South Africa. She is unhappy. She has sold her house; she has sold all her books; the glass on the remaining old photograph of her mother has cracked; her brother is dead. She broods:

'Gwen writes that [the] red honeysuckle is the late Dutch kind that she has planted by the old pump at Tagley Cottage. I used to pump the water from our well in 1934 when we first bought the Cottage. The well was ninety feet deep but much later, in 1950, I think, municipal water and electric light came that way. But by then I had a home in Somerset West forty miles from Cape Town at the foot of the Helderburg mountain with one of the loveliest views I have ever seen anywhere. "Oh, yes!" Gwen said, looking at the Clear Mountain from a window of Klein Helderburg, "Oh, yes! I could be happy here." So I bought the house and furnished it with things I loved and the things I hoped she loved. Three months later, she went back to Tagley and I was left alone with my view and some empty rooms, the room in which she had slept - the house where I hoped she would be happy...My Elias, my cook-boy, faithful to me, went off to marry, so I am alone at Klein Helderburg, as I had called the house I loved...But Gwen loved Tagley Cottage. That was in 1951 and 1952. This Saturday morning in 1962, I have

128

a letter from her here on this desk, telling me of red honeysuckle at Tagley - where she finds peace that passes my understanding as she sits, she writes, by the large open fire-place she and I know so well, with Millen purring on her lap. Millen is Gwen's cat. Chukkie, with the suave black moustache, was my cat, but she was run over and killed in 1961 in the lane that runs by Tagley where the Jennings bus stops in the morning and in the evening...for two years I have not been to Tagley, nor shall not be there again, I think.'[2]

Marda in the black mood despairs of Gwen ever again returning to her in South Africa. Tagley Cottage for her assumed an almost personal power in keeping Gwen from her. But she, too, has felt the pull of Tagley. She returns to England, and once again visits Tagley; this time as a naturalised citizen of the United Kingdom. Her acting career, which had reached a dead end in South Africa, once more began to flourish. Radio, television, and stage work came her way in rapid succession. Gwen also, who had found suitable employment scarce when she first returned to England in 1948, was soon looking forward to an extended phase of work of the most congenial kind, a season at The Memorial Theatre, Stratford-upon-Avon. Both Gwen and Marda would work together again in South Africa, but from 1948 for Gwen, and from 1963 for Marda, home-base was Tagley Cottage.

Playing and Producing (1949-1958)

Gwen's first stage role, following her return from South Africa, was in *Adventure Story* by Terence Rattigan. The play was about the life of Alexander the Great. Gwen played the part of the Queen Mother. Production was by Peter Glenville, with Paul Scofield playing the part of Alexander. Its first night was at the St James's Theatre on 17th March 1949. Writing to Dodie Smith, who at this time was in California, Gwen expressed admiration for the way Dodie disciplined herself to write in that 'sun-filled existence'. In comparison with Gwen, Dodie was extremely wealthy, and Gwen reflected that, if she could afford it, she would contemplate retirement. Eight performances a week of *Adventure Story* were beginning to pall.

'I'm afraid it's the beginning of middle-age - in my mind I mean - [Gwen was 58] in my years I've been in it for some considerable time! Edith Evans was saying the same thing. She has just had the most colossal success in *Daphne Laureola* - she is at the zenith of her career as they say in the papers - and yet she finds complete peace and happiness in a weekend at Tagley! Strange!'[3]

Gwen really had no intention of retiring from the stage in 1949, because she had a contract for 1950 to play a number of exciting Shakespearian roles at Stratford-upon-Avon. Before that season began, however, she was due to return to South Africa to produce in Johannesburg *Macbeth* in Afrikaans.

Marda, who had remained in South Africa, had produced, under the auspices of the new National Theatre Organisation, Shaw's *Arms and the Man* in 1949. André Huguenet, an Afrikaans actor and producer of considerable talent, had been her leading man. Marda's production had been entirely successful, and the administrative arrangements had been undertaken by an able group of lieutenants.

Now, in conjunction with the African Consolidated Theatres Limited, preliminary planning was put in hand for a Gwen Ffrangcon-Davies production of *Macbeth* in Afrikaans, with Huguenet playing the main part. A scholarly translation of the play was undertaken; Marda and Gwen discussed casting, by post, in some detail, but the main negotiations about staging and contracts were left to Marda. Gwen arrived in South Africa at the turn of the year to take over full production responsibilities for an opening scheduled for early February 1950. She was required to be back in Stratford-upon-Avon in the following month.

The first night of *Macbeth* encountered many difficulties concerned with staging problems, all fully detailed in Gwen's report to the African Consolidated Theatres Limited.[4] The resident stage-management team had not allowed sufficient time for the incoming group to hang their curtains or rehearse their lighting plan. Gwen was horrified on the first night to see her Macbeth deliver 'Is this a dagger that I see before me...' lit by undimmed floodlights. She and the cast grieved deeply over the problems encountered on the first night, but for the rest of the performances the high standards of the presentation and acting were warmly applauded. As Gwen left for England she received the following cable:

'You have already won the esteem of the English Theatre in South Africa and with your production of *Macbeth* in Afrikaans you have gained the confidence and appreciation of all the Afrikaans people and captured the imagination of the whole of South Africa. After your production of a Shakespearian play in Afrikaans we trust that this will be an inspiration to you to return to South Africa and give your experience, knowledge and talent to the theatre of this country.
President and Board of Governors - National Theatre.'[5]

After Gwen had returned to England, Marda continued with her work on a number of plays, most notably *Hassan* by James Elroy Flecker. Basil Dean travelled to South Africa to assist her, forming an uneasy partnership, and meeting with qualified success. In 1952, with Gwen once more in the country, they both appeared in *Waters of the Moon* by N. C. Hunter. This was something of a coup because the play was still being performed on the London stage, starring Sybil Thorndike and Edith Evans. Brian Brooke produced the play under the auspices of African Consolidated Theatres Limited in association with The Brian Brooke Company. The selection of appropriate plays for the South African audiences was a constant subject in the correspondence between Gwen and Marda during these years. Plays that had succeeded on the London stage had a certain cachet about them, and to secure the services of producers and stars associated with those plays was an additional bonus. Gwen, in England, spent a great deal of her time canvassing for the rights of the plays with individuals and with theatre managements. Negotiations with Emlyn Williams for *The Wind of Heaven*, and with Noel Coward for *Blithe Spirit* had been relatively easy. However, dealing with Binkie Beaumont or Basil Dean was more difficult. In her selection of plays for Marda's consideration Gwen would be chary of those with subjects that reflected strongly the essential Englishness of family, character or situation. She had to be sensitive to the growing interest in straight drama of the Afrikaans element in the audience. She was also hesitant in recommending to Marda the plays of Christopher Fry in which she herself delighted. *The Lady's not for Burning* (1949) and *Venus Observed* (1950) had met with approval not only from Gwen but from the general theatre-going English public. Yet she hesitated to recommend these plays as suitable fare for the Johannesburg or Pretorian audiences. T. S. Eliot's *The Cocktail Party* she had found baffling. She asked herself 'Is this poetry?' If it was not poetry, she thought it very indifferent prose. *The Cocktail Party*, however, was one of those South African productions for which Marda, her ear as attuned to poetry as Gwen's, was warmly applauded. Indeed, Gwen's own appreciation of Eliot deepened in the course of her taking part in *The Family Reunion*, performed at the Phoenix in 1956 by a brilliant cast. In the following years she was fond of quoting long passages from this play, not from her part but from the Chorus, in particular the passage that concludes Part II Scene I, beginning 'In an old house there is always listening, and more is heard than spoken' and ending 'We must listen to the weather report/ And the international catastrophes.'

The Stratford-upon-Avon season in 1950 lasted seven months. It began on 9th March with a performance of *Measure for Measure*, produced by Peter Brook, with John Gielgud as Angelo. The plays that followed were *Henry VIII*, produced by Tyrone Guthrie, with Anthony Quayle playing the King and Gwen playing Queen Katherine; *Julius Caesar*, produced by Anthony Quayle and Michael Langham, with John Gielgud as Cassius, Harry Andrews as Brutus, and Gwen as Portia; *Much Ado About Nothing*, produced by John Gielgud; in this play he also played Benedick opposite Peggy Ashcroft as Beatrice; and lastly *King Lear*, produced by Anthony Quayle, in which John Gielgud took the main part, Peggy Ashcroft Cordelia, Maxine Audley Goneril, and Gwen Regan.

For Gwen there were many advantages in playing at Stratford-upon-Avon. She stayed for the whole time there at the Arden Hotel. It was just a step across the road to the theatre. The hotel was comfortable: it had a garden; she could invite her friends - and many came to visit her. She was subjected to none of the stress that she had experienced with *The Adventure Story*. She was never required to give eight performances a week. There was, naturally, a heightening of tension as each play approached its first night, but the staging provisions, with one notable exception, were expertly managed.

After the 18th July, when all the planned plays were in production, Gwen found that there were some weeks when she had two days clear of performances. The company was large but friendly, and with all the plays rehearsed and presented, the atmosphere became more relaxed. Many of the actors had returned from war service. They were jolly, companionable, and brilliantly led by their directors and star players. They also proved, according to Anthony Quayle, the very best material for crowd scenes. Tyrone Guthrie, who was noted for his inventive direction of stage crowds, took full advantage of this group feeling in his production of *Henry VIII*. Gwen was among old and congenial friends such as John Gielgud, Anthony Quayle, Harry Andrews, Leon Quartermaine, and Peggy Ashcroft, and while at Stratford-upon-Avon she was to make many new friends such as Robert Hardy. Gwen's friendships, once made, lasted a lifetime.

Perhaps the greatest satisfaction that Gwen derived from this season was the opportunity to play the part of Queen Katherine in *Henry VIII*. Queen Katherine

Gwen as Regan in *King Lear* (left) and as Queen Katherine in
Henry VIII (right) at Stratford in 1950.
She took the part of Queen Katherine again at the Old Vic in
coronation year, 1953

was one of the parts played by Ellen Terry whose performance had made such an indelible impression on Gwen's memory. The other excitement associated with this part in 1950 was the visit of King George VI and Queen Elizabeth to see a performance of *Henry VIII*. This was a notable event, being the first time a monarch had ever been present at a play at the Memorial Theatre.

In the rehearsals for *Henry VIII*, Gwen found that she was more handicapped than usual by her short-sightedness. The trial scene was set with many steeply-stepped rostra which Queen Katherine in her long dress was expected to negotiate smoothly. Gwen complained 'I have already fallen off the throne down some particularly vile steps onto my poor knees'.[6] Although she criticised Guthrie for introducing 'too much funny business which overlays the play', she acknowledged his skill in harmonising a high-powered engine (his demobbed soldiers) with immense vitality in the crowd scenes.[7] For her performance of Katherine she could not have been more warmly supported by her friends. On the first night she received a great number of telegrams of good wishes from her admirers including Ivor Brown, Michael Redgrave, Diana Wynyard, Peggy Ashcroft, Laurence Olivier and Vivien Leigh. After the first night's performance a supper party was given in her honour by Edith Evans and Cecil Williams. When the King, Queen, and Princess Margaret attended the matinée on 20th April, John Gielgud, who normally would not have taken part in this play, spoke the prologue. This particularly grand occasion was not without a pronounced family feeling. As the King and Queen with one of their daughters sat watching the play, Anthony Quayle had his youngest daughter, aged three weeks, carried on in the last scene as the infant Elizabeth to be blessed by Archbishop Cranmer, who foretells great things for her and for her nation:

> 'In her days every man shall eat in safety,
> Under his own vine, what he plants; and sing
> The merry songs of peace to all his neighbours.'

Warming words to the war-weary, the monarch and his people. Quayle's other daughter, a two-year old, also appeared in the play 'in a ravishing white frock looking like a miniature Tudor lady', as one of the crowd, 'and when Tony [Quayle] entered resplendent in velvet and ermine [she] piped up to everyone's delight (including the King and Queen who knew the children were going to appear) "There's Daddy!"'[8]

This visit of the King and Queen to Stratford-upon-Avon meant so much to Gwen that she wanted to convey to Marda as many details as she could recall of the whole day, including the civic events attended in the morning. She wrote her letter the same evening during the parts of *Henry VIII* in which she did not appear. The following days, she explained, she would be unable to find time to write because they were so taken up with a visit to London to be fitted for a wig, which she was to wear as Portia in *Julius Caesar*, and on the Saturday there were two further performances, and on the Sunday Shakespeare's birthday celebrations. She described how attractive the town had been made with its flowers, its flags, and its grove of artificial cherry trees placed outside the Birthplace. Work had gone on all night in the theatre to create a 'royal box' in the centre of the dress circle, wreathed with flowers and in every available space there were tulips, lilac, and daffodils. Towards the end of the morning the royal party had visited the theatre workshops, spoken to the technicians, and watched a crowd scene rehearsal of *Julius Caesar*. After the performance of *Henry VIII* the cast had been introduced to the royal party in the theatre restaurant.

'They couldn't have been sweeter. They all remembered me and were apparently delighted with the play - the Queen said 'I cried a tear or two' and the King said 'I do congratulate you' as if he really meant it. They both came across to talk to me and the Queen said what news do you have of South Africa, so I told her about *Macbeth*...I suppose we were with them about ten minutes but they were just as easy and unforced as that time in Pretoria. The King said to Tony when he saw the garter on the table that it was wrongly fastened - the King told me this with great amusement, and that he'd shown him how to fasten it properly. "Yes", he said "I told him to come to me. I'm the expert!"'[9]

Gwen, towards the end of her letter, commented on how much more cheerful the King looked when he left them – 'gay as a bee and full of smiles'. Sir Alan Lascelles, who had accompanied the royal party, assured Gwen that her performance of Queen Katherine was the finest thing she had done. That day as she wrote her letter she had much to glow about.

Gwen's part as Portia in *Julius Caesar*, she said, 'was so small that I didn't feel that I was in the play at all'.[10] Such a statement masks the detailed attention she gave to the part, however small. She was prepared to spend a day in London being fitted for her wig, and she was delighted when Alix Stone, the gifted costume designer, jewellery-maker and creator of magnificent and imaginative properties, presented her with a fan. That season Alix Stone had been assigned to work at the Memorial Theatre. Gwen praises her work on a number of occasions. Now she writes to Marda, who would readily have pictured the quality of the work:

'Alix Stone...has just made me a fan to carry on as Portia that might have been dug up in Pompeii.'[11]

During rehearsal for *Julius Caesar* Gwen gives us an insight into some of the background tensions at the Memorial Theatre.

'Even here where we do our work under as ideal conditions as are possible, we can't have the stage and set as often as we should because of the constant change of programme. The evening performance must start being set about 2 p.m., and the previous night has to be struck after the show to make it possible to set the one we're working on in time to rehearse in; so of course we can only have the full set for two dress rehearsals, and usually we have the Monday before production off as well as the Sunday. But with *Julius Caesar*, through an oversight while the company was away in Australia, the Monday was booked for *Measure for Measure*, and by the time Tony got back it was too late to change it. So we were rehearsing lights and the storm until about 2 p.m. on the day we opened, and the crowd through being overtired and nervous got out of hand in the Forum and drowned poor Tony's Antony. He didn't play as well as usual nor did Harry or indeed any of us - because we were all tentative - all except Johnny [Gielgud] who having "hammed" his way through rehearsals gave a magnificent performance sans ham on the first night and collared all the headlines.'[12]

All went much more smoothly on the second night when Binkie Beaumont and John Perry were in front and afterwards warmly congratulated Gwen on her Portia.

When *Much Ado About Nothing* was in rehearsal Gwen reported that the cast was in despair because of the endless changes that John Gielgud was making to the production, but once staged she thought it delightful. She would have loved to play Beatrice herself, she confessed, but she thought Peggy Ashcroft in the part 'adorable', and John Gielgud as Benedick, looking like Danny Kaye in a ginger wig, 'Superb!'[13]

In the past Gwen had shared rooms with Peggy Ashcroft and had acted with her in very many plays, some of them with long runs. She had, naturally, felt saddened when John Gielgud had chosen Peggy for his productions of *Romeo and Juliet* in 1932 and 1935, in preference to herself. Indeed, she would have wished to be preferred for the part of Beatrice for the 1950 Memorial Theatre production of *Much Ado*, but such disappointments did not cloud her judgement about Peggy Ashcroft's considerable acting ability, and she responded to Peggy's success with great generosity of spirit. For instance, she wrote to Marda about rehearsals for *King Lear*:

'The three sisters are coming out wonderfully contrasted. Peggy is absolutely exquisite as Cordelia - heart-breakingly tender and true in the tent scene - and with a stubborn integrity in the first scene that does not shirk being almost unsympathetic - but such deep feeling behind the stubbornness that one's heart aches for her and you long to say as to the early Christians "Oh do sacrifice the pinch of incense!"...[she] has a divine dress when she comes back at the head of her army - dirty pink, with sky-blue cloak - a darling little gold breast-plate and Greek sandals - she looks like the winged Victory or a particularly adorable ship's figurehead.'[14]

Towards the end of the season Gwen was asked to take on the role of Beatrice in *Much Ado About Nothing*. John Gielgud and Peggy Ashcroft withdrew from the production with other commitments. Gwen was delighted to have the opportunity of playing the part, even if it meant doing so with another Benedick, Anthony Eustrel, whom she described as 'nice and quite good but a bit in the Robert Atkins' School of acting'.[15] Peggy Ashcroft, writing also from the Arden Hotel, congratulates Gwen on securing the part:

'Darlingest Gwen, sister, and room mate,
        I shall be thinking of you so much when you open this and the old Beatrice will be wishing the new Beatrice great happiness and fun! I only wish our dear and one and only John were with you for none knows better than you or me how inspiring he is. But I know also with absolute conviction that YOU have the spirit and the heart that will make it go on your own.

Our time together has been so lovely and unforgettable
                With deepest admiration
                        Your loving
                            Peggy'[16]

A postscript refers to an accompanying present of candlesticks for which use might be found at Tagley Cottage. Gwen knew too well the difference that having any Benedick other than John Gielgud would make to the play. The Benedick whom she was to play opposite was relatively unknown. Yet she must have gained comfort from the reviews and her fan mail. Robert Donat saw the production and wrote to her on 27th October 1950.

'Dear Gwen,
        Renée [Asherson] and I were in Stratford for one night this week to see *Measure* and *Much Ado*. It was all we could manage and even then we had to dash for a train after the matinée.
        May I say how enormously we enjoyed your Beatrice? She is absolutely enchanting and completely real. You convinced us not only that Beatrice was completely alive, but entirely credible in all her actions - a feat I have never before seen equalled. Neither have I seen so loving and so lovable a lady.
        Forgive this. I have written but two or three fan letters to a fellow pro in my whole life. This one I can't help sending.
                Very sincerely,
                        Robert.'[17]

In 1951 Gwen was to play the part of Beatrice in *Much Ado About Nothing* in South Africa. And she was invited to repeat in England another of her Stratford-upon-Avon parts which meant even more to her. On Wednesday 6th May 1953 there was a gala presentation of *Henry VIII* 'in the presence of Her Majesty the Queen in Honour of the Coronation'. The performance took place at the Old Vic. Once again Tyrone Guthrie directed, and once again Gwen played Queen Katherine, but the cast was greatly changed from the 1950 production. Timothy Bateson and Robert Hardy from the earlier cast were included, but this time Robert Hardy took the role of the Lord Chamberlain. Archbishop Cranmer's speech, at the end of the play, over the infant Elizabeth, was printed in full in the programme. The implication was that the reign of Queen Elizabeth II was being doubly blessed, through this production at the Old Vic and again, in a month's time, at Westminster Abbey. Gwen had always taken her royal 'duties' very seriously. She had sent Princess Elizabeth a present on the occasion of her marriage and received a gracious reply; she had written a letter of condolence to Queen Elizabeth on the death of her husband, and again received a royal reply; she had waited hours in the rain at the funeral of King George VI, and she was to attend the Coronation of the new Queen on 2nd June 1953. In her time she had played the part of so many queens and, indeed, encountered a number of queens in person, that it was understandable that she should have a deep-seated feeling for queenliness. She had met Queen Mary in 1933 when playing Richard II's Queen in *Richard of Bordeaux*; in 1950 she had played Queen Katherine before King George and Queen Elizabeth, and now she was playing the part once again, but in front of their daughter Queen

Elizabeth II. Gwen made such an impression in this part that for long afterwards she was asked to give extracts from *Henry VIII*: the trial scene, Act II Scene IV and, in particular, the scene with Griffith, the Queen's Gentleman-usher, Act IV Scene II. Robert Hardy so cherished the memory of playing Griffith to Gwen's Katherine that forty-one years later he was pleased to tell her what a joyful chance it was for him to have had that privilege.[18]

The Gala performance at the Old Vic took place on 6th May 1953, a month before the Coronation. The Old Vic, on the Waterloo Road, was then the home of the embryonic National Theatre which was about to be built on the South Bank. *Henry VIII* had been deliberately chosen as the theatre world's offering to celebrate the Coronation, and the Queen had graciously consented to attend the first night's performance. The nation at the time was in a fervour of patriotic excitement, and the Queen, on her way to the theatre, was met by dense crowds of Londoners. On the approach of the royal car, containing the Queen and the Duke of Edinburgh, the air rang with Cockney cries of 'God bless your Majesty' and 'God save the Queen'. As the Queen stepped from the car, Caroline Hunt, the nine-year old daughter of Hugh Hunt, the Theatre Director, who had been waiting in the lobby, came nervously down the steps and presented the Queen with a Victorian bouquet of roses, forget-me-nots and lilies of the valley, given by the florist across the road; she then burst into tears. Inside the theatre the royal box had been created, as earlier at the Memorial Theatre, in the centre of the dress-circle. The Queen and the Duke sat on two regal yellow satin chairs, and were surrounded by flowers. As they took their places the whole of the audience, who were in evening dress, turned towards them and sang 'God Save the Queen'. From the start of the evening there was evident a warmth and enthusiasm which passed from the players and audience to the Queen and the Duke.

Henry VIII is of questionable penmanship with troughs of potential boredom, but in the hands of Tyrone Guthrie it became for this occasion a fast-moving colourful pageant. A number of analogies could be drawn between parts of the play and events in England in 1953. A grand coronation, that of the Queen, Anne Boleyn, is described in what must be one of the finest passages in the play. A splendid procession passes slowly across the stage. The eye-witness account of the three Gentlemen describing the procession and succeeding events (Act IV Scene I) served as a foretaste of what most of the nation would hear as a radio commentary, in somewhat less poetic language, on Queen Elizabeth II's coronation in a month's time. The trial of Queen Katherine and her final scene with Griffith emphasised those queenly qualities of dignity, loyalty, charity and grace. In 1950 at the Stratford-upon-Avon production of the play before King George VI and Queen Elizabeth there had been an almost palpable sigh from monarch and audience when Archbishop Cranmer, in blessing the infant Elizabeth, had spoken of peace. Three years later, with the imminence of Queen Elizabeth II's coronation, the mood had changed. Holding the young child in his arms William Squire, playing the part of Cranmer, said:

> '........................all princely graces,
> That mould up such a mighty piece as this is,
> With all the virtues that attend the good,
> Shall still be doubled on her: truth shall nurse her,

Holy and heavenly thoughts still counsel her:
She shall be loved and fear'd: her own shall bless her;
Her foes shall shake like a field of beaten corn,
And hang their heads with sorrow: good grows with her....'

As these words were spoken a thrill went through the house and there was an audible murmur of assent from the audience. After the final curtain-call the cast grouped themselves together on the stage and sang the National Anthem. And so ended an evening devoted to communal patriotism. During the following few days the press reports praised the show of patriotism, applauded the pageantry, bemoaned the inadequacies of the play, scolded Tyrone Guthrie for his wayward egocentricity, congratulated Paul Rogers on his red-haired Henry, and gave the prize to Gwen for her luminous performance and her ability to speak the verse as though it was music.

In November 1953 Gwen was invited to spend ten days in Denmark, sponsored by the British Council, to give her recital performance of Shakespeare's Women. These recitals were given both to adult audiences and to children. The advertisement indicated the selection:

'Lady Macbeth's Sleepwalking Scene, Juliet's Poison Scene, the Nurse's honest humanity, Portia in the Trial, Desdemona's Handkerchief Scene, Beatrice's verbal duels with Benedick, Ophelia's madness, the nobility of Queen Katherine before the King, Cardinals, and Bishops....'

When Professor Wallis had attended one of these recitals in Johannesburg he had taken away with him the lasting memory of Gwen's portrayal of Shakespeare's Cleopatra in the scene where she receives the messenger from Rome and hears from him of Antony's marriage to Octavia.[19]

Early in 1954 she was playing at the New Theatre as Donna Lucia D'Alvadorez in *Charley's Aunt*. Such a part was as far from the roles she presented in her recital of Shakespeare's Women as it was from her next role, that of Madame Ranevsky in *The Cherry Orchard*, which opened at the Lyric, Hammersmith in May, 1954. The last Chekhov play she had appeared in had been *The Three Sisters* in 1938, produced by Michel St Denis. It had been hailed as a masterpiece of theatre direction and ensemble playing. The accolades that were showered upon this production of *The Cherry Orchard* were almost as lavish. John Gielgud had played Colonel Vershinin in the previous Chekhov production; now he directed *The Cherry Orchard*, but did not act in it. In order to achieve the mood-music and the high degree of ensemble playing required of a Chekhov production perhaps it is imperative that the director, however accomplished an actor he might be, should not also involve himself as one of the actors. Gielgud, with his Lithuanian background, had an intuitive understanding of Russian plays and literature and, contrary to Shaw's disparagement that he 'couldn't possibly play anything by Chekhov, being a Terry',[20] achieved some of his most brilliant successes playing in and producing Chekhov's plays. Unlike *The Three Sisters* in which there is no single character that stands out above the others, in *The Cherry Orchard* the most important role is that of Madame Ranevsky. In casting Gwen for this role Gielgud was giving the lead to an actress who he knew was highly skilled in this genre of playing, someone he and his company could work with, creatively and sympathetically. His choice of Trevor Howard to play Lopahin, the wealthy peasant with serf ancestry, was thought extremely risky. The risk was worth taking, for Howard worked extremely well with the gifted cast which included Pauline Jameson as Varya, Patience Collier as Charlotta Ivanovna, Shirley Roberts as Anya, Esmé Percy as Gaeff, and Robert Eddison as Epihodoff. Gielgud had taken pains to adapt the play himself, thus removing many of the infelicitous and repetitive phrases of the earlier translation. The reviews were varied, but most of them warm and appreciative. Harold Hobson for *The Sunday Times* enjoyed the play and many of its delightful moments, but found 'Mr Howard's Lopahin too gruff for the play's fragile beauty: possibly Miss Ffrangcon-Davies's Madame Ranevsky is too much an exquisite recitation. Something, at any rate is missing, though what is found is rich indeed.' If that review made Gwen ponder on the effectiveness of her Madame Ranevsky, receiving a note from Alec Guinness dated 18th July 1954 would have been of some comfort. Guinness was usually conservative in his comments, and chary of extravagant praise.

> Dear Gwen
> I cannot tell you how impressed I was by your performance last night. It is a creation of rare beauty - deeply moving and tender and witty. I have never seen the part played before (though I've seen it acted many times) so truly - and never before have I believed in the lover in Paris or that the Cherry Orchard really *belonged* to Madame R. The London theatre has much to thank you for but for this performance above all.
> Yours sincerely,
> Alec G.'[21]

Gwen valued Alec Guinness's judgement. She had played with him on a number of occasions; indeed, he had been one of the company that had enjoyed such a notable success in the 1938 production of *The Three Sisters*. He had also spent the best part of a week in Stratford-upon-Avon in August of 1950, seeing all the plays. He praised Gwen in all her parts, but made a special point of telling her 'that her performance of Queen Katherine made him proud of being an actor'.[22]

Summertime followed in 1955 in which Gwen starred with Dirk Bogarde, *The Mulberry Bush* in 1956 and, later that year, the brilliantly cast and produced *The Family Reunion*, so enthusiastically reviewed by Alan Dent:

> '...it is magnificently produced by Peter Brook, and...flawlessly well acted in every part and every particular...The performances of Paul Scofield, Dame Sybil Thorndike and Gwen Ffrangcon-Davies, as Harry, his mother, and his aunt, make us realise that the play has never before had the deeply and subtly imaginative acting which it deserves.'[23]

The Chalk Garden, written by Enid Bagnold, produced by John Gielgud and starring Edith Evans and Peggy Ashcroft, after touring the provinces, had opened at the Haymarket in April 1956. It proved a great success. When Peggy Ashcroft left the cast in January 1957, Gwen replaced her in the role of Miss Madrigal. The play is about an eccentric Mrs St Maugham, played by Edith Evans, who is looking for a governess for her neurotic granddaughter and also for some help in managing her unruly garden. Miss Madrigal, a lonely silent woman with a mysterious past, applies for and secures the post of governess, and proves that she can manage the garden, the grandchild, *and* Mrs St Maugham. Enid Bagnold had married Sir Roderick Jones, who for many years had been the chairman of the news agency Reuters. She was wealthy, gifted, energetic, and tenaciously concerned that no actor should, in performance, alter one syllable of her text. A short while after Gwen had joined the cast of *The Chalk Garden*, she, Marda and Enid enjoyed a social meeting together, after which Gwen sent Enid a generous sheaf of flowers, for which she received a thank-you response, typed on both sides of two post cards. The thank-you was not just for the flowers, but also for Gwen's performance in the part of Miss Madrigal:

'*You* have given it a depth and reasonableness and spirituality and poetry (and yet stiff common sense) which is what I have always wanted. The best of the Madrigals...let me say it flat out. The fourth - to me. I mean I've seen four. But you the nearest to what I want. So near you are there! I suppose no one could ever persuade Edith not to take such a time before she says "What do women do in my case?"...In any case I know it's too precious a moment to her to touch it. She was really wonderful. But the whole cast was radiant that night. I sensed the play swelling as I watched it. Shall I ever be able to cope again?...Bless you and thank you and I will ring and try and get you to come here. I wish you were free on Sunday night to come to family supper but you never are?
    Love Enid'[24]

Then on 8th February 1957 she writes again to Gwen, beginning with the sentence 'I thought it *splendid* last night. I thought at the end of Act Three you had *got* it.' She proceeds to correct Gwen at length in the minutest details of her part. Three examples suffice from a two-page letter:

'A few word things. Do you mind?...
"I was put in charge of...
What?
A garden."
(You said "*of* a garden" and it makes it too practical...It loses the poetical quality of what it meant to her. I expect it was a slip because I was there!)
When will you learn you live on chalk? (not *that* you live on chalk)...Page 87 in book.
It matters because it again makes it too practical.
I missed the smiling certainty in "What learned men at the top of their professions" etc. You said it with anxiety as though you minded whether or not she knew. I think it should be said with a sort of smooth certainty and a smile and all in one piece...'[25]

Actors and actresses, not to mention the directors, involved with productions of plays by Enid Bagnold, needed infinite patience in dealing with a playwright who attended rehearsals and performances with so proprietorial a passion. As her popularity as a playwright faded, Enid Bagnold became progressively more jealous over the inviolability of her script. In 1964 after the first night at The Arts Theatre of her play *The Chinese Prime Minister*, in which Edith Evans played Mrs Forrest, Enid Bagnold entered Edith Evans's dressing-room 'with her mouth set in a grim smile, the smile on the face of a tiger. "How clever of you darling," she said, "to invent so many new words for my play."'[26]

Gwen played Miss Madrigal when Enid Bagnold's star as an author was in the ascendant, but even so she would have had to exercise a measure of self-control to deal with the pleased, but pernickety playwright. Among the letters of congratulations on her performance came one from Rayne Kruger, himself an author, and an age-old friend.

> Darling Gwen,
> May I record - I would wish for posterity - how entirely delighted we were with and for you last night?...you gave us a truly lovely performance, carrying...all the burden and the anguish and the courage and the sharpened but unembittered humour (I suppose this sincerity saw you through those years) of those 15 years: expressed in poise, restraint, voice and, especially face. Especially face because that is the chief register upon which a long incarceration must write. Second, because I can't see how this part and performance can fail to place you very firmly in your rightful place among our real stars - which managements and public have tended lately to overlook: now you can be overlooked no longer. For Gwen, you're back with a bump! Third - and this an extremely personal sense of satisfaction - because you demonstrated quality far superior to Peggy A. I have been in the minority who have consistently denied her a throne in the celestial courts of the theatre and we have here the perfect proof of my contention, when a truly great actress plays the same part and shows what *can* be done with it. There being neither envy nor malice in your soul you won't feel as pleased as I am: my pleasure being the purely vain one of having been proved right...
> > All love
> > Rayne'[27]

This letter was written on 23rd January 1957. The following year Gwen Ffrangcon-Davies was, publicly and with great acclaim, placed 'among the real stars'.

Friends and Funerals

Gwen's absence from the country during most of the war years had made a difference to her being invited to play the roles in classical and new drama that otherwise might have come her way. There was no overt statement of prejudice. Playing the Queen-Mother in *Adventure Story* for nearly six months certainly helped to pay a few bills and brought her once more into the congenial fellowship of colleagues, particularly Paul Scofield, but she found the work less than fulfilling. The 1950 season at Stratford-upon-Avon, on the other hand, gave her the feeling of at last being rehabilitated within her profession. John Gielgud of all her friends during this period, 1948-1970, was most anxious that Gwen should be re-established as one of the greatest actresses on the English stage. Following that

141

notable Shakespearian season of 1950, he had invited Gwen to take the lead in *The Cherry Orchard*, welcomed her as a superb replacement of Peggy Ashcroft in *The Chalk Garden*, and acted with her in Graham Greene's *Potting Shed* at the beginning of 1958.

In *The Potting Shed* Gwen had played the part of Mrs Callifer; Gielgud had played the son. Gwen was a little more than thirteen years older than Gielgud. When they had first played *Romeo and Juliet* together at the Regent Theatre in 1924, she had been thirty-three and Gielgud just twenty. She was then the more experienced, helping a much younger actor through the intricacies of a great classical role. Theirs was never a mother-son relationship, but one of colleagues, mutually committed to their art. By the time they played in *Richard of Bordeaux* together in 1932, Gielgud was fast becoming acknowledged as an acclaimed director as well as the most accomplished classical actor of the period. The balance in their relationship was changing. Now, where Gielgud led, Gwen was content to follow. She was always most ready to rejoice at his success and give full credit to his brilliance, without trace of envy or resentment, apart from that time when, having planned with her another *Romeo and Juliet*, he chose Peggy Ashcroft for the part. Gwen was a sounding-board for many of his plans for production. He valued her judgement as well as the staunchness of her friendship. During the 1950 Stratford-upon-Avon season when, following the opening of *King Lear*, he had the feeling that the standard of performances was flagging, he would deliver such opinions in a very forthright manner to Anthony Quayle, the overall director. Quayle thought that Gielgud needed to be more relaxed about the issue. Each in turn would visit Gwen's dressing-room, as she says, 'letting off steam' and seeking counsel.[28]

There was a deeper tie between Gwen and John Gielgud than just their art. Associated with that art was the Terry dynasty. Gielgud's family history was very much part of that dynasty, and he fully realised that many of his great talents were genetically derived. Gwen's parents had been on very friendly terms with Ellen Terry, who personally had encouraged their daughter to become an actress. She became the lodestar of that daughter's early life, and an influence that Gwen never ceased to recognise. Both John Gielgud and Gwen would regularly offer their services for the annual Ellen Terry Anniversary Performances held each summer at Small Hythe. Gwen's contribution in 1949 included the material from one of Ellen Terry's letters to her father in which she gave him sound advice concerning the making of artistes' contracts. The letter of thanks, dated 27th July, came from Christopher St John:

'....You had splendid material for your address in that letter of Ellen's to your father, but what a splendid use you made of it! I sat entranced by the magical word-music of the speech, and its sense was as lovely as its sound - in the far distance, in fact in another world not here. I could hear both Edy and Ellen chuckling with pleasure, as they did in the theatre when anything was done superbly well, at your performance...'[29]

The Small Hythe celebrations were viewed by both Gielgud and Gwen as pilgrimages in which they paid homage to one of their greatest theatrical forebears. Correspondence from Ellen Terry's children, Edith and Gordon Craig, was also cherished. Gwen was a frequent visitor to the Gielgud's family home, and counted herself a personal friend of Kate, Gielgud's mother, who died at the age of ninety in 1958. The whole of Gielgud's correspondence with Gwen treats her less as a colleague and more as one of the family. He tells her news of his mother, father, and his sister, Eleanor, and confides in her his thoughts about his brother Val's matrimonial problems. He and Gwen exchange frequent visits when in Essex: she at Tagley Cottage, Stambourne, and he a mile away at Foulslough Farm, Finchingfield. He allows her to use his home in Westminster, 16 Cowley Street, to entertain her guests, including Edith Evans, to a supper party after the gala performance of *Henry VIII*, and when he is settled in his palatial new home, South Pavilion, Wotton Underwood, Buckinghamshire, Gwen is invited to stay. A deep friendship, based on love and respect, by 1970 had lasted forty-six years. It had many more years yet to run.

Edith Evans, three years older than Gwen, had first acted with her in *Back to Methuselah* in 1923, since when they had appeared together in such famous productions as *The Lady with a Lamp* (1929), *The Importance of Being Earnest* (1939), and *The Chalk Garden* (1957). From their first encounter Gwen had deferred to Edith's greater experience, and was full of admiration for her unbounded energy, and the command, imagination, and individuality she showed in the interpretation of the parts she played. Edith's talent and flair had secured for her a great following of fans, and she had always been prepared to undertake tiring tours of the provinces. During the war she had acted for some time at the Garrison Theatre in Salisbury, but had also travelled the country and performed to troops in Gibraltar and India. In 1946 she was awarded the Order of Dame of the British Empire. The following year she was to have, what she maintained, was the most enjoyable holiday of her lifetime, the three months with Gwen in South Africa. At moments of stress Edith would stay with Gwen at Tagley Cottage. As mentioned earlier, although trained as a milliner, she had none of Gwen's practical skills in that field, nor her friend's zest and ability in housekeeping, cookery, and gardening. For a short time before the 1939-45 war, Edith and Gwen set up house together in London, when Marda would scold Gwen for doing all the work. She referred to Edith as 'that lazy elephant'.[30] The experiment was short-lived, but the two friends did not fall out, and during the war Edith let Gwen use her flat, L4 The Albany, Piccadilly W1, a fitting address for Lady Bracknell. This was in the late summer and autumn of 1942, when Gwen was performing as Lady Macbeth at the Piccadilly Theatre. They had shared plays, houses, dressers; they also shared a firm belief in Christian Science. In their letters they referred repeatedly to 'CS', the set readings they were undertaking, and the degree to which they found these readings relevant to their immediate lives.

Edith Evans shared with Gwen some critical moments in her life. When Gwen revisited England at the end of the war it was Edith who met her at the Savoy Hotel. Gwen gave an account of this meeting in a broadcast to South Africa. She was anxious for her rehabilitation. Edith, through some string-pulling, had booked her five nights accommodation at the Savoy. Gwen had been met by her sister at the airport and together they had driven to the hotel. Publicity given to her return was of some importance.

'It was wonderful to be met there with all the pomp and circumstance of pre-war days. Dame Edith Evans was waiting for me at the Savoy, and we went up to a charming suite filled with flowers. After sitting up in an aeroplane for two nights, I imagined I should have been worn out...but that evening I went to see *Crime and Punishment*. You can't imagine what a thrill it was for me to be back in the London theatre again...We went round to see John Gielgud afterwards, then out to supper at the Ivy, and so to bed...'[31]

Gielgud played Raskolnikov, Edith Evans Katerina Ivanovna, and Peter Ustinov the Interrogator in this 1946 production of *Crime and Punishment*, directed by Anthony Quayle. It was important to Gwen that she should not only return to England, but be seen to be with her most distinguished friends, still stars on the London stage. Edith was there to lend her what help she could. Ten years earlier she had also stood by her. It was the night after Gwen's mother had died. She had come straight from her evening performance to that Hampstead church where Annie lay at rest, to keep vigil with Gwen and a small group of friends.

Dodie Smith, four years younger than Gwen, counted her among her friends from their time together at the Three Arts Club in the Marylebone Road. Although both had stayed at the Club repeatedly during the First World War, they did not meet each other there until 1920. Dodie, with strong Mancunian roots, had trained at RADA, but found difficulty in earning her living as an actress. She took a job as an assistant at Heals, the furnishing store. While there she wrote her first play, *Autumn Crocus*, which proved a great success on the London stage. In the 1930s the London theatres clamoured for her work. Success followed success, until *Dear Octopus* seemed to epitomise her ascendancy over all other contemporary dramatists before the onset of the Second World War. She went to America at the beginning of 1939 with Alec Beesley, her manager, and there they married. Despite her writing many more plays, none was accepted for the English or American stage, but a novel, *I Capture the Castle*, and a children's book *The Hundred and One Dalmatians*, proved extremely popular. Walt Disney's two film versions of her children's book ensured that Dodie was never without large royalties payments.

However, in those earlier days at the Three Arts Club, Dodie was often very hard up. She managed to keep her head above water with the allowance she received from her uncles in Manchester. But when she resolved to leave the acting profession and apply to Heals for a job, Gwen let her have £10 to help her with a new wardrobe. It was at a time when Gwen was establishing a name for herself as Etain in *The Immortal Hour*. The loan was duly repaid. Dodie, who had some musical talent herself, recalled how magical it was for the girls at the Three Arts Club, when Gwen of an evening would sit at the piano and sing.

'I liked it best when Gwen Ffrangcon-Davies sang. She had belonged to the Club for some years, but I only met her around this time, when she had already acquired some celebrity. This was the year she played Etain in *The Immortal Hour* at the Old Vic: she got me a seat. I thought she was exquisite and loved the music.

Gwen brought back memories of my schooldays at St Paul's, singing lessons with Gustav Holst...I had always loved folk songs and Gwen sang them admirably, very simply and unaffectedly, accompanying herself with Cecil Sharp's settings. I must say that the Gang, so often noisy and ribald, appreciated her fully and would listen for as long as she would sing.'[32]

144

Gwen took Dodie to concerts, shared bus rides with her, and on one occasion, that fixed itself in Dodie's memory, sang to her in an old Hendon churchyard at sunset. When Dodie had a part in which she was required to sing, she came to Gwen for singing lessons in the Club's Practice Room, but to little effect. They were both Christian Scientists and thought at first that their belief might help in overcoming this singing problem:

> 'We finally decided I had better sing in the way that came naturally to me and put our trust in Christian Science. Gwen was a very good Christian Scientist and I a very vague one. She assured me that to God all things were possible and there were cases where people had been able to accomplish feats that seemed physically impossible.'[33]

It would seem that Gwen, both on and off the stage, had something of an other-world aura about her, because Dodie recounts that when Gwen was present the 'ribaldry', so freely bandied about at the Club, became very much subdued.

A close friend of Dodie's was Phyllis Morris, actress, playwright, and author of children's books. They had trained together and were frequent inmates at the Three Arts Club. When they decided to rent a house together, they looked for a place in the Baker Street district and found a flat in Crawford Street. It comprised the top floors of two old houses but was too large and too expensive for them. They needed someone to share the flat and the expenses with them. They considered which of their friends they should approach, and lighted on Gwen, who was then living in a hotel in Portman Square. Gwen chose the two large front rooms; Phyllis had two rooms and Dodie one at the back. The expensive outlay remained a worry, and so Gwen agreed to take on the main responsibility for the flat and to rent out the rooms to Dodie and Phyllis. On Sundays there were parties in the flat, hosted by Gwen. The two younger women were very pleased to meet such a variety of men friends, and on these occasions the preparation and clearing up was undertaken by the maid, Ann, who stayed over.[34]

It was about this time that Phyllis Morris was getting a variety of her work published. Also, in the autumn of 1926, one of her plays, *Made in Heaven*, about two girls in London who shared a bed-sitting room, was accepted for production at the Everyman Theatre. Raymond Massey directed, and the cast included Claude Rains, Marda Vanne, and Gwen Ffrangcon-Davies.[35]

Dodie Smith, a little rueful at Phyllis's success when her own efforts were being ignored, at last broke through with a West End hit. In October 1930, after the enthusiastic reception of *The Barretts of Wimpole Street*, Gwen wrote to her mother asking if she had seen in *The Observer* that Basil Dean

> '...had a new play by an unknown woman author, of which he thinks very highly? It is Dodie Smith! Isn't it exciting for her. I do hope it's a success. She tells me she has written it for me, but of course I shall be tied up for some time now and anyway Basil doesn't like me!'[36]

The play was *Autumn Crocus* and set Dodie off in the direction of wealth and celebrity which she was to enjoy for many years. One outcome was her purchase of a house in the country. In 1934 she had sent Alec Beesley and Phyllis to search in

Essex for a suitable home. They came across The Barretts, Finchingfield, a large thatched house in a very dilapidated condition. Dodie, with some misgiving, paid £425 for the house and three times as much in having it renovated. They knew at this time that Gwen was also looking for a country house and recommended that she should have a look at Tagley Cottage, Stambourne, only a short distance from The Barretts. Gwen and Marda saw Tagley Cottage and bought it between them for £300, although Dodie records that the advertised price was £200. The extra £100 probably was spent on improvements. Neither in Finchingfield nor Stambourne were electricity and mains water available until 1953. Even without these facilities both properties required a great deal of attention. Gwen and Dodie, who

Dodie Smith in America

had shared a house together, were now near neighbours in the country with a number of their theatre friends also living near at hand, or coming as visitors. Gordon Daviot, for instance, came to stay with Dodie in 1938, and at the beginning of 1939, before Dodie and Alec sailed to America, Dodie held a Christmas party at The Barretts which included Gwen, Marda, John Gielgud and his house party, Nadine March and her husband Stephen Thomas. She and Alec were away from England for the best part of fourteen years. Dodie herself returned once or twice after the war to discuss with theatre managements the production of her plays, but the two of them did not take up residence again at The Barretts until 1953. In the meantime their house had been let to Binkie Beaumont, whose mother lived there throughout the week, while Binkie came only at weekends. When Gwen and Marda returned to Tagley Cottage after the war they found that they had different, but familiar neighbours. Christmas 1953 was celebrated at Tagley Cottage, with Dodie and Alec as the special guests. Such friendship and neighbourliness, which had lasted over thirty years, had nearly another forty to run, with Dodie becoming increasingly crotchety, and Gwen unbelievably forbearing.

Laurence Olivier was never as close a friend to Gwen as John Gielgud, but she marvelled at his astonishing and versatile gifts in performance. He, in turn, was appreciative of her accomplishments. She had acted with him in *Queen of Scots,* but in little else. Marda had starred with him in James Bridie's *King of Nowhere,* and

Olivier would often mention Marda in his letters to Gwen. The difference in the quality of the correspondence between Olivier and Gielgud is very marked. Gielgud's letters are detailed, informative, often long, with reflections on their colleagues, usually of a benign, even avuncular, kind. Olivier's letters, of which there are nearly as many, are, on the whole, brief to the point of being perfunctory, recording effusive thanks for a gift, a telegram, a parcel, good wishes for an imminent performance, or congratulations on an honour. There are one or two letters in which he opens his heart about the health, condition, and treatment of Vivien Leigh. Generally in his letters he gives the impression that he has scarcely time to make a courteous acknowledgement before turning again to those thousand and one things that preoccupy both a radiant star and director of the National Theatre. Gielgud, on the other hand, will write a letter to Gwen, thinking primarily of Gwen and what within his letter will most interest or please her. Gwen recognised clearly enough such letter-writing differences. These two great actors, however, are remembered not for their letter-writing but for their stage and screen performances. Gwen tried to recapture the impact of Olivier's 1946 *King Lear* in a broadcast to South Africa:

'As we follow Lear, through the growing storm and terror that his own act has unleashed upon him, we are almost unbearably moved. Few actors would dare to make of themselves the tattered scarecrow that this King Lear shows us in the heath scene, with naked bleeding feet and a wreath of field flowers set at a crazy angle over one ear; yet when he says "Every inch a king" we know it to be the truth. Two moments in his performance were for me almost unendurable: the first when for an instant his disordered brain clears and he recognises his faithful old follower, Gloucester, whose eyes have been put out by the fiendish Regan; I'll never forget the picture of Lear comforting the weeping Gloucester, the two old men like children, sorrowing over each other's griefs. And again at the end of the play, when the Lear enters with the dead Cordelia in his arms; madly he tries to bring her to life, putting her arm round his neck, and as it falls down each time, replacing it with growing frenzy until it seems like the disjointed arm of a marionette. I can still hear the desolation of his voice as he said "No, no, no life! Thou'lt come no more. Never, never, never, never, never." One felt that the sorrows of all humanity were fused into that one word. It's not often in our modern theatre, we experience the catharsis, or purging of soul, through pity and terror that great tragedy gives us. This was one of those memorable occasions.'[37]

This extract is taken from a talk which begins with an account of the post-war plans for developing the Old Vic and also creating the New Vic as a training centre. Laurence Olivier leads a team of producers that includes Michel St Denis, Glen Byam Shaw, and George Devine. While the Old Vic building is being repaired after the extensive war damage it received, temporary headquarters have been shifted to the New Theatre. It was here that Olivier and Richardson were to offer packed houses many of the most 'memorable occasions' of their lives. Yet theatre management, play production, and playing the star role can be uneasy bedfellows. In addition, during 1946 and 1947 Olivier was planning, directing, and playing the lead in the film of *Hamlet*. In January 1948 Vivien Leigh wrote to Gwen saying how hectic life was. She and Larry were packing for their nine-month tour of Australia and New Zealand. It was such a long time to be away and they would miss their lovely new house in the country, especially the garden with all the spring flowers. The film of *Hamlet* was due for release after they started on their tour.

'I've seen bits of it and I really think the boy has done alright - Pray God it will be a success for him for he's practically killed himself over it - but I think *enjoyed* it too - hugely - He absolutely loves directing films.'[38]

Vivien Leigh ends her letter by saying that she is just about to put on a pair of stockings that Gwen has sent her from South Africa. She and Gwen were to meet two months later in the Cape, when Gwen acted as host to the touring party during their brief stay on their way to Australia.

During the 1950 Stratford-upon-Avon season Gwen was anxious to see as many plays on the London stage as possible, so that she could pass on to Marda in South Africa suggestions for performance there. She had seen Christopher Fry's *The Lady's Not for Burning* in 1949 starring John Gielgud and Pamela Brown, and been very impressed. The following year Laurence Olivier produced and acted in Fry's *Venus Observed*. Gwen sees it and reports to Marda:

'...went up for a night to see *Venus Observed* - an enchanting play - but I think would be caviar to the general in S.A. Larry's production is, I think, too elegant - the play when I read it has an elegiac quality - something of the nostalgia one finds in Chekhov - but I dare say he thought the play needed all the visual style he could give it. It's not the success *The Lady* was – tho' as a play I like it better - if Vivien had been free to play it - it would have run forever of course. I think Larry is too *avid* for success and power at the moment and is wearing himself out. He is so busy being a manager he hasn't the time to remember he is an artist and, as he told me himself, is playing his part with his mind on his next production, worries of casting and what have you - which is hardly fair to Christopher Fry!
I spend next weekend with them at Notley and fear I am not grand enough – "We dress for dinner to impress the parlour maid" says Larry. Oh dear, oh dear, my undies and accoutrements will not I fear pass muster!'[39]

Gwen's assessment of Vivien Leigh's ability to fill a theatre for a long run was fully endorsed by Binkie Beaumont, who was confident she had more pulling power than her husband.[40] This fact might have put an added strain on that famous marriage. The couple lived grandly and entertained with awesome splendour. Gwen spent the next weekend at Notley Abbey, but she need not have been apprehensive about the state of her undies. She wrote to Marda that although her stay had been 'luxurious' it had not been 'a bit grand'. She admired the fourteenth century abbey and the way that Vivien had furnished it with the most exquisite taste - every piece is an

'objet d'art and yet it does not look like a museum. Most of the things she collected while on tour in *Skin of Our Teeth* - bed linen and furnishing perfect, and wonderful tableware - and glass. She has a cordon bleu cook, and really I would be sorry to stay too long as one would not get into one's clothes - we also had thick, thick cream - yellow and luscious - at every meal - as they have three Jersey cows. The place has 65 acres most of which they let to a farmer - but they are mad about the garden - and have planted hundreds of trees and know each one by name and fuss over them just as we do...Hamish Hamilton, the publisher, was there with his wife - They spent the day but drove back to London for the night, so I was the only one staying. We had a lovely restful evening listening to records. They have a whole record room and a perfect instrument - I am so impressed by the knowledge they both have of the arts other than the theatre - they know about pictures and music and literature, and I feel so ill educated beside them.'[41]

When Gwen was at Notley Abbey Laurence Olivier had told her of his management and production plans and the problems that attended them. An acute anxiety was shortage of funds. She was being entertained most generously in a stately setting, but the system that supported this style of living was strapped for cash. Her realisation of the severe strain under which he was working, that which she had sensed a week earlier, when she had seen *Venus Observed* and talked to him afterwards, was confirmed during the weekend. She had felt that the augurs for the future were not good. Her sense of unease at the time was well-founded. The couple's lives drifted apart. Laurence Olivier's career continued and diversified, under ever increasing tension, but the marriage failed. Vivien Leigh's last few years were the stuff of tragedy. She died in 1967. A service was held in the parish church of St Martin-in-the-Fields. Emlyn Williams read an extract from 'Of the Progresse of the Soule' by John Donne; John Gielgud gave the address. The Donne passage began:

> 'Look upward; that's towards her, whose happy state
> We now lament not, but congratulate.
> Shee, to whom all this world was but a stage,
> Where all sat harkning how her youthfull age
> Should be emploi'd, because in all she did,
> Some Figure of the Golden times was hid.'[42]

After John Gielgud had delivered the address, the congregation sang the Battle Hymn of the American Republic, 'Mine eyes have seen the glory of the coming of the Lord...Glory, glory, Hallelujah.' The evocation of Scarlett O'Hara in *Gone with the Wind* was inescapable. Gwen was one of the singers.

Gertrude Norman, one of Gwen's dearest friends, died on 12th March 1961, at the age of eighty-one. She had acted for many years with Minnie Fiske in New York and then had joined Sir Henry Irving's company in England. She was eleven years older than Gwen but her friendship for both Gwen and Marda was warm and long-standing. Gertrude Norman was known to all as 'Toto'. She was extremely well-read, knowledgeable about all the most recent developments in the theatre and in opera, and accustomed to attend each new production two or three times so that she had a full grasp of the play or opera, and the performers' prowess.[43] Among the letters addressed to Gwen and Marda is one dated less than a year before she died. She begins 'Darling, great, loyal and wonderful little Gwen...' and goes on to thank

Gwen for the generous gift of eggs and flowers, and for the invitation for her to stay at Tagley. She cannot accept because she is so busy with work for the Musicians Benevolent Fund, also she has a sister to keep an eye on, but she promises to visit for a day. She is just off with two friends to see Gielgud perform in a play. 'How marvellously he has enriched the lives of millions...by his dedicated, disciplined, rare and glorious art'[44] - a sentiment that Gwen would have most warmly endorsed.

On the night of Toto's death Gwen and Marda had invited her to dinner. When she did not come, they made enquiries and discovered she had died peacefully in her home. The funeral was arranged for the afternoon of Thursday, 16th March, at Golders Green Crematorium, and Gwen was invited to conduct it. She devised a simple service with some Bach organ and choral music as an introduction, followed by her reading short passages from two Psalms and the Book of Revelation. She then read from the Christian Science Textbook, *Science and Health with Key to the Scriptures*, by Mary Baker Eddy. There followed a prayer, and a hymn was sung during the committal. She finished with the Blessing: 'The Lord bless thee, and keep thee: the Lord make his face to shine upon thee.' Her conduct of this service must have had a profound effect, because she received many letters, some from people she had not known, who expressed their deepest appreciation. An acquaintance wrote:

'I couldn't say much to you yesterday so now may I write to tell you how you lifted us out of our desolation into happiness that our beloved...had been spared so much suffering and pain. She would have said thank you to you with outstretched arms in that dear loving voice...And I suppose we shall not meet at Smallhythe anymore - but we can remember always.'[45]

Toto, with Gwen and John Gielgud, had always tried to be present at Small Hythe for the annual Ellen Terry celebrations. The celebrations would continue, but with one pilgrim less.

Another death, that of Marjorie, occurred a few years later. Gwen, with her endless parcels, had tried to keep Marjorie fed and warm in battered and freezing post-war Vienna. She had nursed her at Tagley Cottage when she was ill, and had continued to send her money on a regular basis throughout her life. In May 1964 she received a sad and desperate letter from her sister, then living in a flat in Torquay. She thanked Gwen for her cheque and for the offer to pay for a telephone in her flat. The gist of this long letter was that she felt near to death. Her Christian Science practitioner had approved her seeing a doctor, who had recommended that she should be visited and, if possible, looked after by her family. She had written another book about singing but had been unable to interest a publisher. Perhaps after her death her children would 'cherish the manuscript' and get it published. She asked Gwen to visit her as soon as possible; she was wretched that her children did not seem to want to have anything to do with her. This was the main reason she had taken herself off to Devon.[46] She died later that year, not in Torquay, but near her birthplace in Conway, north Wales - a sad death following an unfulfilled life. Her sister had done what she could.

Perhaps no one had a more fulfilled life than Sybil Thorndike. She was buoyant, busy, successful, happily married, with a close and loving family. Her Christian beliefs embraced pacifism and the championing of the underdog.

Throughout her life she carried a banner for the deprived and underprivileged. She had created the part of Shaw's St Joan in 1924, and for the rest of her life she was forever leading her troops into one kind of moral battle or another. She was greatly gifted, with abounding energy, much loved, and was made a Dame of the British Empire in 1931. From the time that Gwen wrote to her wishing her well for the first night of *St Joan*, and she replied appreciative of the many West End performances of Gwen she had already seen, they were bosom pals. They wrote to each other very regularly over a fifty-year period, visited each other's homes, shared the same friends, and sometimes acted in the same plays. They also shared a love of music to an unusual degree. Sybil had trained as a concert pianist at the Guildhall School of Music, but was forced to relinquish that profession when she suffered from hand-cramp. Gwen was able to share her musical interests with Sybil in their concert-going. When Gwen was in South Africa during the war, and hungry for news of the theatre in England, Sybil would tell her in detail who was in what, and how well they were doing. She wrote in May 1940, when things were particularly grim in England, replying to an earlier letter from Gwen. She praised the work that Gwen and Marda were doing in South Africa, was laconic about 'the awfulness of the war', but expanded with news of the theatre and her ENSA activities with Lilian Braithwaite –

'as the hospital work has grown hugely (sadly); Edith Evans is on tour with Cousin Muriel; Alec [Guinness] is waiting to be called up any day now – he's hoping to be exempted till *The Tempest* is over – he's Ferdinand. Edith and Peggy's and Alec's poetry recitals were such a joy and they made £100 for theatre charities – wasn't it splendid? *King Lear* was such a thrill - and did so well - of course it dropped when things became so acute. Jessica [Tandy] was beautiful and Fay [Compton] and Cathleen Nesbit wonderful as the two nasties! Jack Hawkins made a huge hit as Edmund and Lewis's [Casson] Kent was just real Kent - honest, sincere and a darling person. John [Gielgud] was superb - always exciting - bits better than other bits - but what he didn't get in huge power he made up in other ways and moving, oh! so moving - he is a thinking actor. *Tempest* is enchanting. Oliver Messel has done a fine job so has George Devine producing. Jack H[awkins] Caliban - amazing- Jessica Tandy so so lovely and new Miranda - and John - well you know his Prospero - but this is so much more than before and looking such a splendid Italian Elizabethan this time.'[47]

This sort of letter to Gwen in her self-imposed exile was food and drink as Sybil knew full well. She was diligent in maintaining the service.

Sybil and her husband, Sir Lewis Casson, celebrated their diamond wedding in 1968. The following year, at the age of ninety-three, Lewis died. His memorial service was held in Wesminster Abbey. The readings were by John Casson (a poem by William Henley 'A late lark twitters from the quiet skies'), John Gielgud (from *The Tempest* 'Our revels now are ended'), and Canon Edward Carpenter (Revelation xxi, 1-7 'And I saw a new heaven and a new earth'). At the end of the service, as the procession withdrew, the bells of the Abbey were rung, half muffled.

At the time of Lewis Casson's death Gwen wrote a number of letters to Sybil, and she replied briefly, mostly on cards. One of them reads:

'How lovely, Gwen darling - Such a beautiful reminder - Yes, Lewis would be so cheered by the Abbey - he never thought anything of himself really. Oh! I'm so glad you will be there...Thank you for the lovely thought...'[48]

Many find it very difficult to respond in any truly helpful way to other people's bereavement. Gwen seemed to have no such problem. Time and again, as here with Sybil Thorndike, she was able to write giving comfort and support, judging imaginatively how her response might prove most helpful. Moreover, she would know how to follow up expressions of sympathy with most practical suggestions, such as invitations to Tagley Cottage for a period of recuperation.

No one laid a greater claim on that well of sympathy than her friend, Marda Vanne. Whether together or apart, there was between them a flow of love and mutual concern. Marda's happiness and poise of mind hinged on the physical proximity of Gwen, without which she seemed unable to function satisfactorily. Gwen, while wishing to be loving and supportive, required sufficient space in which to exert her freedom and independence. From the time when she came to England late in 1941 to begin rehearsals with John Gielgud for *Macbeth*, until the time that she returned to South Africa, late in 1942, Marda was distraught. During Gwen's Stratford-upon-Avon season in 1950, although Marda managed somewhat better with her play-management, she was constantly racked with the thought that Gwen would not return to her in South Africa, and she conveyed such anxieties in her correspondence with Sir Barry Jackson, Scott Sunderland, and the South African artist, Le Roux Le Roux. All three visited Gwen while she was in England in 1949 and 1950. They saw her Stratford-upon-Avon performances and talked with her afterwards. Barry Jackson and Scott Sunderland came together, and Scott reported back to Marda that although he and Barry had always thought that Marda and Gwen were inseparable, it seemed now as though Gwen could manage quite well without Marda.[49] Le Roux Le Roux wrote, describing Gwen as serene and quiet, savouring her independence, and he advised Marda to leave her for the moment and make no demands on her.[50] These friends had been briefed by Marda to spy on Gwen and report back. It was again one of those periods when Marda was at a very low ebb. A friend, from the United Kingdom Information Office in Johannesburg in April 1949, tried to comfort her:

'I know that there have been days when you've given up and grabbed the brandy bottle and when the anguish within has translated itself into a hellish mood without, when small irritations never noticed in the ordinary way, become hot pins. But, darling, what else can you expect?'

When one is utterly bereft, agony of mind cannot be stilled in a day or a week or a month...and it has to come out somehow.

And now there is the beginning of hope and a job to do. The first will begin to give you life again and the second - the job well done, as you will do it - will give you back some sense of security you have lost.'[51]

Later that month Marda wrote to Gwen saying that she had discarded alcohol once and for all.[52] She managed to pick up her production work again, and achieved a success with *Arms and the Man* in 1949, and then became involved with the presentation in 1950, in collaboration with Basil Dean, of Flecker's *Hassan*; but it proved less than an unqualified triumph. The production had artistry and panache, but audiences were thin, and her drinking problems again beset her.

Gwen returned to South Africa on a temporary basis in 1953 and then came back to England for a series of engagements, some of which were of significance. Marda also visited England on a number of occasions during this decade. But in 1962 she asked for all her things at Tagley Cottage, including books and clothes, to be sent to her house on the Cape.[53] Earlier Gwen had negotiated for the remortgaging of Tagley Cottage in order to repay Marda for her initial investment in the property.[54] In 1963, Marda changed her mind yet again and decided to apply for British citizenship and leave South Africa for good. On her return to England she took up residence in Kensington. She remained on affectionate terms with Gwen and the two friends met regularly and also maintained the flow of their correspondence. Marda had complained in 1939 that whereas there would always be interesting parts for John Gielgud, Edith Evans, and Gwen, she would be excluded.[55] She now found that she was in regular employment for jobs in radio, television, and on the stage. Her work was greeted with acclaim, as her fan mail testifies. In particular, her performance as Mrs Avery in the stage adaptation of E. M. Forster's *Howard's End* elicited a great deal of praise. The part was small, but Marda's mastery and magic in portraying eccentric character parts had not been lost. The last part that she played was that of Anfisa, the old nurse in Frederick Messina's television production of Chekhov's *The Three Sisters*. This was transmitted in February 1970. Soon afterwards her emphysema, from which she had long suffered, took its heavy toll, and she was taken to hospital, where she died on 27th April 1970. Father Ambrose, the Prior of the Carmelite Priory in Kensington, had for many years been pastorally concerned for Marda. Gwen wrote to him asking that a requiem mass might be arranged. It was duly sung with organ and choir on the morning of Tuesday, 16th June.[56] Instructions were given for the burial to be in Gunnersbury Cemetery. Gwen paid for a Portland stone memorial tablet with an inscription and agreed to an annual payment for the maintenance of the grave.[57]

In the autumn of 1962 when Marda was trying to decide whether to stay in South Africa, where there was no work for her, or risk returning to England, she received a long letter encouraging her to return. It came from Ronnie Adam, who was the same age as Marda and a former flame of long ago. Ronnie Adam had moved from South Africa to England to work in theatre management. He continued a friendly association with Gwen and Marda but, with increasing family commitments, relinquished his theatrical business. In his letter he compared his own background with Marda's, pointing out how she had been blessed with material benefits which had not come his way:

'Now you - you with your generosity, your intelligence, your warmth, with the dear "woman" side of you, your integrity, your charm, your simplicity - bedevilled, churned up with your bodily appetites, your physical laziness, your combustible desires - ending in loneliness and frustration. Darling, this must not be. There *is* comfort in growing older if others can save one from turning in upon oneself.'[58]

He went on to assure her that there would be work for her in England, and ended with reference to Gwen:

'...she sent us two seats for a matinée of *Penny for a Song*. We saw her in her dressing room for 7 minutes of quiet, surface chatter. I feel that she has filled her life quite satisfactorily. The cottage - the friends that visit her - the excitements of work and the possibilities of work - Gwen learnt, years ago, to live for herself and herself alone. I feel that she has no wish to be burdened with the demands of others - no wish to feel responsible for anyone else's well-being - I feel that she has always been the immaculate gazelle, ready to have its ears tickled, its flank gently stroked, but with ears and nostrils twitching with the apprehension of capture, and ready to bound into the bush at the first sign of involvement.

You were always the better actress - with greater versatility, greater humanity, - but Gwen had, and has, the ruthless egotism that makes the star. Don't base the rest of your life on her...'[59]

In 1963 Marda returned to England, she returned to work, and she returned, against Ronnie's advice, to Gwen. They kept separate homes, but were frequently together when their professional commitments allowed. Tagley still drew them together, and after Marda's death, until her own, Gwen always designated one of the rooms 'Marda's room'. Of the two thousand and more letters in the Ffrangcon-Davies archive Ronnie's is the only one that speaks disparagingly of Gwen. There is no evidence that Marda gave credence to his view. She had written for Gwen a simple lyric in 1956, which she refrained from sending her until she was sailing to South Africa in 1962. At the bottom of the poem she wrote 'Candlemas: (Feast of the Purification of Our Lady, and the lighting of the Easter Candles):

Tagley Cottage, Tagley Cottage,
Are the roses still as red,
As they were when first we saw them,
New and proud, and when you said,
Let's go out together, dearest,
On Life's long unchartered way. -
Dear, my love, of all the fairest,
May the roses last your day.'[60]

Here was her heart, and here it stayed.

Evening Star (1958-1970)

Eugene O'Neill's *Long Day's Journey into Night* was written in 1940-41. It is the playwright's masterpiece. He died in 1953, and the play was first performed in 1956. It contains a great deal of painful autobiographical material. In the autumn of 1958 the American director, José Quintero, presented the play in England first at the Edinburgh Festival, then at the Lyceum, and later at the Globe. The play is the story of a day in the life of the Tyrone family. James Tyrone, the father, has been an actor of talent, but he has betrayed that talent in seeking 'popularity'. He has turned to concerns with real estate. His meanness has been the source of much family unhappiness. His wife, Mary, was denied sound medical advice after the birth of Edmund, her second son, when a hired quack gave her drugs. Her subsequent drug-dependence, her hands crippled with rheumatism, and the uncertain balance of her mind, throw a shadow over this day. The elder son, Jamie, is a drunkard, a womaniser, and a ne'er-do-well; the younger son Edmund, who has a poetic flair, has to come to terms with the fact that he has tuberculosis. In this family love and recrimination are intertwined. Quintero cast Anthony Quayle as James Tyrone, Gwen as Mary Tyrone, Ian Bannen as Jamie, Alan Bates as Edmund, and Etain O'Dell as the maid.[61] The impact of the play was immensely powerful. Kenneth Tynan, who had seen the earlier productions of the play in New York and Berlin, captured the intensity portrayed:

> 'The family goes round and round in that worst of domestic rituals, the Blame Game. I blame my agony on you; you blame yours on her; she blames hers on me. Father blames his past; mother blames father; elder son blames both; and younger son blames all of them. If the play has a flaw, it is that O'Neill, the younger son, lets nobody blame him: though I recall, as I write this, the moment when his mother cries out that she would not be what she is had he never been born. The wheel coming full cycle runs over them all...By West End standards all these performances are exceptionally good. That of Ffrangcon-Davies is magnificent. In this production the mother is the central figure, a guileful, silver-topped doll, her hands clenched by rheumatism into claws, her voice drooping except when drugs tighten it into a tingling, bird-like tightrope brightness. Her sons stare at her and she knows why they are staring, but: "Is my hair coming down?" she pipes, warding off the truth with a defence of flirtation. At the end, when the men are slumped in a stupor, she tells us in a delicate quaver how the whole mess began. "Then I married James Tyrone, and I was happy for a time..." The curtain falls on a stupendous evening.'[62]

Critics mention the ovation that was especially given to Gwen after the fall of that curtain, and many subsequent curtain-falls, of this production. The letters she received from distinguished and discriminating correspondents reiterate the 'groundbreaking' or 'definitive' nature of her performance. Her portrayal of Mary Tyrone etched itself into the mind. Many years later, in 1984, Gwen sent a note to Glenda Jackson, congratulating her on an accomplished performance. She received the following reply:

> 'Dear Miss Ffrangcon-Davies,
>   Your letter gave me so much joy! I have admired your work for as long as I can remember and your performance in *Long Day's Journey into Night* is one of the few truly great performances I have seen. To know someone you admire likes your work is the greatest of all possible tributes and I do thank you most sincerely...'[63]

The 1958 Evening Standard Drama Award for the best performance by an actress was made to Gwen Ffrangcon-Davies for her part in *A Long Day's Journey*

Gwen as Mary Tyrone in *A Long Day's Journey into Night*
with Anthony Quayle as James Tyrone, 1958

As Mrs Candour in *School for Scandal* with Peter Barkworth, Geraldine
McEwan and Malcolm Keen, 1962

into Night. It was made without dispute: there was no close challenger for those laurels. Two years later she was invited to play the same part in Toronto with a Canadian company. Again, she performed to great acclaim. On returning to England there followed what she termed 'tiny parts to pay the frightening bills': Queen Isolde in *Ondine* by Giraudoux (January, 1961); the Queen Mother in *Becket* by Anouilh (June, 1961); and *Penny for a Song* by Whiting (August, 1962). What Gwen greatly enjoyed at this time, that made the participation in these small parts so tolerable, was her being part of the Aldwych Theatre Royal Shakespeare Company. The fellowship was a reward in itself.

For the October 1962 Haymarket production of *The School for Scandal* she was offered the part of Mrs Candour. She read the play and thought that it was not the part she would have chosen for herself, but she accepted, because it meant her joining once more a distinguished cast led by John Gielgud and Ralph Richardson. Gielgud was also the director. An added incentive was that the company had been invited to perform in the United States and Canada. The tour was extensive and lasted several months. When they performed in Washington D.C., President Kennedy and his wife came to the theatre, enjoyed the play, and later met the cast; and Gwen was one of those invited by the President to attend the White House ceremony on 9th April 1963 to witness the signing of the resolution of Congress designating Sir Winston Churchill an Honorary Citizen of the United States.

After the gaiety and glitter of the tour, life back in England, especially without much work, seemed rather humdrum. In the autumn of 1964, however, Gwen found herself performing with Sybil Thorndike in *Season of Goodwill*, a comedy by Arthur Marshall, destined for a provincial tour before opening in London. It was a slight piece of work without a future. Sometimes the laughter came in unexpected places.

Sybil and Gwen played the parts of elderly American ladies from the northern state of Minnesota. When performing in Leeds, Gwen, probably because of her short-sightedness, tripped over and fell out of view behind a sofa. Sybil, who was renowned for coping bravely, if not brazenly, with any stage mishap, came right out of character and leaning over the back of the sofa said in a very English, jolly-hockey-sticks voice: "Are you all right dear?" Gwen struggling to get up behind the sofa, and realising that the play needed to be brought back to America, answered with a Deep South response: "Ah sure am. Ah didn't hurt mehself none". The audience roared with laughter, at which the play, and the accents, returned to northern America.[64]

That deep south accent Gwen was to make use of once more as Amanda Wingfield in *The Glass Menagerie* in 1965. The small cast included Ian McShane, Anna Massey, and George Baker. It proved the beginning of a deep and lasting friendship with Anna Massey. They collaborated in a number of memorable broadcasts.

Gwen's very last performance on the English stage was as Madame Voynitsky in Anthony Page's production of *Uncle Vanya* at the Royal Court in 1970. Paul Scofield played Vanya. Also in the cast were Colin Blakely (Dr Astrov) and Anna Calder Marshall (Sonya). Performing in plays by Chekhov had meant a great deal to Gwen, and she was pleased to quit the London stage in such a trumpeted production. Paul Scofield, in his blending the tragic-comic elements of his part, was proposed as the greatest actor of his age by Martin Esslin, writing in the *New York Times*.[65] Of another performer he wrote:

> 'In the tiny part of Vanya's mother, Gwen Ffrangcon-Davies, one of the great old ladies of the English stage, gives a lovely image of a dotty senile bluestocking - a performance in the Edith Evans class.'[66]

Gwen, perhaps, would have preferred to be in a class of her own, and that reference to 'great old ladies' might have acted as a timely reminder that retirement should be contemplated. She was in her eightieth year. The broadcasting and television work that still lay ahead of her were not as exacting as that grinding requirement of eight shows a week, even for an actress with a small part. Yet there was a surprise still to come. Gwen had bidden farewell to the English stage with her performance as Madame Voynitsky in *Uncle Vanya*, and now she would bid farewell to the South African stage with her performance of Carlotta Alexandra in Anouilh's *Dear Antoine*, presented as a première performance in Cape Town on 24th May 1971. The play was set in Bavaria in the winter of 1913. There was some nostalgia in Gwen turning back the clock to her own time spent in Germany as a young girl with her family in Berlin, and later as an eighteen-year-old assistant teacher at Watzum. In the Cape she was also returning to a community that honoured her work, as an actress and as an ardent missionary for the cause of a South African National Theatre; in that field of work they would always associate her with the name of her friend, who had died just over a year ago, Marda Vanne.

Marda Vanne

158

Chapter Six: The Long, Slow Sunset
(1970-1992)

In Sickness and in Health

Most people who live into their eighties have problems of health to face. They have also to confront the loss of relatives and friends. The making of new friends becomes more difficult. It is time for stocktaking. Gwen was not exempt from such problems. Her short-sightedness as an actress had been a handicap to her even in the 1920s. Gielgud had recognised the problems this had created for her during rehearsals for *Romeo and Juliet* in 1924. It was necessary for her always to have her spectacles handy. She herself had complained about the cumbersome, high-stepped staging of Guthrie's *Henry VIII* at Stratford-upon-Avon in 1950, and Dirk Bogarde, when starring with her in Peter Hall's production of *Summertime* in 1955, had described the undulating stage set as being a perpetual hazard to her. In rehearsal she fell over so many times that her unsteadiness in negotiating the hazardous terrain was deliberately incorporated into the performance for comic effect.[1] In the course of the years she had to cope not only with increasing short-sightedness but also with strabismus, a turn to the eyes, resulting in her eyes seeming to be focused in different directions. With or without spectacles such a condition for an actress, however distinguished, would prove a severe drawback in securing parts for the stage, film-work, or television.

Two other afflictions, which in her old age affected her work as an actress, were her hearing problems and the agonies she had to endure at her London dentist's in his endeavour to fit a satisfactory bridge in her mouth. This latter problem of 'fighting the battle with her ill-fitting teeth' was never properly resolved.[2] The former was greatly helped, aided by the generosity of friends, through the purchasing of the most suitable and efficient hearing-aid.[3] Throughout her life her financial affairs had never received priority treatment. Even when she was receiving handsome sums of money for those leading roles that filled the West End theatres, her generosity to family and friends often resulted in an overdraft at the bank. She held many investments, some through family legacies, but the timing of her buying and selling seldom resulted in a profitable outcome. She frankly acknowledged her inadequacy in the field of business. She consulted her friends, and they responded positively both with advice for her investments and also with the ready money that might directly improve some of those health problems which she was facing.

From the time of her last stage appearance in *Dear Antoine* in 1970 in South Africa until virtually the time of her death nearly twenty-two years later, Gwen was always concerned to know what her next performance would be. When would the next offer of work come along? From her earliest years she had cherished the ambition of being a great actress, and through patience, hard work, and innate accomplishment had achieved that ambition. But there was always more to be done, more to be achieved. There could be no resting on her laurels. When her physical disabilities restricted the offer of parts for stage and television, she accepted with added alacrity contracts for radio. Of course there were bills to be paid and such contracts were helpful in meeting them, but much more than the payment of bills was the drive to fulfil her vocation. This was felt with something of the force of the Puritan work-ethic. Her acting work was not merely for the plaudits, but more as a fulfilment of her life and her religious beliefs. It was her given destiny to be an actress, and she must play this role to the end. And when no work was offered, not even broadcasting, what was to be done? An entry in her diary for 26th December 1979 reads

'1979 - not very pleasant - This is the first year I can remember when I've had no work at *all*.'

Yet her diary entries throughout the year show how busy in so many other ways she has been; in caring for invited guests; exchanging visits with her neighbours; journeying to family and friends in Yorkshire and Northumberland; and, the year round, tending that beautiful Tagley Cottage garden. Her ageing bones begin to complain about kneeling on the damp ground;[4] the ground elder assumes qualities of personal animosity; but the honeysuckle is there, smelling sweeter than ever; her precious, scented roses are rich in their profusion and in season she can lie in her hammock and feel the blessing of the sun upon her. It is those sunless days at Tagley, especially in the winter, that she most dreads.

'The cold in this cottage is unbelievable. £700 worth of heating a year, and every time I touch the fridge my hands are so numb I have to warm them in hot water. At my age to open the garage and bring in the logs and coal for the fire is not funny. But I managed with God's help.'[5]

From the 1980s there are few days when she is entirely free from physical pain, often of an arthritic kind. An entry for 17th January in her diary for 1980 reads:

'...not pleased to find my hip niggles when walking. We go as far as the Hardings [neighbours] - then I turn back. I *will* walk over the waves of error. I will, I will.'

Her Christian Science had instilled in her the belief that she could overcome feelings of physical discomfort by a supreme effort of will power. There is no doubt that in this she was largely successful. Her friends drew on her strength, and felt themselves the better fortified to cope with their own last few years. Among that great number who might have joked with Gwen about her 'Tagley Clinic'[6] were George Howes, Mercia Relph, Caroline Ramsden, Mavis Walker, Cecil Williams, Clive Robbins, Edith Evans, Sybil Thorndike, and Mrs Aubrey Pyke. The last, nicknamed 'Boosie', after a stay at the cottage when she was feeling very poorly, wrote to Gwen: 'I went to the Tagley Clinic all tied up in knots and you ironed them all out.'[7]

During this last period of Gwen's life her nieces, Heather, and Nan [Doreen], did what they could to help her at Tagley, particularly with those heavy physical chores that were exacting such a heavy toll of her. Heather would visit with her husband, Colin, travelling from their home in Herefordshire, and Nan would come with her husband, Roger, from near Ripon in Yorkshire. Roger's tragic death in a road accident had a deep and depressing effect on his wife, and in a way deprived Gwen of a great deal of that energy that she had previously found so helpful.

Less than three miles away, on the road to Finchingfield, lived her oldest friend, Dodie Smith. Dodie, on her return from America to her Essex home, had achieved yet another giant success with the Disney filming of *The Hundred and One Dalmatians*. Although she had written many new plays for the stage, the West End theatre management showed very little interest. She became reclusive and bitter. She and her husband, Alec, would frequently visit Tagley Cottage, and Gwen would less frequently be invited to The Barretts. Invariably Gwen would enter into her diary such visits, and invariably remark how pleasant they had been. On the other hand, when Dodie wrote her version of the day's events in her journal she would usually find something disparaging to say about Gwen. In 1957, after spending Christmas Day with Gwen, she recorded that they had smoked salmon and champagne for supper. Gwen who had entertained with style and generosity, was now playing Gielgud's mother in Greene's *The Potting Shed*. 'I know that she doesn't like playing old women but she's glad to earn £100 a week.'[8] During the 1969 Christmas at Gwen's, Dodie was disgusted at Marda's drunken behaviour. This was shortly before Marda died. 'My poor Gwen,' Dodie wrote, 'hated age more than anyone: with her dressing up and her false hair, she looked like a fortune teller in a tent, yet despite her deafness she continued to get film and television work.'[9]

In September 1987 Dodie, when Alec had failed to bring her breakfast, found him dead on the floor of his bedroom. As soon as the news reached Gwen she came to comfort Dodie, but Dodie was in no mood to listen, and laid down strict instructions that no one was to attend Alec's funeral - nor hers. When she died towards the end of 1990, ninety-four years old, Gwen attended her funeral with other mutual friends, David Spenser and Vic Pemberton. Julian Barnes, Dodie's literary executor, was also present. This was shortly before Gwen's one-hundredth birthday.

A short while after Dodie's death a television programme was made of her life and achievement.[10] It was produced by Victor Pemberton and directed by David Spenser. In the programme Gwen spoke of her friendship with Dodie, dating back seventy years, and of Dodie's great success as a playwright. Her reflections on the succession of boisterous, exuberant, almost out-of-control Dalmatians, are less than enthusiastic. She noted a marked change in Dodie's character and behaviour on her return to The Barretts after her long stay in America. There might have been some cooling in that long friendship. Certainly, Dodie was less preoccupied with play-writing and the theatre, and more absorbed in other literary forms. As she became more reclusive her comments in her journals on Gwen's excursions - for instance to America and Canada as Mrs Candour in The School for Scandal in 1962, her filming in Tangiers in 1967[11], and her holiday with Cecil Williams in Italy in 1976 - became more acerbic. Both women had left England during the war, and each for the person they loved. Alec was a conscientious objector, and Dodie was anxious that in the event of war he should not receive his call-up papers. They therefore sailed for America in January 1939, and stayed away for nearly fifteen years. Gwen embarked for South Africa with Marda Vanne in the spring of 1940. She had returned to England by sea at the end of 1941, risking the enemy mines and tor-

161

pedoes, and faced again those hazards on her way back to South Africa a year later. But the reputation of both Dodie and Gwen had suffered by these absences. Dodie had yearned to be back in Britain so that she could write from first-hand experience of 'Britain at war'. The magnet pulling Gwen back to Britain was her patriotism and her concern that theatrical standards there should not be eroded by wartime restrictions. She regretted not being able to stand shoulder-to-shoulder with her fellow actors and actresses who had stayed in Britain.

The careers of Dodie and Gwen took rather different directions after the 1939-45 War. Dodie became more noted for the Disney film of her Dalmatian story than for her pre-war theatrical successes. Gwen's work in South Africa continued to be extolled, whereas her return to the English stage was little noticed until her breathtaking performance in *A Long Day's Journey into Night* (1958). Health problems afflicted both women as they grew older. Dodie became more inwardly absorbed by herself, her writing, Alec, and the dogs. Gwen extended herself in travelling, in her personal care of her garden, in her hospitality to friends, and in increasing radio work. Shortly before she died, Dodie had to be taken away from The Barretts because she was no longer able to look after herself. She had clung to the garden gate, unwilling to be moved. Gwen, too, had no wish to be moved into a home. She stayed at Tagley Cottage until she died, which was two days after her one-hundred-and-first birthday.

Memories and Memorials

Gwen's friendship with Cecil Williams had begun to flourish in the 1940s when he took a leading part in her work for the theatre in South Africa. It matured over the years, changing in its depth and quality. In 1942, following Germany's invasion of Russia, Cecil had, largely for political reasons, joined the South African Navy. At the end of the war he returned to the stage, more interested in producing than acting, with an ambition of achieving a measure of racial integration through his stage work. After the war he kept in touch with Gwen from his home in South Africa, and ensured that he visited Gwen in England regularly, especially when she was at a critical phase of her career, such as the 1950 Stratford-upon-Avon season. During the last part of his professional life, when he was banned from returning to South Africa, he acted as an external examiner of speech and drama for Trinity College, London, travelling the world extensively, and from its far-flung quarters writing letters to Gwen of his various activities. In 1976 he and Gwen travelled to Italy together, visiting Venice, Assisi, Florence, Rome, and then returning to Venice. They travelled by car. Gwen kept a record of the places they visited, the churches, cathedrals, museums, and art galleries. Her notebook shows her alert, percipient, tireless. She was eighty-five years old.

Cecil Williams had learned much about the craft of the theatre from his association with Gwen and Marda in the 1940s, and he was to become a prominent theatre director in Johannesburg during the 1950s. His growing fame, however, was fostered also by his political activities in South Africa. He had an affiliation with the Communist party and identified himself with the anti-apartheid struggle. In his productions he endeavoured to include both black and white actors and actresses. Furthermore he became a champion of gay rights. Consequently in the 1950s and

Cecil Williams
(signed on the back, 'Dearest love and very best wishes from Cecil')

1960s he was a prime target for the attention of the South African police. But never more so than when he became a close friend of Nelson Mandela. He had enabled Mandela to travel widely in South Africa by allowing him to pose as his chauffeur, so eluding the police and providing the black leader with the opportunity of rallying support for the growing anti-apartheid rebellion. In 1962 on the 5th April Cecil Williams had relieved Mandela of the driving by taking the wheel himself. The police took notice of the unusual sight of a white chauffeur at the wheel and a black man reclining in the left-hand passenger seat. Cecil Williams and Nelson Mandela were arrested on a dirt road in Howick. They were taken to Pietermaritzburg and locked up in separate police cells. Williams was freed the following day; Mandela was subsequently tried and sentenced to life imprisonment. In 1998 Jezebel Productions made a film of Cecil Williams' life in which Corin Redgrave took the main part. The film, a documentary, was entitled *The Man who Drove with Mandela.*

In the 1979 diary there is an entry for 8th March relating to Cecil's bringing to Tagley Cottage Nan (?Hunter). They have an excellent lunch at the Moot House, Castle Hedingham. In April of that year Cecil stayed at Tagley for three days in April, 6th -9th. On the 5th May Gwen received a telephone call from a friend to say that Cecil had passed away in his sleep. There follow two further references to Cecil in this diary:

'Still stunned and bereft, but am holding on to reality as best I can. (7th May 1979)
'8.30 leave for London. Cecil's funeral - a wonderful uplifting service - no gloom or sadness - all of us united in loving gratitude for all that Cecil has meant to us. I read Psalm 139.' (11th May 1979)

In the 1970s Gwen lost many other friends. Peggy Webster died in November 1972. She was the daughter of Ben Webster and Dame May Whitty, who had dedicated their lives to the theatre. Peggy and Gwen had acted together, holidayed together, and corresponded copiously over half a century. Peggy had directed many operas at the Metropolitan, New York, including *Aida*, and had also directed Paul Robeson in his ground-breaking performance of *Othello*. She was author of *Don't Put Your Daughter on the Stage*, a cautionary tale for the aspirant actress, and of the play *Royal Highness*. She was acknowledged as one of the foremost producers of the plays of Shakespeare in the world. Although an American citizen, she returned to England to die in St Christopher's Hospice, Beckenham. At the Service of Thanksgiving, held in St Paul's Church, Covent Garden, the readings by Sybil Thorndike and Gwen Ffrangcon-Davies had been especially chosen by Peggy Webster before she died. Gwen read from the First Epistle of St Paul to the Corinthians: the basis of apostleship. A missionary zeal informed the work of all three women.

Noel Coward died in 1973, and the Memorial Service was held on 24th May in St Martin-in-the-Fields. Some of his music, 'London Morning', was played as the Prelude, and some of his verse was read by Laurence Olivier: Yehudi Menuhin played a Prelude and Gavotte by J.S. Bach; John Gielgud read Shakespeare's Sonnet XXX 'When to the sessions of sweet silent thought/I summon up remembrance of things past'; the congregation sang Psalm 100 'O be joyful in the Lord', 'Mine eyes have seen the glory of the coming of the Lord...Glory, glory, Alleluya!', and this was followed by an Address from the Poet Laureate, John Betjeman. The last hymn was 'For all the Saints'. After the Blessing 'London Pride' was played on the organ. This was yet another service that was anything but gloomy. Indeed, it smacked of a sanctification.

Gwen had been very fond of Noel Coward. She and Marda had toured South Africa with *Blithe Spirit* and been greeted with unbounded enthusiasm. They had also given Coward hospitality when he visited them at the Cape. In 1950 when Gwen was engaged at the Memorial Theatre, she found time to see Noel Coward's latest play *The Ace of Clubs* being performed in Birmingham. She then wrote to Marda:

'...we were very sad because it was so common and old-fashioned - but I'm glad that [Alan] Dent has given it a good notice - because the others were very mixed - I hope it will be a success because everything he has done since the war has been a failure – He's such a tormented soul - this thing has been written to exploit his last great love, Graham Payne - who is very charming though not in any way outstanding. On the first night Noel was misguided enough to go on and make a speech - whereupon the gallery promptly and rudely booed - which would not have happened if Noel had not gone on himself. He came to see *Henry* [*VIII*] a week ago and was so sweet and generous about Katherine - he absolutely raved - and I felt so truly sad that I hadn't liked his *Ace of Clubs* - but of course I perjured myself and said I *had*. There is something so loveable and touching in him - and then the other devilish side that makes so many people hate him.'[12]

Edith Evans in her later years, when her memory was losing its sharpness, was one of those who thought not too kindly of Noel Coward when, in rehearsals as

Judith Bliss in *Hay Fever* at the National Theatre in 1964, he had exploded at her slowness in learning her part. Memory retention was no problem for Gwen. She used this faculty not only as a primary aid to her acting, but also as a means of consolidating her relationship with friends and acquaintances. She would remember important dates in their lives; she would recall who were friends of friends; and when there was a bereavement she would write to those nearest, expressing her sympathy. When Noel Coward died she had written to one of his closest friends, the artist, Cole Lesley. After the Memorial Service she received the following reply, dated 26th June 1973:

'Dear Gwen,
After all the turmoil a little peace in which to thank you for your dear kind letter when Master died. I was infinitely touched that you should think of me. A great comfort at that dreadful time. Thank you, thank you, from my heart. I was so happy to see you at the Service. It was lovely wasn't it? We had dreaded it, and needn't have. It was not sad. Rebecca West said "Do you know what I liked best? - that packed congregation of friends all singing Alleluia at the tops of their voices for Noel - I thought it was lovely." And it was, and moving too because I am sure they meant it. We often talked of you - you know the immense admiration he had of you. "I have never seen Gwen give a bad performance in all the years I've known her."
He particularly treasured your Queen Katherine that lovely afternoon we came to Stratford. I treasure it too. How fortunate we all were to have known him. I thought you might like to see what the house is like - it has a lovely garden, which is a joy. Inside it is very gay, welcoming and full of Master's spirit. So Graham and I begin to feel less sad, which is what he wanted - he forbade us to grieve.
Once more my thanks for your loving sympathy,
Always
Coley'[13]

This note is written on two sides of a card on the front of which is affixed a coloured photograph of Cole Lesley's oil painting of a large chalet with extensive lawns to the front and mountainous forestry at the back. Beneath the photograph Gwen has written 'Noel's home in Switzerland'.

In 1972 and 1973 two noble lords, William John Montagu Watson-Armstrong, 2nd Baron Armstrong of Bamburgh and Cragside, and Terence Edmund Gascoigne Nugent, 1st Baron Nugent of West Harling, died. Both had distinguished military careers, both were Gwen's dear friends over very many years, both industrious correspondents, and both directly instrumental in ensuring that Gwen received a reasonable pension at just the time when her income as an actress was in decline. William Armstrong was a year younger than Gwen. He had served in the 1914-18 war with the Northumberland Fusiliers, and it was as a member of that regiment that he first was introduced to Gwen. After the war he had a number of consular appointments that took him to many different parts of the world. In 1941 he succeeded his father to the peerage. Built on a bare and rugged hillside above Rothbury in Northumberland, Cragside was famous as a great Victorian house, which, in the 1880s, could boast of hot and cold running water, central heating, fire alarms, telephones, a Turkish bath suite, a passenger lift and, most remarkably, it was the first house in the world to be lit by hydro-electricity. The first Lord Armstrong had been an engineer and an inventor of some genius. His inventions extended to armaments and munitions. In that field, at the end of the nineteenth century, there were large sums of money to be made. With part of his considerable wealth he bought and restored the decaying Bamburgh Castle. Gwen visited and stayed many times at both Cragside and Bamburgh. At Cragside special guest quarters were reserved for her. She maintained a warm relationship with Lord Armstrong, his wife, Zaida (Zidi), their son, William (Wia), and his wife, Maria-Teresa, a baroness. Other of Gwen's friends were also regular guests at Cragside: Nan Munro, Rayne Kruger, and Edith Evans. William Armstrong's letters to Gwen spanned many years. More than fifty remain, covering the period 1950-1972. Many were written from abroad: Canada, Egypt, and Switzerland. Family skeletons were shaken. Gwen was never addressed as a lover, but always as a confidante. Some of the letters contained expression of thanks for the quiet and restorative time he had spent at Tagley Cottage. Zidi also wrote to Gwen in affectionate terms. Both Lord Armstrong and his wife were ardent theatre-goers, and in his letters there was much about the contemporary theatre-scene. When Lord Armstrong died, his son wrote to Gwen thanking her for the good influence she had over his father and especially for her concern for him during his final illness. He told her that his father had left Gwen 'a very modest annuity' of £200.'[14]

Terence Nugent died in the following year and his Memorial Service was held in the Guards Chapel.[15] He was five years younger than Gwen. Like William Armstrong he had been to Eton, but he would have been in one of the lower forms when Armstrong was a senior. After Sandhurst he joined the Irish Guards and served with distinction in the 1914-18 war, winning the M.C. However, his military career came to an end when he was required by royalty to attend them on their various overseas visits. In 1936 he became Comptroller to the Lord Chamberlain, in which post he was required to read play-scripts, visit theatres, and uphold the laws and regulations governing public entertainment. Like Lord Armstrong he had a passion for the theatre and, through his work, a thorough understanding of the range of dramatic material that was presented to the public. He and his wife, Rosalie, had long admired Gwen as an actress, but they met her for the first time shortly before she left for South Africa in 1940. This was the starting point of a long, courteous correspondence punctuated by a number of meetings, such as when he accompanied King George VI, Queen Elizabeth and their two daughters to South Africa in 1947. After he retired he was made President of the King George's Pension Fund for Actors and Actresses. On 5th November 1965 he wrote to Gwen:

'...As you may know this fund was started in 1911 (in honour of King George V's Coronation!) to provide annuities to actors and actresses who have rendered such service to the Profession as to merit recognition. Your position in the theatre is so distinguished that we all feel that you are in every way worthy of this mark of respect. We also hope that the added income will be of use to you in these difficult times. It is good to know that you are playing in *The Glass Menagerie* and we all hope that we shall have the pleasure and privilege of seeing you act for many years to come, but we realise that work is less easy to come by nowadays...'[16]

Terence Nugent goes on to tell Gwen that his Committee formally asks her to accept a pension of £400 per annum, and to notify him of her acceptance, so that the first quarterly payment may be made to her on 1st December. Perhaps, as Gwen agreed to accept this pension, her mind went back to the production of *Hamlet* to celebrate Shakespeare's birthday in 1930. Henry Ainley had taken the lead, and she had played Ophelia. At the end of the play Henry Ainley had informed the audience that the King and Queen had commanded a repetition of the play on 19th May. The performance was to be given in aid of the King George V's Pension Fund for Actors and Actresses. She probably also remembered that wet morning in February 1952 when she waited long hours in the street with her maid, to see King George VI's funeral procession pass through a rain-swept London. On the first page of her largest and most treasured scrapbook is a newspaper cutting; it stretches across the first two pages of the book. It is a black and white photograph of the guards, who have removed a coffin from a gun-carriage. The coffin is draped with a cloth bearing the royal arms. On top of the coffin, at one end, is a wreath of flowers; in the centre, on a cushion, is the crown of England. The bearers with the coffin are about to pass a group of three women, all veiled, and all in black, and all queens. On their right is a tall, erect, military figure, prepared to act as an escort. At the bottom of the page Gwen has written: the Queen (Mother), Queen Mary, Terence Nugent.

In 1976 Gwen lost a further two friends: Sybil Thorndike and Edith Evans. Sybil died in June, and Edith in October. Sybil's Memorial Service, like her husband's, was held in Westminster Abbey. Gwen was unable to attend. She was given an account of it in a letter from Freda Gaye. Freda was an actress who had toured with Sybil Thorndike and Lewis Casson during the 1939-45 war; she later edited *Who's Who in the Theatre* and became the first curator of the British Theatre Museum. She wrote to Gwen on 7th July, following a stay at Tagley Cottage:

'Darling Gwen,
    I am truly sorry not to have written since leaving you, after that happy and restoring week-end, which gave me so much peace and refreshment and always the right kind of stimulation!
    I journeyed home very comfortably having been warned to sit on the LEFT side of the bus, to dodge the western sun. Your lovely herbs are still being so useful, and the roses gave me two days of ecstasy...Then, of course, there was the Abbey Service for Sybil. How much I wish you could have seen and heard it. Joyce Grenfell said she had sat next to Robert Morley who had pronounced the occasion "Really a Coronation - not a Memorial Service!!"
    First the procession of clergy and choir - then the family - Such singing, with Trumpets!...Ralph R. [Richardson] read the 91st Psalm without - for me - feeling it had much meaning for him, but Joyce G. didn't agree! Paul S. [Scofield] gave us the *Cymbeline* "Fear No More" from and by his heart...Then J.G. [John Gielgud] gave his marvellously right address, comparing Sybil to Ellen Terry. It was so just and loving and *right*. While the family went to the Interment, we all sang the Metrical Psalm 23 from the Scottish Psalter...John Casson read Mr. Valiant-for-Truth very well. After a fanfare of Trumpets we were all quiet - and then we had "Now Thank we all

our God". The muffled Abbey Bells, and the standard at half-mast. One really felt the size of everyone's love for her, everyone with his own relationship to her. No tears but such thankfulness. I am thrilled to have been given the drawing of Lewis which Sybil loved and had over her bed. Dear Kathleen [carer] came to lunch on Sunday, and said how marvellously kind you'd been to her. It was just what she needed. Ann [daughter] also said she'd heard how marvellous you'd been, and how Sybil and Lewis had loved coming to Tagley.

Thank you again, darling, for such loving-kindness to me - and I hope to see you again soon...Freda'[17]

As Freda mentioned in her letter, at the Memorial Service John Casson had read that passage from Bunyan's *Pilgrim's Progress* in which Mr Valiant-for-Truth prepares himself for his last journey. It was a passage near to the heart of Sybil, Edith, and Gwen:

'My sword I give to him that shall succeed me in my pilgrimage, and my courage and skill to him that can get it. My marks and scars I carry with me, to be a witness for me, that I have fought his battles who now will be my rewarder. When the day that he must go hence was come, many accompanied him to the river side, into which as he went he said, "Death, where is thy sting?" And as he went down deeper, he said, "Grave, where is thy victory?" So he passed over, and all the trumpets sounded for him on the other side.'[18]

The trumpets certainly sounded for Sybil, as they were to sound a few months later for Edith. At her Memorial Service the only hymn sung was Bunyan's pilgrim-call 'He who would valiant be'. And the dirge for Fidele from *Cymbeline* was also said, but it was given not by a single voice but by two. In the play it is a farewell refrain for a lost sister. The two actresses who had been closest to Edith for more than fifty years, Gwen and Peggy Ashcroft, recited the lines alternately. No threnody over Edith could have been more telling. It was, of course, more than a threnody; it was an incantation to secure the quiet passing of her soul by the two women with whom she had shared the greater part of her professional and personal life. Bryan Forbes gave the Address. At this stage he had nearly completed his biography of Edith Evans.[19] She had wished him to undertake this work, and had been intrigued to hear him read to her the story of her life as he progressed in his task.

In contrast to Peggy and Gwen, Edith had lived a solitary life, feeling the loneliness, and often engulfed in sadness. Her husband, Guy, had died forty-one years previously. She enjoyed the company of men, but her life never took on that pattern. Even when married, her husband spent most of his time away from her, working abroad. Judith Wilson, a very wealthy friend, bought The Gatehouse, Cranbrook, Kent in 1955, and invited Edith to live with her there, sharing the household expenses. Judith died in 1960, but Edith was able to regard The Gatehouse as her own home until she died. In her later years she was neither easy to direct on the stage nor to live with on very agreeable terms as her secretaries, gardeners, and house-servants discovered. But she would listen patiently to Gwen and heed her advice as far as she could. When she was finding it hard to learn her stage lines, Gwen would visit her, even when she was on tour, and settle down in her dressing room or hotel room to hear her go over her part. This Edith found enormously encouraging. Just as in the past she had looked to Gwen for advice about her dresses and her hats, so now she needed Gwen's presence to see her through these last professional crises. After her death Gwen had written to William Houghton and his wife. William had stayed with Edith at The Gatehouse following Judith Wilson's death. He and his wife lived nearby, and since Judith Wilson had bought The Gatehouse they had been employed to do the household chores. William, unused to expressing himself in any literary form, replied how much he would miss Dame Edith, because he had come to think of her almost as a mother. Yes, she was sometimes hard to get on with, but she had pleaded with him not to leave her, and so he had stayed at The Gatehouse, sleeping there night after night. He then recalled how when Edith and Gwen were both acting in *The Chalk Garden* at the Haymarket, Edith's car would bring them both back after the show to The Gatehouse. William's letter is placed in its envelope in one of Gwen's scrapbooks.[20] Next to it is another envelope marked 'Edith's last letters 1975, 1976'. The address is The Gatehouse. Edith is nervous whenever she feels that she has been left alone. She feels poorly: her thumbnail has broken; she cannot find things, particularly envelopes, so she continues writing to Gwen, day after day, until someone can find her some envelopes. She is shocked that her oil bill has gone up to £1,200 and resolves to make some savings. Her handwriting, never pellucid, degenerates to a scrawl. She ends 'God Bless you duckey, always. Edith'. One hears her voice clear enough! Generations of playgoers have gone on hearing that voice.

Sybil Thorndike was created a Dame Commander of the British Empire in 1931; Edith Evans in 1946; Peggy Ashcroft in 1956. Gwen was not so honoured until she had passed her hundredth birthday. When she received the news that such an honour was to be conferred she was obliged to keep silent on the matter until the honours list was made public. She so much wished to tell her news to her dearest friends, especially Peggy Ashcroft.[21] But she could not. Peggy died on 14th June 1991; the citation was dated 15th June 1991. Dame Gwen Ffrancgon-Davies's celebrations were tinged with sadness.

Shovelling snow in the winter of 1979

The Tagley Diaries: (1979, 1980, 1981)

Three diaries were found among Gwen's papers when she died. They cover the years 1979-1981. Each diary is beautifully illustrated: 1979 was issued by The Metropolitan Museum of Art, New York; the other two by the Victoria and Albert Museum. All three were given to Gwen by Mavis Walker. Mavis had been an actress, performing with Gwen and Edith in *The Chalk Garden* at the Haymarket, and had then been employed by John Gielgud as his secretary and aide during his many trips abroad on film work. At the time of these diaries she was living in St Albans Grove, London W.8. The diaries might have been deliberately given to Gwen, at a time when work was not coming her way, to encourage her to set down the daily details of her life as a routine task to alleviate the anxiety she felt when her artistic talents were going to waste.

The diaries contain relatively few references to plays and performances, although Gwen was always listening to the radio or switching on the television in the evenings, hopeful of hearing or seeing something of interest. There are few visits to see plays or attend concerts in London. The visits to London are mainly to see her dentist, or receive other medical attention, usually associated with her hearing aid. Yet these visits give her the opportunity of staying with friends and enjoying a few convivial dinner parties. Travelling about in London was greatly facilitated by Rayne Kruger's offer of putting a taxi service at her disposal. The substance of the diaries covers her shopping, cooking, gardening, dress-making, furniture repair, worry about bills, entertaining guests, visiting neighbours, preparations for Christmas, and the passing of that festival. There is, of course, 'the unloved and unloving' Mrs Drew to keep an eye on. Mrs Drew worked for Gwen at Tagley Cottage in the very early days, and helped to keep it in good order when Gwen was in South Africa. She was three years older than Gwen, who was not above making purchases for her and fetching her coals. When Mrs Drew's husband died in 1950 and Gwen went to Stambourne to commiserate with her, she found that Mrs Drew grieved more for her husband's lost sugar rations than for her husband! Gwen had help in the garden from Colin Rawlinson and, in the house, from his wife, Mary. Doris Hatton, originally appointed as a cook, became her stand-by in most domestic emergencies and also a stalwart in the garden. Whenever Doris was unable to come, for whatever reason, life became distinctly more difficult. The diaries are certainly not written for subsequent publication to astonish the literary world with the diarist's accomplishments. The entries are plain, mundane, but because of the character of the writer never without interest and seldom without a touch of humour. There were times when Gwen felt too ill to make any entry for days on end, and sometimes she covers a whole week's events well after they have passed. But one never feels that the keeping of these diaries is boring or tiresome for her. She recognises it as a discipline to which she should subscribe. The following extracts from the diaries illustrate the texture and pattern of her domestic life.

'1979

January 1. Came in... ice age nothing like it since 1963. It all looks very pretty but the house is icy even with all forms of heat on at full blast. I am alone as Nan and Roger [her niece and her husband] left on Friday.

2. continued efforts not to freeze to death! Deep everywhere and Doris has to

walk as it's too slippery for her to bike - write some letters and pay bills.

5. Decide to cancel Twelfth Night Party and have a lunch instead. The lunch very pleasant and friendly - I so glad to feel more at one with the locals - Take down Xmas Decorations at night.

8. am not very energetic and don't do much - except tidy the paint shed - thaw has come and snow and ice gone - TV documentary about Afrikaaners - excellent.

9. Doris has a cough and stays home. I walk to Strebers with Xmas cards and back to Doris - enjoy the beauty and feel vigorous – make lunch - quite *beastly!* Do nothing after.

12. No Doris - lovely cold winter day. All to do - so get cracking. Fetch in wood - make bed, feed cats, clean floors etc. Walk in the freezing but sunny weather to see Doris - make lunch then a sleep - and no more work, but nice T.V. especially Delia Smith.

13. Hardings to lunch. Still no Doris. I cook the pork too much but the leeks à la Delia Smith are a success. Then went shopping in Sainsburys with Irene and home exhausted!!

17. Cecil for lunch. Cooked a shoulder of lamb and vegetables. Spiced peaches not very good!!

18. shopping in Haverhill. Late lunch roast pork, sleep by the fire, very cold, snow and ice return.

19. Roger and Nan for tea and overnight. 2" of snow and ice.

20. Roger leaves after helping to sweep etc. very sweet and kind all my men friends.

20. *Hair* - gallant little souls - I have made a lamb stew. v. good! They leave early. [Two hairdressers visit, usually on Mondays]

February

16. and 17. [having returned from a few days in London] Return to Tagley with Westrops by roads like jagged glaciers - but happy to be home with KATS - walked to Doris to tell her not to come - visit Mrs Drew - delighting in calamity! Deep snow.

26. Hair - quite forgot this so took the hairdressers to lunch at the Red Lion - cottage pie - appalling but glass of wine surprisingly good!

28. Fish arrived 1st time for 7 weeks lunch Dodie very nice and peaceful. Now they shop only in Finchers!

March

1. Kats delighted with fish at last. Did some cutting out and sewing of chiffon blouse.

20. Kats in disgrace. Someone has eaten a mouse and been *sick*.

27. David phones to say that Ronnie Adam has died.

April

2. Doris away so busy with chores - went down to compost heap, icy cold - and poor crocuses all shut up. Picked daffodil buds from bed under window - blessed creatures seem unperturbed - Fingers frozen stiff!! April!!

June

1. Drinks with the boys [David and Vic]

2. Dodie and Alec to lunch

20. Summer at last we *sit* on the hammock and central heating off! Garden begins to burgeon in spite of ground elder.

21. Go to Nan and Roger [Yorkshire]

26. Go to London stay with Nan [Munro] Nan's for supper

27. Lunch with Wendy Hiller - Lovely! *Lady from the Sea* controversial

28. Nan's birthday party. She so kind and lovely. See Prue and Rayne and Wendy *again.*

July

20. and 24. I wake early, make my tea at 5 a.m. Cloudy start to day but sun breaking thro' Smoky (cat) off her food - and sleeps all day. Very misty morn - but warmer - do some phoning about my will and the septic tank!! - after sleep and tea garden madly in slight thunderstorm.

August

8. Leave for Yorkshire

9. Great gathering of clans at Shoulder of Mutton [former pub near Ripon where Roger and Nan live] and baby worship for new member.

10. Dine with William Armstrong and wife in Spanish restaurant

13. We go to Chollerford for the night to see the Roman excavations. Gorgeous drive back in heavenly sun over the Pennines and Swaledale and Wensleydale - Heavenly- dine with the Armstrongs and Miss Cecil Lewis...

November

18. Go to London by car with Mavis. Straight to dentist - nice Mr Carpenter very helpful but bridge still not possible. Then decides to look in my ear and finds it full of hard old wax. Why did he not look in my ear a year ago!! However arranged Dr Abel to syringe ears at vast cost - again most charming elderly doc. Who remembers being taken to see me in *Richard of B* when he was *twelve.* This shakes me rather, but he makes amends by refusing to believe what I tell him is my age.

24. Marda's Mass and party *very* sweet

December

16. Went to church with the Hardings and to carols by candlelight. I read the wise men lesson as usual

Decorations

23. Mercia and George [Howe] arrive for tea

26. 1979 not v. pleasant - The first year I can remember when I've had no work at *all.*

1980

January

6. Very nice lunch party with Peggy Lawton and meet Mrs Seth Smith who I like very much. I wear my new red hat and feel a sense of guilt at having spent £35 on it.

9. The usual busy day when I'm on my own. One might think I'm really wasting the rest of my life - but no one seems to want me to work in the art world so I guess I'm useful keeping the home fires burning and making a small *peace* in a naughty world!

15. I look hopefully for the post but never anything but *buff envelopes...* usually bills.

February

8. Yesterday was assailed by panic over my financial state - but am now more composed tho' still sad at loss of £2000 on shares! This inflation is past a joke and the weekly housekeeping approx £50.00!!

March

21. Busy morning as always on Friday *but* we manage - Doris and I are a good team - Mavis arrives by bus so light all the lights and candles to welcome her.

22. I regret so much that I don't keep this diary every day - forget for a week and then can't remember so far back!

November

8. I don't feel 100% and so cosset myself and do nothing much - I feel guilty at not rising above physical trials - which are in themselves fairly trivial - I just drift - very wrong!

9. Well I have to pull up now as Doris is away for two days - so I cope with the KATS and the fire - I become a perfect Nibelungen dwarf - a slave to the fire - I wash and iron two blouses "weiter nichts" [no more]

December

2. and 3. Snow melting and everything "mucky"! Went to Mrs Drew with a small snack and a chat - poor soul so unloved and unloving! If only she had taken the bungalow offered her last year - a cosy warm place and now it looks as tho' she'll have to go to a home after Xmas. The winter jasmine is a shower of gold and coming out in the house - After a restless night awake to bitter cold and icy winds - get up after my meagre breakfast and come down to feed the KATS and start the day's chores. Light the fire and wash up and tidy kitchen. Then up and dress. Fishman comes so I emerge in winter boots and a red shawl over my head and old quilted grey coat. Could play any old Chekhov woman at the drop of a hat! Get fish and some veg and think it a kindly act to take fish etc myself to Mrs Drew - she not pleased as she wanted the fish man to fill her coal scuttle and now he has not come. I battle with the sack of coal in scullery - she weeps, full of self-pity - I feel a pig to feel so irritated. So make a hot oxtail dinner carried in large thermos. She approves of enterprise.

1981

January

23. My birthday - in the T.V. rehearsal rooms all day - 85? *The Times* says so! [This was her 90th birthday: the public thought she was 85.] Supper with Mavis and Geoffrey and Nan [Munro] who brings champagne - The children at T.V. were adorable to me - never was I kissed by so many.

26. Bobby Norman and Alec [McCowen] for drinks. Very nice to see them all. Went to Anna Massey's new and superb flat. She is a dear girl.

27. My marathon 10 - 11.30 p.m. a bit of a nightmare - disappointed in end scene - conditions too tough.

28. Home again to a lovely welcome. Doris had made the most enchanting flower decorations everywhere.

February

10. Doris and I decide to make Marda's room a single one again - are frustrated by not being able to move large chest of drawers. Must wait for Colin on Sunday. Day cloudy and cold - fire unamiable!

16. Electrician repairs radiators...he came to mend a plug in my room and stayed all afternoon.

18. new red curtains for Marda's room.

20. I start upholstering a chair. It takes longer than when I did it 10 years ago. Colin comes and does fire and wood - early start on upholstering chair - Good T.V. film about Gordon of Khartoum. Larry wonderful as mad Mahdi.

February

21. lunch Dodie cold cold. No Doris still - called in on way to Dodie and she looked pretty wretched. I felt concerned - Dodie and Alec sweet and kind.

March

1. and 4. I feel a bit low as I broke a tooth last night - shall have to go to London on Thursday - such a bore and expense! Watch *Hedda Gabler* with Diana Rigg - a surface performance and production - Still no Doris but she comes and returns the money I sent her. I very touched.

8. Busy all morning washing and cooking and then the Budget!! However lovely Lent lilies in bloom and crocuses. Fish etc and laundry, then start on yellow chair cover - This make-do-and-mend!! Who would have thought we'd have all that to do again!

14. Watched silly early film of darling Dirk's Doctor series. He is so adorable.

23. Lunch Terry Thomas 12 ocl. And very nice it was - I did my stuff I think and amused them. Then home at 4. Tired watched Glenda Jackson in *Elizabeth* a splendid series - magnificent acting and décor.

April

5. and 6. Mercia leaves after lunch. V. delicious roast chic. And sprouting broc from the *garden*, - which is quite something! Also my famous choc. mousse.

Heather at tea time - But cold, cold, cold. Heather a marvellous help. We spray and feed the roses. I full of aches and feel rather low!

9. a catastrophic bill of £292 *surcharge* for Electricity. This has nearly given me a heart attack. However shall fight it tooth and nail! A lovely day of hot sun tea in garden. Heather leaves after final spray on roses on trellis which have suffered from blackspot.

11. David and Victor to lunch. Lovely to have them to myself. Elec. Bill still haunting me! But still hope to prove the Board wrong.

18. Did a little more feeding of roses magnolias are beautiful...like gigantic...butterflies in the sun but oh - the mind!!

May

11, 12. and 13. Caroline and Ann stay to lunch so I busy in kitchen. They so kind and cheerful - leave at 2.30 - I sleep - then tea and read the lesson - feel v. uninspired - and guilty...after a grey mist start by tea time a heavenly May day - I out in the garden to feed peonies and delphs - and to hand pick ground elder from their roots - was out 1hr 30 mins not bad for kneeling and bending! Oh bliss to be out...halcyon day and I alone which halves my joy -

household chores all morning and I pretty stiff after yesterday! I shall finish painting furniture and hope to spray roses. Weather deteriorates...The Pope has been shot, but not killed. Oh! Oh!

August

4, 5. and 6. Evening on the terrace exquisite!...Hotter than ever. So shall stay v. still. Pam SS. [Seth-Smith] To drinks this eve. A most lovely evening and so enjoyed having someone to *share* the beauty -...a thunder storm - it was a terrific one all over the county...dark as pitch at 1 ocl: I thought how terrified Marda would have been. So I did some C.S. work about it and slept as usual.

November

6. Very busy - early start cook fish for Kats - usual chores arrange food for supper and leave at 10.30 (with Clive Robbins) for concert at The Maltings - Good concert - but alas! Ben B[Britten] is not for me but *Firebird* wonderful! A long day and pretty tired at bed time.

December

24. No buses so Mavis arrives by train. Robin will fetch her. Doris and I do the decorations in record time - all up and place tidy and swept by lunch when Mavis comes.

25. We have a happy Xmas morning very unusual! And go in freezing cold to David and Victor. Nice party 8 in no. and super food cooked by Vic very very lovely day!

January 1982

1. Doris and I cook like mad She wonderful and cheerful but won't come to the party. I don't know why. Clive arrives with Mavis.

It is clear from her diary entries that at times Gwen became deeply upset by her financial situation. That large electricity bill preys on her mind. A generous friend, hearing of her plight, paid the whole bill. When the Electricity Board wrote to her proposing to debit her account by £50 a month, she replied, saying that she would not accept such an arrangement, and instead of so increasing her electricity charges intended to reduce them. Other worries beset her apart from payment of bills. There are frequent references to a sense of guilt: at sleeping too much; at not being sufficiently 'mindful of the needs of others'; at neglecting her garden; at spending too much on a hat. It is her Garden of Eden but, alas, it is threatened not by the Serpent, but by ground elder. There is a philosophic entry on 17th May 1981: 'Have decided to take Geoffrey Smith's advice and waste no more money on weed killer but have the ground elder.' The extracts quoted mention only few of the many friends who came to see her from afar, and those staunch local friends, who were concerned for her happiness and well-being. She did not attend church regularly, but usually read at the Christmas carol service. During her last years at Stambourne the development of the church choir was a cause of great joy, and she remarked on its excellence. The choir was later to be invited to London to take part in her Memorial Service. That low point which she had reached at the end of 1979, when she lamented that for the entire year there had been no offer of work, extended to the beginning of 1980 when her post seemed to bring nothing but buff envelopes. But as 1980 progressed the buff envelopes gave way to more attractive letters with offers of work in a variety of fields. She responded with gratitude and high spirits.

Until the late 1970s Gwen had been given only a small amount of television work but a great deal of radio broadcasting. Her broadcasting began in 1925 and included, for example, a Hospital Appeal (1925); Scenes from *Tess of the D'Urbervilles* (1925); Song Concert with Nellie Chaplin (Harpischord) (1926); *Othello* - Desdemona (with Godfrey Tearle and Malcolm Keen) (1933); World Theatre - *Cyrano de Bergerac* (1938); Calling South Africa (on her return to England) (1941); The Brains Trust (1943), Curtain Up: *Victoria Regina* (1949) Stars in their Choices: *Romeo and Juliet* (1954). Her broadcasting continued well into the 1970s with talks about Rutland Boughton (1956) and Walter Sickert (1961); readings from the Letters of Elizabeth Barrett (1961); Desert Island Discs (1962); and in the 1970s a ten-part reading of *Period Piece* by Gwen Raverat; and playing Miss Havisham in a serialised version of *Great Expectations*. Such a sample of her broadcast work is the merest fraction of the total. Gwen was accustomed to receive fan mail following her stage performances, but she also heard from a number of admirers who appreciated her broadcasts. For instance, Bernard Miles, who had in 1975 listened to the broadcasting of *Great Expectations*, typed a note to Gwen expressing his admiration for her performance of Miss Havisham.

> 'You are marvellous in *GREAT EXPECTATIONS*. Precision, <u>style</u>, phrasing, rhythm – it's all there! - and so very rarely heard...Many congratulations.'[21]

In the note he has underlined the word style, and linked the underlined word to what he has written in long hand beneath his signature: 'That's what it boils down to!!'

Theatre critics in retirement found themselves spending more time listening to the radio than going to the theatre. Two such were T. C. Worsley and Alan Dent. Each had followed Gwen's career for more than fifty years. Alan Dent in 1973 had heard her in a broadcast reflect on some of her theatrical experiences.

> 'This is your old friend, and critical admirer, and colleague - Alan Dent.
>
> It is just to say...how much I admired your talk, last week on sound-radio, on your rich theatrical feast.
>
> You delivered it with the professional expertise - not a single *um* or *er* - of Johnny [Gielgud] himself. And I was particularly glad that you dwelt, towards the end, on the Saint-Denis production of Chekhov's *Three Sisters* which I still think the best production ever of that particular masterpiece...
>
> Johnny gave me the record of the music when the army march away at the end of that *Three Sisters*. It is nearly worn out, but I treasure it.'[22]

T. C. Worsley, too, wrote, having heard her on the radio.

> '...I must send you a note of gratitude for two superb radio performances I have been enjoying: Miss Havisham in the Dickens is masterly! Aunt Mant in the *Wings of the Dove* [Henry James] - exact to the last degree. I wish I still had the opportunity of trumpeting them publicly.

Reminiscing about the theatre of yesterday I often refer to your mother in *Long Day's Journey into Night* as one of those definitive pieces of acting that I was lucky enough to see when I was still a theatre critic. In fact much though I wanted to see Larry as the father I couldn't bear the thought of my smudging of your heartbreaking performance...'[23]

Both Worsley and Dent, when they wrote to Gwen about her most recent performance, wished also to recall past performances. This was a characteristic of a great deal of her fan mail. As aged ears heard her voice on radio in poem, play, or novel, a response would be forthcoming. An arthritic hand would take up pen, and the ensuing letter would thank Gwen for her most recent performance and then reminisce about *The Immortal Hour*, or *Romeo and Juliet*, or *The Lady with a Lamp*, or *The Barretts of Wimpole Street*. It is striking, too, to note how many, as they listened to her on the radio, were, by her magic, stopped dead in the midst of their ironing or washing up. Dirk Bogarde admits to being one of these. And there were tears: tears of joy and tears of sadness, for magical moments remembered, when their own lives had been illuminated by a stage presentation in which Gwen had appeared.

After the death of Edith Evans in 1976, Gwen was asked to take part in a broadcast programme, paying tribute to her friend. It was transmitted on November 5th. She received a note from the director, John Gau.

'How joyfully you spoke about Edith on Monday - your affection and admiration shone through it all - a splendid sharing with us of your feelings and thoughts.

Thank you also for a delicious lunch and the excellent company...We shall see each other at the end of the month when you are here with Henry James and the *[Aspern] Papers*: To that I look forward.'[24]

John Gau was the son of her friend, Nan Munro. His wife, Susan, also worked for the BBC, as a presenter of televised programmes. In January1983 the BBC made a striking programme about Gwen, presented by Susan Gau, entitled 'A Life in the Theatre'. It traced Gwen's career from her first appearance on the London stage as a member of the chorus in 1911 in Beerbohm Tree's *A Midsummer Night's Dream*, her success in *The Immortal Hour*, and her partnership with John Gielgud in *Romeo and Juliet* in 1924, to her last appearance on the London stage as Madame Voynitsky in *Uncle Vanya* in 1970. The interview between Susan Gau and Gwen took place in the sitting-room of Tagley Cottage, and the programme itself lasted thirty minutes. There were no outdoor shots. Susan Gau took Gwen through her professional career, filling in some of the gaps in the interview with commentary and shots of some of the performances not specifically covered in the interview. John Gielgud gave his comments about his early association with Gwen, especially their coming together for the first time in the 1924 London production of *Romeo and Juliet*. No one else appeared in the programme as Gwen recalled the various stages of her career. When, finally, she was asked about her philosophy of life, she ended the programme with Lilith's speech which completes the last part of *Back to Methuselah*: 'Of life there is no end...' The programme was well-made, gripping, and the inescapable effect was that of bringing the viewer close to an actress of genius, with a golden story to tell. Over and above that, was the strongest of impressions that there was more of the story still to be unravelled. Gwen was so alert, sharp and persuasive, that the viewer had no doubt that there were yet more parts for her to play. Before the programme was transmitted Susan Gau wrote to her:

'Just a little card to thank you for all your hard work over the last few days. You were so completely splendid. All the crew were completely bowled over by you - that Gwennie Magic casting its spell again! I am sure that when the BBC sees the rushes they'll be very impressed.'[25]

The BBC was duly impressed, but it was not until five years later that it devoted a series of programmes to Gwen, which alerted millions of people, who had never heard of Gwen Ffrangcon-Davies, to the variety of her accomplishments, and how, because of her distinction and longevity, she had walked hand-in-hand with the history of the English theatre for the best part of a century.

Early in February 1988 a radio programme entitled 'Still a Juliet' was transmitted. It comprised a conversation between Nigel Hawthorne and Gwen. Nigel Hawthorne's early years had been spent in South Africa. He recalled having been spell-bound by seeing Gwen and Marda Vanne in a performance of *The Merry Wives of Windsor*. In a very self-effacing way he let Gwen tell the tale of her life in the theatre, and of particular influences such as Mrs Manning-Hicks and, especially, Ellen Terry. She explained how stage movement, so signal a part of her performance as Etain in *The Immortal Hour*, was based on the work of a French-man, Delsarte. She performed Juliet's speeches from *Romeo and Juliet*: first the potion speech, and later the balcony scene, and she gave Portia's speech from the Fourth Act of *The Merchant of Venice*: 'The quality of mercy is not strained...'.

The audience's response to this programme was remarkable. Gwen, Nigel Hawthorne, and the BBC were deluged with letters of keen appreciation. People in their homes were brought to a halt not only in their ironing and washing up, but in dusting, reading, cooking, and drawing. Hearing the passion and the poetry of Juliet's heartache seemed to bring everything to a stop. A complete stranger wrote to Gwen:

'I am aged 45 years old and fell romantically in love at 16 and then suddenly emotionally passionately at 41...Last night your performance of *Romeo and Juliet* "stopped my heart". I have never been so affected by anything. It was so beautiful a masterpiece...Thank you for the great privilege you gave me and many others to be able to hear it...'[26]

The overriding tenor of the letters that came to Gwen in great abundance, following this programme, was of thanks for having reawakened feelings of love that had been lost, forgotten, or unarticulated. The consequent need for expressing gratitude seemed well-nigh compulsive, as one example illustrates:

'February 16. 1988.

Dear Miss Ffrangcon-Davies,
        On Sunday morning my husband came down from his studio unable to draw for the tears in his eyes only to find me crying into the washing up.

They were, in both cases, tears of joy for we had been listening to the Radio and your incomparable Juliet. It was an experience so rare and transcendent for which I can only say, Thank you. Thank you.'27

The Sunday morning programme had included the 'Juliet' extract in 'Pick of the Week'. Tribute was paid to Nigel Hawthorne's handling of the dialogue. He let Gwen tell her story at her own pace without constant interjections, and when she brought to an end her speeches, he allowed pauses of some length to bring home the more effectively the emotional impact she had made. Far from presaging a breakdown in the service, the pauses and silences were moments of intense feeling.

Later that same month Gwen appeared as a guest on the Terry Wogan television programme. Many millions watched, bewitched by the interview, but when it came to an end, because there was no more time for Gwen to speak any Shakespearian lines, the post-bag arriving at the BBC in the next few days contained so many protests that a further appearance of Gwen on another Wogan programme was arranged. It was fittingly scheduled for 26th April, the Monday after Shakespeare's birthday. It also happened to be the 500th Wogan programme in that series. Gwen was the last guest to be interviewed. A member of the cast of 'Eastenders' came first, followed by a former member of the cast of 'Neighbours'. The third item was the singing of three Bulgarian ladies in their traditional folk costumes. The studio lighting was garish; the décor tinselly. When Terry Wogan came to sit by Gwen, she knew that she had to transfix an audience which had little knowledge of her craft. She recited first 'The quality of mercy....', and then the potion speech from *Romeo and Juliet*, for which she had to set the scene for the audience. She wore a black dress with puffed sleeves; a silver brooch at her throat; and a lime green shawl over one shoulder. She sat cross-legged. After her preparation piece for the Juliet scene, and before she began her Juliet speech, she said to the audience, almost as an aside, 'Don't look at me now'. It was the moment when she was changing from Gwen to Juliet. If they took their eyes off Gwen for a moment, when they looked back they would be seeing and hearing Juliet. She gave the speech, drank the potion, and dropped her head on her breast. Thank goodness, the programme ended there without another word being uttered! She had transcended the conditions of that television studio in the most stupendous way. The applause that echoed round the studio was quite outdone by the applause that echoed round the country. The presenter, the producer, the BBC, the studio audience, and much more, the wider audience, had witnessed a ninety-seven year old actress capture the hearts and minds of her viewers with her consummate artistry. Her triumph might be summed up by a note she received from Tom English, who for many years had been secretary to Sir Barry Jackson:

'...your Juliet Potion Scene is now the supreme theatrical experience of my life. You were, indeed you *are*, superb. My scalp contracted to the size of a postage stamp. There can be few who can project such emotion as you have to-night - before the biggest audience of your wonderful career.'28

In June 1988, for the second time, Gwen appeared as a castaway on 'Desert Island Discs'. This time the interviewer was Sue Lawley. The programme was transmitted on Radio Four, and repeated a few days later. The story line followed the familiar pattern of reference to Mrs Manning-Hicks, Ellen Terry, Sir Barry Jackson, and Rutland Boughton. She was asked whether there was any actor with whom she preferred to act more than any other. She refused to answer this question, but among her eight choices of records was John Gielgud's reading of T. S. Eliot's 'The Journey of the Magi'. Other records chosen included, her own singing of Etain's faery song from *The Immortal Hour*, and to end with, Kiersten Flagstad singing the 'Liebestod' from Wagner's *Tristan and Isolde*. That last record she chose to take with her to her desert island. She also said that she would like it to be played at her funeral. Her attachment to it derived from its supremacy within its genre, and also from her personal acquaintance with the singer, and her precious memory of hearing her give a concert performance of the 'Liebestod', at which she and Sybil Thorndike listened, holding hands, with tears streaming down their eyes. When Sue Lawley asked if she would recite some Shakespeare, Gwen chose the balcony speech from *Romeo and Juliet*. It was immensely moving. After a brief silence Sue Lawley said, 'I think all the palms will quiver when you sit on the island and perform that'.

Before the programme was broadcast Gwen received letters from Sue Lawley and Gillian Hush, both thoroughly delighted with the interview and confident that the public would receive it with acclaim. The public did, and showed their pleasure in the spate of letters that followed.

In the February 1988 Radio Four programme, Nigel Hawthorne had mentioned Gwen's taking some master-classes. These she had directed in the previous year for the benefit of members of the National Theatre and those of the Royal Shakespeare Company. She so excelled at this work, and left such an indelible impression both on the students and those others who watched her, that the idea was born to make a longer and more detailed study of Gwen's life in the theatre, built round her taking a master-class. The programme was to be the work of an independent company, Saffron Productions, with Victor Pemberton as producer, David Spenser as director, and Nigel Hawthorne as presenter. In consequence a magnificent 60-minute programme was made and transmitted by the BBC in October 1988. In 1989 in New York the programme was given an Emmy Award for the Best Arts Documentary.

Most memorable about the programme was seeing Gwen in the context of Tagley Cottage: making a salad in the kitchen with Nigel Hawthorne; lying back with him in the swinging garden-seat, with his arm around her; walking in the waist-high cornfield, where she stops to demonstrate the Delsarte technique of movement; her sitting at the dining room table with Nigel Hawthorne, talking about death; and, finally, in her sitting room chair, reciting 'The Oxen' by Thomas Hardy. The filming of the figures moving in the cornfield, being seen through trees and shrubbery, and seated in the garden was, as Tanya Moseiwitsch described in a letter to Gwen, 'like the best of impressionist paintings'.[33] Gwen this time was accompanied throughout the programme by Nigel Hawthorne. The distinguished supporting cast included John Gielgud, Peggy Ashcroft, Alec McCowen, Anna Massey, Wendy Hiller, Alan Bates, Peter Hall, Dirk Bogarde, and others. The master-class was central to the programme. Four young, aspiring actresses, drama school students, had each learnt a different speech of Juliet's. They sat in a row on the stage of the Aldwych Theatre facing Gwen and Nigel Hawthorne; either side of them and behind were other students and members of the National Theatre and Royal Shakespeare Company. The girls delivered their speeches from a seated position. Each in turn then crossed over to Gwen, and sat next to her, while Gwen reviewed what she had heard and offered suggestions for improvement. The management of this master-class with the four Juliets was made the thread that bound the programme together. The camera moved freely from the master-class to other aspects of Gwen's theatrical life. By the end of the programme we had not only charted some of the main events of Gwen's career, but had also measured the mileage between the four young Juliets and the ninety-seven year old.

When each of the four Juliets came to sit next to Gwen, she held their hands, gave colour and background to the scene they had been concerned with, and spoke some of the lines herself. She urged each to take more time, to think more deeply about the dramatic situation, and about what they were saying. It was done very lovingly, but it was demolition work, and needfully so. The progress of the master-class was interspersed with comments about Gwen's acting career by the supporting cast. John Gielgud admitted how he had broken faith with Gwen when he chose Peggy Ashcroft as his leading lady for the 1937/8 season instead of Gwen - the one hiccup in their long friendship - but he went on to say how relieved he had been when Gwen, with some encouragement from St Denis, had consented to join the cast of *The Three Sisters*. He had been nervous about whether the two actresses would get on well together, and he was greatly relieved to discover that they formed a friendship that was deep and lasting. This was borne out in the Omnibus programme by Peggy Ashcroft herself, as she recounted her many appearances with Gwen, showing an unstinted admiration for her. Gwen's triumph as Mary Tyrone in *Long Day's Journey into Night* was analysed by Alan Bates, who had played the younger son in that production. His was probably the most telling tribute to her genius.

The second Juliet was Emma Cunningham, a LAMDA student. Hers was the speech which begins 'Gallop apace, you fiery footed steeds...' (Act III. ii). Juliet is longing for the nightfall, which will bring Romeo to her arms. When this Juliet had reached the fifth line 'Spread thy close curtain, love-performing night' a worried look came into her eyes, and she said 'Line?' The cue was not given her by any of the other Juliets; instead it came directly from Gwen 'That runaways' eyes may wink, and Romeo/Leap to these arms, untalk'd of and unseen.' It was a moment of awe – Gwen's quickness to help this Juliet in distress. When the award was made in New York to the producer and director of this programme, the clip that was shown to the assembled guests was of that moment.

Once more, following the programme, the 'thank-you' letters came in great numbers:

> 'Thank you. Thank you for all the joy and beauty you have given, and still give. I watched 'Omnibus' on TV last night! Once more I was a child of eleven, with stars in my eyes, and deep love of poetry, and for the theatre, and Shakespeare in particular.
>
> Today I am a 67 years old Grandmother and widow. But when I went to bed last night I could not sleep. I was on a 'high' after seeing and listening to you earlier. Eventually I had to read a very dull book to bring me down to earth again!...'[29]

Another fan, who saw *The Immortal Hour* nearly sixty years earlier, wrote:

'...I find I cannot resist writing to thank you for the joy you have given me. I did not see your Juliet, but through that Radio programme I feel I *have* seen it. I was transported, as in the rarest evenings in the theatre, by this young girl's emotion - it was wonderful. I did see you in *The Immortal Hour*, and it was pure magic - one of the loveliest evenings I've ever spent in the theatre...And to round it all the Omnibus - riveting, and leaving a host of beautiful memories. Please forgive my horrible handwriting - arthritic hands. I shall never forget these treasures, and so thank you and wish you happy always.'[30]

Men as well as women wrote to congratulate Gwen. Some were anxious that she should write a book about her life:

'7th October 1988
I have just watched the Omnibus programme about you and feel I want to write and thank you for the best hour's viewing I've had in a long time. You were wonderful.

So good in fact as yourself, that it must make many of your new fans very sad to think we must make do with second-hand accounts (albeit many of the best kind) of your performances on stage. Have you any more plans for further television or radio work? Or perhaps a book we may look forward to?...Please continue to enthral us...'[31]

An enthusiast from a neighbouring Essex village was delighted that such a distinguished lady lived so close to him.

'I just wanted you to know that I have so very much enjoyed all the various broadcasts you have made during this year, including the two appearances on 'Wogan', 'Desert Island Discs', and now - this jewel in the crown - last Friday's 'Omnibus' combining a theatrical portrait of you with your Juliet masterclass. What a joy it all was, and what a great inspiration you are for everyone who sees you and listens. It was especially thrilling too, to hear mention of *The Glass Menagerie* as I hold such wonderful memories of seeing you in that production, when it played at the Arts Theatre in Cambridge some years ago.

My dream now is that some enlightened publisher will come along and manage to persuade you to write a book about your life and work and memories!'[32]

That book was never written in Gwen's lifetime, despite the best efforts of Vic Pemberton and David Spenser to persuade Gwen to do so. She would say 'Yes, I should like to write a book about my life in the theatre, one day.' But it did not happen, and when fully-loaded tape-recorders were left with her, for her recordings to form the basis of such a book, nothing was forthcoming. In this regard it was some considerable achievement on Vic and David's part that they managed to secure on film and in sound their splendid 'Omnibus' programme. The programme

Gwen with Nigel Hawthorne in the garden at Tagley 1986

had ended with talk of death. Nigel Hawthorne and Gwen were seated at the round dining-room table; the large wooden salad bowl was empty; empty the plates; knives and forks were in repose. Beyond them there was a vase of flowers on the window-ledge. Through the window one could see the garden shrubs and trees, spreading into the distance. Nigel asked Gwen, 'Do you fear death?' She replied 'I am always afraid of doing anything for the first time. I don't consider it the end.' As she continued talking about 'struggling humanity's search for the thing that makes everything worthwhile', the camera took us once more to the cornfield, ripe for harvest, as the two of them walked through it hand in hand. The programme closed with her sitting in her fireside chair, speaking, incomparably, the lines of Hardy's 'Oxen'. In the young and even in the very old, hope cannot be quenched.

The series of radio and television programmes about Gwen in 1988 aroused great interest in her past career from many who, naturally, had never seen her perform on the stage. That interest was to focus now on what else she might now perform. There was also curiosity about whether she would live to be a hundred. A number of papers published reviews of her life and work. Julius Eichbaum, in 1989 for *The Theatre*, wrote a long and detailed account of her professional life. He quoted from Zoe Randall, who was a member of the first group of players Gwen had worked with in South Africa:

'At an audition in Johannesburg just after the war, Gwen proclaimed. "This young man will go far". How right she was. He went on to play the lead in over twenty British films - that loveable rascal, Sidney James!...July 1946 saw the Company stage Emlyn Williams' play *The Wind of Heaven*, the cast of which included Sidney James in his first professional role.'

In his subsequent career Sid James was not associated with dramatic material of such a spiritual nature.

Eichbaum, writing his article to celebrate Gwen's forthcoming 100th birthday, also quotes John Gielgud on the lack of any official honour being conferred on her:

'I have twice written in past years to ask the Prime Minister why she has been so sadly overlooked, but without success I am sorry to say.'

The Tate Gallery invited Gwen to be photographed in various poses beneath Sickert's great portrait of her as Isabella of France, La Louve. She reached the age of 100 with a telegram from the Queen, but no accolade. However, on Christmas Day 1990, a few weeks before her hundredth birthday, the BBC broadcast at 2 pm a programme 'With Great Pleasure'. It comprised readings from poems and plays. The readers were Anna Massey, Alec McCowen, and Gwen. It was exquisitely done, with taste, judicious selection of material, variety in the ordering, and above all, a sense of joyful camaraderie emanating from the three friends - a fitting tribute to Gwen Ffrangcon-Davies.

It was Gwen's vigour and sense of jollity that so impressed Valerie Grove when she visited Tagley Cottage. Her account, which appeared in *The Times* the next day, 26th January 1991, began:

'To live to the age of 100 is rare enough; to be as full of joie de vivre and surrounded by friends, as Miss Gwen Ffrangcon-Davies - 100 yesterday - manages to be rarer still. She greets the visitor at the door of her cottage, and it is all too picturesque for words: the log fire, the old sofas, the cat snoozing gently, the coffee cups. Everyone who walks into this Beatrix Potter scene exclaims that they feel at home here at once.'

It was in this interview that at last, publicly, the obfuscation was removed from the account of her age when she played Juliet to Gielgud's Romeo in 1924. She had always claimed that it was an actress's privilege to conceal her true age. In the 'Omnibus' programme her true age was manifest, but the age at which she had played Juliet was not. Now, at last, she tells Valerie Grove that when she played the 'child Juliet', as her performance was termed at the time, she was thirty-three years old.

On the day following this interview the theatrical profession held a dinner at the Café Royal to celebrate Gwen's 100th birthday. It had been organised by Vic Pemberton and David Spenser with infinite care. The response to the invitations was very gratifying: most of the leading stars of the profession attended, together with others of Gwen's friends and family. Towards the end of the dinner Donald Sinden gave a short resumé of Gwen's career and read the many messages and telegrams of good wishes. He then introduced the guest speakers, Sir John Gielgud,

Dame Peggy Ashcroft, and Dame Wendy Hiller. Gwen spoke last; finishing by quoting the last part of Lilith's speech, which brings to a close *Back to Methuselah*. The post that reached David and Vic in the following few days attested to yet another superb performance on her part. Notes from two of the distinguished diners illustrate the success of the evening.

> 'Just a thank-you for letting me be part of that most special night. I knew she was a great actress, I didn't know how great a woman she is. Her speech was astonishing and inspiring - I went straight home and read the last act of *Back to Methuselah* with so much more understanding...'[34]

> 'That was such a very special evening last night and I just want to thank you both for making it happen.
> What a remarkable woman Gwen is - an inspiration to us all.
> A joyous occasion.'[35]

Gwen's ability to bring joy to others through her stage performances had long been recognised. As a result of the personalised approach of recent radio and television programmes her remarkable gift of spreading joy among her friends also became evident. The Queen in her birthday greetings had included her best wishes for an enjoyable celebration. The Café Royal occasion was all that Gwen, the organisers and the guests could have wished. More good wishes came pouring in. The Secretary for State for Social Security, Tony Newton, sent his congratulations, and Tim Renton, Minister for the Arts, published a handsome tribute to her work which, more than a formal gesture, had the tenor of something personally felt:

> 'Gwen Ffrangcon-Davies' contribution as an actress has been of the rarest quality. Her style on stage was particularly her own. Her capacity both to touch the heart of an audience and to move it is a memory held dear by all who saw her. She enhanced the British stage with her art and the high respect in which the British stage is now held internationally owes not a little to the work of such a fine performer. Many more will benefit indirectly, because of her skill and generosity as a teacher - as clearly demonstrated in her recent master-classes. It is simply a delight to be able to congratulate her on her 100th birthday and to pay tribute to the art with which she has so outstandingly adorned the theatre.'

John Gielgud could not have put it more succinctly. Of more singular importance was the message she received on her birthday from John Major, the Prime Minister:

> 'It is a great joy to congratulate such a doyenne of British theatre as Gwen Ffrancgon-Davies on her 100th birthday. Her contribution...has raised the spirits of all who saw her...Her contribution to British theatre is unlikely to be matched in its particular quality and I offer her my warmest birthday wishes.'

There was no precedent for a Prime Minister writing to an actress on such an occasion. The Government, the acting profession, and the media had all rejoiced

The Party at the Garrick Club in 1990
Standing, left to right: Alan Bates, Wendy Hiller, Alec McCowen, Peggy
Ashcroft, Nigel Hawthorne, Dirk Bogarde, Anna Massey
Seated, left to right: John Gielgud, Gwen Ffrangcon-Davies

with Gwen on her reaching her hundredth birthday. The village in which she lived also wished to mark the occasion. The 'Gwen Ffrangcon-Davies 100th Birthday Celebration' was held in Spains Hall Finchingfield, the home of Sir John Ruggles-Brise, on 17th February 1991. The concert, in which the Stambourne Singers played a prominent part, was given in the afternoon for Gwen's benefit. The instrumental and vocal items were interspersed with readings by David Spenser.

With such national and local publicity being given to the hundred-year-old actress, particularly at Government level, it was not totally unexpected when in the Queen's birthday honours list, the first of John Major's premiership, Gwen Ffrancgon Davies was made a Dame Commander of the British Empire. She was the first centenarian to be made a dame. It was 35 years after Dame Peggy Ashcroft had received her honour. The honours list was published on 15th June 1991; Peggy had died the day before. Gwen received the accolade at Buckingham Palace accompanied by Heather and Nan, her two nieces. It was a proud day for the whole family; the great nieces and their families also came to London for the occasion, and later that fine summer's day Tagley Cottage was the scene of countless photographs of Gwen and her family - and the award.

From her schooldays Gwen had been a dedicated letter-writer. She had written regularly to Geoffrey when he was at boarding-school, and to her father when he was abroad and, later, in hospital. When, at eighteen, she spent the best part of a year in Watzum, Germany, she wrote letters home to her mother, Marjorie, and Geoffrey with great regularity and in profusion. She was lonely, unhappy, and she needed letters from home to comfort her. The letter-writing pattern of those early days, coupled with her mother's gift and assiduity in writing, had instilled into Gwen the importance of always replying to letters. There was also in her the innate feeling that any letter received required the courtesy of a reply. From the days of

Dame Commander of the British Empire in 1991

her early stage successes she had been diligent in answering her fan mail. It was a matter on which she and Edith Evans saw eye to eye. If an actress wanted a sympathetic public, such small courtesies should be observed. Towards the end of her life she had received a letter from a retired clergyman in North Wales who, as a young man, had seen *Richard of Bordeaux* and written to John Gielgud and Gwen asking for signed photographs. Gielgud duly obliged, but Gwen who did not have a photograph to hand at the time, sent him a letter and a copy of the *Theatre World*, in which there were many photographs of the play, one of which she signed. The clergyman felt that she had gone the extra mile, and never forgot it, but having seen her on the 'Omnibus' programme more than fifty-five years later, thought it time to mention it.[36]

That habit of replying to letters never left her. She received many letters after the Café Royal dinner. On each of those received she has written 'replied'. Letters came to her from students of drama from different parts of the world who were writing up their higher degree theses on some aspect of the theatre in Britain. Dennis Elkins, from the University of Colorado at Boulder, for instance, was completing some research work on the Birmingham Repertory Theatre and wished to interview Gwen. This was in October 1991. She was approaching her 101st birthday. He wrote to her twice, and his tutor also wrote in support. Gwen has noted at the top of his second letter, dated 12th October, 'Mr Elkins coming to lunch Tuesday 29 October.'[37]

At the beginning of January 1992 she appeared in yet another television drama, *The Master Blackmailer* (Granada). It was a dramatisation of a Conan Doyle story. Jeremy Brett played Sherlock Holmes, and Robert Hardy played the master blackmailer. An account of the first rehearsal describes how, because of her failing eyesight and hearing, Gwen was quite at a loss, but she found by coming close to Jeremy Brett and watching his lips move she could more easily pick up her cues. Rehearsals from that moment went smoothly. Nancy Banks-Smith reviewing the programme in *The Guardian* on 3rd January, wrote:

'It is an astonishing moment in *The Master Blackmailer* when Gwen Ffrancgon-Davies appears, encrusted in black jet and sporting a rather insouciant widow's cap. She will be 101 on January 25.

She leaned her chin on her hand with the index finger running up her cheek. It was a tender, flowing gesture and she must have used this, or something very like this, for Juliet:

"See how she leans her cheek upon her hand.
O! that I were a glove upon that hand
That I might touch that cheek."

There is a certain playfulness about her performance which suggests she is, perhaps, too young for the part.'

Gwen felt less young as her 101st birthday approached. She took to her bed. Heather and her daughter, Ann, came to be with her. On her birthday David and Vic asked if they might visit Gwen; Heather insisted that they should come only one at a time. When David came to her bedside she spoke, brokenly and cryptically, about the bridge between this world and the next. The following day she was restless and asked Ann to telephone her Christian Science practitioner, Barbara Brighton. In the course of this telephone conversation Gwen entirely regained her composure as though she had been assured that the right moment was approaching for her to depart. She died the next day, the 27th January. Her funeral service was held in Stambourne parish church, and she was buried close to the church on the north side. It was not the end.

Epilogue: 'Death no more hath dominion'[1]

The obituaries that were written after Gwen's death had a great deal of material to call on, especially as so much of it had been printed in reporting her 100th birthday in 1991 and, a few months later, in articles concerning her DBE award. In *The Independent*, her obituary notice was in two parts: the first written by Nigel Hawthorne, and the second by John Tydeman. Nigel had known Gwen only recently, when she was well into her nineties. John Tydeman, working for the BBC sound programmes, had known her for many years more, but mainly in association with her broadcasting. They both wrote less about her acting career and more about their personal knowledge of her. Nigel Hawthorne recounted his astonishment at first watching her take a master-class at the National Theatre when she was in her ninety-seventh year: 'Six aspirant Juliets were made to seem brittle and unprepared as the dynamic, totally committed little lady with the thick spectacles and restless hands took over.' He recalled that when she was suffering from a severe attack of bronchitis, especially after a period of extreme discomfort, instead of calling the doctor and accepting a bottle of pills, she dosed herself with hot water and lemon, and promptly recovered. Her Christian Science routine not only kept her happy, it kept her well. John Tydeman also alluded to her extraordinary will-power:

> 'Gwen Ffrangcon Davies was one of the world's great life-givers. Her connections with Bernard Shaw and her admiration for his works were no accident. She was the Life-Force incarnate and life pulsated through that grip which anyone close by her in her later years is bound to have felt. She would not grip a neighbour's arm for support, but to give and to enthuse. It was fire. Her powers of mind and heart outran her physical faculties. Towards the end her sight and hearing were poor and her small body frail, but the will was strong and memory formidable, especially for texts.'

During the master-class that was part of the 'Omnibus' programme, when each of the Juliets had said their piece and sat beside Gwen, she had held them by the hand, lovingly, firmly, but inescapably. It was as though through such physical contact her power and genius might pass to them. The hand-holding with Nigel Hawthorne in the same programme served a somewhat different purpose. Her eyesight and her hearing were poor, and she was given to falling over. Nigel's holding of her hand was as much to support her in the movement of those outdoor scenes, as to show affection.

Both obituarists mentioned her will-power; both had experienced it at first-hand. Both had been uplifted by her friendship and her cheerfulness. Her fondness for finishing programmes, or even after-dinner speeches, with Lilith's last words from *Back to Methuselah*, 'It is enough that there is a beyond', or with Hardy's 'Oxen' was an attempt, in a cynical world, to keep ajar the door of hope.

A distinguished life was to be celebrated. The Church of SS. Peter and Thomas, Stambourne, held a service on 30th January 1992 in loving memory of Gwen Ffrangcon-Davies. Plans for a service of thanksgiving in London were soon in hand. Gwen's nieces had asked Vic Pemberton and David Spenser to undertake the preliminary inquiries and the subsequent arrangements. The two friends did not spare themselves in this task. The result was a Service of Thanksgiving for the Life and Work of Dame Gwen Ffrangcon-Davies in the Church of St Martin-in-the-Fields on 18th June 1992. The service was so crafted as to reflect and recall the quintessential qualities that went to make such an extraordinary human being. It proved both a joyful and a profoundly moving occasion.

The service was conducted by the Vicar, Canon Geoffrey Brown. The introductory organ music consisted of a Bach Prelude, followed by Wagner's Liebestod from *Tristan and Isolde*. The hymns were cheerful and well-known. Paul Scofield read St John Chapter I, verses 1-14. Gwen so frequently quoted 'In the beginning was the word' adding, in a provocative manner, 'In the beginning was the *thought*'. There were further readings by Anna Massey, Wendy Hiller, George Baker, and Dorothy Tutin. The 'Faery Song' from *The Immortal Hour* was sung by Hilary Jenkyns. Nigel Hawthorne gave the Address, the Stambourne Singers performed stoutly, followed by prayers, and then John Gielgud, aged eighty-seven, delivered Romeo's final speech from *Romeo and Juliet*, 'How oft when men are at the point of death/Have they been merry!...' He had first performed the part sixty-eight years earlier, when Gwen had been his Juliet. The poignancy was palpable. Then the Gloria from Mozart's *Mass in C Minor*, the Blessing, and Vivaldi's 'Spring' from *The Four Seasons*. The church bells, unmuffled, rang out across Trafalgar Square, Charing Cross Road, and Theatreland.

There was a pointed propriety in each part of the service, the music, the readings, the hymns, the prayers, even the bells. Particularly telling, and not printed on the service sheet, was the hearing of Gwen's voice, recorded, reciting some of the verses of Psalm 139:

> 'O Lord, thou hast searched me, and known me.....
> If I take the wings of the morning,
> And dwell in the uttermost parts of the sea;
> Even there shall thy hand lead me,
> And thy right hand shall hold me.'

This was followed by a snatch of the conversation with Nigel Hawthorne, at the end of the 'Omnibus' programme, when she replied to his question 'Gwen, are you afraid of death?'

Nigel Hawthorne's Address followed Gwen's answer. All who were present found his words about Gwen immensely moving. The many letters to Vic and David after the service testify to this and also shower thanks and praise on them for their great care and diligence in helping to arrange such a fitting tribute to Gwen. Place was found in the church for a splendid display of Tagley Cottage roses. Heather later remarked 'the formal arrangements were beautiful, but the informality of the basket was more Gwen'. Anna Massey, too, mentioned the flowers in her note to Vic and David:

> 'The basket of Tagley roses was so touching. She was, of course, there - and oh how she loved it! I shall remember it all forever.'[2]

Many others had also felt quite strongly Gwen's presence at the service. Kate Stephens wrote:

190

'Thank you both for last week's exquisite occasion. The organisation of such an extraordinary event must have required so much time, energy and skill - it was so beautifully orchestrated.

I can only imagine Gwen sitting on her sunbeam holding an expression of delight and pleasure!

You did a great lady justice and your love for her shone through.

Thank you again from a still stunned   Kate'[3]

Gwen had said at the end of her 'Omnibus' discussion with Nigel Hawthorne, that men and women in their search for what is worthwhile in life which might, for instance, be typified by the sun, are always reaching upwards, and it does not matter which sunbeam they go up on. She was certainly a great lover of the sun herself. The happiest entries in her diary are when she describes herself swaying in the hammock with the sun upon her. She wanted to bring the sun to others, and in this she was abundantly successful. They thanked her in their lives, their letters, their tribute to her at St Martin-in-the-Fields. The applause of her audiences was helpful, but not essential, and she knew she would have her failures. Mrs Drew, her neighbour, 'unloved and unloving', was one of them. In her nineties, Gwen would call on her, fill her coal scuttle, bring her a thick soup in a thermos, and receive no plaudits, only tears, and those tears of self-pity. Gwen was saddened by this response, but not deterred from calling again and again. She had a need to share with others the gifts she had been endowed with. Sometimes they came in the form of great performances and sometimes in the bringing of coal and soup. She felt acute loneliness when there was no one to share with her the glory of her garden on a sunny day. And she passed through troughs of uncertainty when her artistic talents were not being called upon. Those troughs largely disappeared in the last three years of her life. In September 1988 she wrote to Irene Worth, who was then in New York:

'...Well my news is that after almost total oblivion - your little friend has blossomed into a late summer flowering - to wit - David, Victor, and Nigel have engineered me into a massive "Omnibus" TV - with the B.B.C. - and we have just finished a whole week's shooting - part in London and two days here in the cottage. It's called "Juliet Remembered" and they all seem very excited about it and pray heaven they're right! I have truly tried to know it *is* the Lord's doing not mine - I am but the humble servant and deeply grateful to have what I have learned from such a long life!!

So darling that's why no word from me - but I think of you every morning when I brush the powder from my face with your brush!

We had a heavenly day for shooting in garden and cornfield!'[4]

The work that came to Gwen in that 'late summer flowering' very probably helped to extend her long life even further. When Nigel had asked that question about death she had begun her reply with 'I am always afraid of doing anything for the first time. I don't consider it the end...' She had spent many hours in her life caring for the sick, comforting relatives and friends in their bereavement, and partaking in, and sometimes conducting, funeral services. Her unwavering mien in all these circumstances was to be positive and cheerful, never submitting to gloom and despondency. Death was not to be allowed its victory. Death itself was to be overcome. She carried with her the stoicism her mother had shown in the face of Geoffrey's death. Geoffrey had died within the first year of the 1914-1918 Great War. A year earlier he had been a schoolboy. Annie had chosen as an inscription on his headstone in a foreign land THERE IS NO DEATH.

Close to the Church of SS Peter and Thomas, Stambourne, on the north side, is a burial place with a headstone on which the inscription reads:

Dame
Gwen
Ffrangcon-Davies
Actress
1891 - 1992

The headstone is of dark grey granite. The inscription is in white. In the morning sunbeams dance on the lettering.

The gravestone in the churchyard at Stambourne

Appendix One. Gwen Ffrangcon-Davies: Chronology of parts played in the Theatre

1911 April	His Majesty's	*A Midsummer Night's Dream*	Walk-on fairy
1911-13	On tour with the Gaiety Girls	A variety of musicals	Chorus girl
1912	Church House, Westminster	*Eager Heart*	Eager Heart
1914	On tour	*The Glad Eye*	Kiki
1916	On tour	*Tonight's the Night*	June
1916	Glastonbury	*Everyman*	Everyman
1917	On tour	*The Arcadians*	Sombra
1917-18	Concert Halls	Concerts (for the troops)	Singer
1919-20	Glastonbury Festival	*The Immortal Hour*	Leading soprano
		Bethlehem	Virgin Mary
		The Birth of Arthur	
		King Arthur	Nimue (soprano)
1920	Birmingham	*The Immortal Hour*	Etain
1921	Old Vic	*The Immortal Hour*	Etain
1922	Birmingham	*The Admirable Crichton*	Lady Mary
1922	Regent	*The Immortal Hour*	Etain
1922	Birmingham	*Romeo and Juliet*	Juliet
1923	Birmingham	*Quality Street*	Phoebe Throssel
1923	Birmingham	*Mary Stuart*	Queen Mary
1923	Birmingham	*The Professor's Love Story*	Lucy
1923	Regent	*Back to Methuselah*	Eve & The Newly Born
1923	Regent for The Phoenix Soc.	*The Immortal Hour*	Etain
1923	Regent	*Edward II*	Queen Isabella
1923	Regent	*Bethlehem*	Virgin Mary
1923	Court	*Back to Methuselah*	Eve & The Newly Born
1924	Regent	*King Lear*	Cordelia
1924	Regent	*Romeo and Juliet*	Juliet
1924	Birmingham	*The Master Builder*	Hilda Wangel
1924	Drury Lane	*A Midsummer Night's Dream*	Titania
1925	Kingsway	*Caesar and Cleopatra*	Cleopatra
1925	Kingsway	*The New Morality*	Betty Jones
1925	Barnes/Garrick	*Tess of the D'Urbevilles*	Tess
1926	Kingsway	*The Immortal Hour*	Etain
1926	Birmingham/Kingsway	*The Marvellous History of St Bernard*	Marguerite
1926	Shaftesbury	*Martinique*	Zabette
1926	Everyman	*Made in Heaven*	Olga Lessiter
1926	Kingsway	*The Doctor's Dilemma*	Mrs Dubedat
1926	Ambassadors'	*Riceyman Steps*	Elsie
1927	Kingsway	*Pygmalion*	Eliza Dolittle
1927	Kingsway	*Man and Superman*	Ann Whitefield
1927	Prince's	*Might Have Beens*	Juliette
1927	Svoy	*The Cage*	Ena
1927	Gate	*Maya*	Bella
1928	Court	*Back to Methuselah*	Eve
1928	Court	*Harold*	Edith
1928	Arts	*Prejudice*	Myra Flint
1928	Prince's	*Contraband*	Tommy
1928	Arts	*Easter*	Eleanora
1929	Arts /Garrick	*The Lady with a Lamp*	Elizabeth Herbert Florence Nightingale
1929	On tour	*The Lady with a Lamp*	Florence Nightingale
1930	Oxford (OUDS)	*Macbeth*	Lady Macbeth
1930	Arts/Criterion	*A Doll's House*	Nora Helmer
1930	Haymarket	*Hamlet*	Ophelia
1930	New	*Magda*	Magda

1930	Queen's	*The Barretts of Wimpole Street*	Elizabeth Barrett
1932	Queen's	*The Immortal Hour*	Etain
1932	St Martin's	*Precious Bane*	Prue Sarn
1932	New	*Richard of Bordeaux*	Anne of Bohemia
1932	Wyndham's	*The Way of the Stars*	Marquesa de Casa Reya
1933	New	*Richard of Bordeaux*	Anne of Bohemia
1933	Cambridge	*The Lady of Belmont*	Portia
1934	New	*Queen of Scots*	Mary Stuart
1934	Whitehall	*Flowers of the Forest*	Naomi Jacklin
1935	Piccadilly	*The Barretts of Wimpole Street*	Elizabeth Barrett
1935	Playhouse	*Justice*	Ruth Honeywill
1935	Arts	*The Benefit of Doubt*	Theophila Fraser
1935	Savoy	*Close Quarters*	Liesa
1936	Ambassadors'	*Out of the Dark*	Diana Huntley
1936	Lyric	*Charles the King*	Henrietta Maria
1937	Queen's	*He was Born Gay*	Miss Mason
1938	Queen's	*The Three Sisters*	Olga
1938	Drury Lane	*Henry V*	Chorus
1938	Richmond	*Gaslight*	Mrs Manningham
1939	Apollo	*Gaslight*	Mrs Manningham
1939	Globe	*The Importance of Being Earnest*	Hon. Gwendolen Fairfax
1940	Pretoria, S. Africa	*I Have been her Before*	Director
1940	Johannesburg, S. Africa	*Major Barbara*	Major Barbara
1941	Pretoria & on tour	*Twelfth Night*	Director/Olivia
1941	Pretoria & on tour	*Quality Street*	Director/Phoebe Throssell
1942	Piccadilly	*Macbeth*	Lady Macbeth
1942	Phoenix	*The Importance of Being Earnest*	Lady Bracknell
1943-6	South Africa Plays on tour	*Flare Path/Watch on the Rhine* *What Every Woman Knows* *Blithe Spirit/A Month in the Country* *Merry Wives of Windsor/Milestones* *The Taming of the Shrew*	Director/Lead role Director only
1949	St James's	*Adventure Story*	Queen Mother
1950	South Africa	*Macbeth* (in Afrikaans)	Director
1950	Memorial Theatre Stratford on Avon	*Henry VIII* *Julius Caesar* *King Lear* *Much Ado about Nothing*	Queen Katherine Portia Regan Beatrice
1950	Denmark	Readings of Shakespeare British Council	Queen Katherine, Juliet, Lady Macbeth etc.
1952	South Africa	*Waters of the Moon*	Director/Lead role
1953	Old Vic	*Henry VIII*	Queen Katherine
1954	New	*Charley's Aunt*	Donna Lucia D'Alvadorez
1954	Lyric	*The Cherry Orchard*	Madame Ranevsky
1955	Apollo	*Summertime*	Aunt Cleofe
1956	Royal Court	*The Mulberry Bush*	Rose Padley
1956	Phoenix	*The Family Reunion*	Agatha
1957	Haymarket	*The Chalk Garden*	Miss Madrigal
1958	Lyceum, Edinburgh Globe	*Long Day's Journey into Night*	Mary Tyrone
1961	Aldwych	*Ondine*	Queen Isolde
1961	Aldwych/Globe	*Becket*	Queen Mother
1962	Aldwych	*A Penny for a Song*	Hester Bellboys
1962-3	Haymarket/Majestic/ New York	*The School for Scandal*	Mrs Candour
1964	Queen's	*Season of Goodwill*	Beatrice Portman
1965	Haymarket	*The Glass Menagerie*	Amanda Wingfield
1966	Lyceum, Edinburgh	*A Present for the Past*	The Baroness
1970	Royal Court	*Uncle Vanya*	Madame Voynitsky
1971	Cape Town, S. Africa	*Dear Antoine*	Carlotta Alexandra

Appendix Two. Chronology of Parts Played in Films and Television

1936	Tudor Rose	Mary Tudor
1939	Gaslight	Cast Member
1959	The Hill	Mary
1964	A Day by the Sea	Laura Anson
1966	The Witches	Granny Rigg
1967	The Burning	Gran
1968	The Devil Rides Out	Countess D'Urfe
1969	The Mark Two Wife	Mrs Ritchie
1970	The Patchwork Quilt	
1972	The Edwardians: Baden Powell	Mrs Baden-Powell
1976	The Picture of Dorian Grey	Lady Agatha
1978	Liza	Cast Member
1982	Aubrey	Reverend Mother
1992	Sherlock Homes: The Blackmailer	Dowager

Appendix Three. Chronology of BBC Radio Programmes

15.6.1925	Hospital Appeal	31.10.1925	Scenes from Tess of the D'Urbevilles
27.2.1926	Concert: Actors' Benevolent Fund	16.5.1926	Shakespeare's Heriones: Juliet
30. 5.1926	Shakespeare's Heroines: Desdemona	10.8.1926	The Maker of Dreams
24.8.1926	Song recital, acc. Nellie Chaplin	19.8.1926	Songs with Holme Valley Choir
21.11.1926	Hassan by James Elroy Flecker	8.4.1927	Concert with D. Wise, violin
27.5.1927	R.U.R. (Rossum's Universal Robots)	9.8.1927	The Bell Flower's Blue
13.10.1927	Wun Tu or The Seventh Heaven	17.10.1927	Faust by Goethe
18.5.1928	Songs for 'My Programme'	20.6.1928	Paolo and Francesca
10.10.1928	Moyen Age	29.11.1928	Love by L. de Gg. Sieveking
27.12.1928	Can Voice be Visualised?	30.11.1930	Week's Good Cause
15.8.1932	As You Like It – Rosalind	8.10.1933	Othello - Desdemona
11.3.1934	As You Like It – Rosalind	2.1.1935	Back to Methuselah by G.B.Shaw
9.6.1935	Much Ado about Nothing – Beatrice	23.6.1935	Justice by John Galsworthy
28.9.1935	Scene from Close Quarters	27.10.1936	Excerpts from Charles the King
31.5.1937	He was Born Gay by Emlyn Williams	25.6.1937	The Silver Box by John Galsworthy
17.10.1937	Candida by G.B.Shaw	6.2.1938	Cyrano de Bergerac
22.2.1938	Readings from Macbeth (Schools)	27.3.1938	Easter
24.4.1938	The Master Builder by Henrik Ibsen	9.12.1941	Radio Newsreel (in South Africa)
24.12.1941	Calling South Africa (from England)	23.7.1942	The Barretts of Wimpole Street
3.9.1942	Calling South Africa (from England)	15.9.1942	Macbeth
20.9.1942	Far from the Madding Crowd	14.11.1942	London Re-visited: Fanny Burney
11.12.1942	Travelling Companions	6.1.1943	The World Goes By
23.2.1943	The Brains Trust	8.12.1948	Gaslight
31.1.1949	Two Generations (Stratford prod.)	16.2.1949	For your Leisure (Re. Adventure Story)
24.4.1949	Adventure Story	14.10.1949	After Dinner by Alwyn Whatsley
1.11.1949	Victoria Regina	21.9.1950	Madame Clara
7.1.1951	Happy and Glorious	4.6.1951	The Importance of Being Earnest
11.7.1951	Evensong	22.3.1953	The Golden Sovereign
6.1.1954	Romeo and Juliet	2.11.1955	Interview re. Summertime by Ugo Betti
27.3.1956	Green Room Cavalcade	5.5.1958	Rutland Boughton
3.12.1958	Woman's Hour: Guest of the Week	4.1.1959	Today: Evening Standard awards
6.9.1959	Tribute to Sir Barry Jackson	18.2.1960	Rutland Boughton
10.2.1961	Walter Sickert	27.4.1961	Tribute to Sir Barry Jackson
25.1.1961	'My dear Miss Mitford'*	30.7.1961	Walter Sickert 1860-1942
3.10.1962	'Playing Hamlet'	8.10.1962	Desert Island Discs
3.11.1962	Desert Island Discs (repeat)	2.4.1963	The Masters : Thomas Hardy
18.10.1965	Woman's Hour	22.10.1965	Pick of the Week (Woman's Hour)
21.8.1966	Dame Sybil Thorndike	25.11.1968	Tess of the D'Urbevilles -Narrator
10.10.1971	Michel Saint-Denis		

* Six readings from the letters of Elizabeth Barrett Browning to Mary Russell Mitford

References

Chapter One:

1. *David Ffrangcon-Davies: His Life and Book* by Marjorie Ffrangcon-Davies, London, 1938, p. 44   2. An extract from a 1949 South African broadcast by Gwen Ffrangcon-Davies on her father. 3. As above.   4. A letter to the Bishop of London from David Ffrangcon-Davies. (Hospital Papers A). 5. Hospital Papers (A).   6. Letters (F16).   7. Letters (B1) 8. Letters from Watzum, (BC)   10. Letters (B9)   11. Letters (B4)   12. Letters (B9)   13. Marie Tempest: *The Honeymoon* at the Royalty Theatre, October 1911-April 1912   14. Letters (V28)   15. Letters (A13)   16. Letters (A5)   17. Letters (A11)   18. Letters (A4)   19. Letters (A6)   20. Letters (V22)   21. Letters (B8)   22. Hospital reports (Letters A)

Chapter Two:

1. *Daily Telegraph,* 20 March 1920   2. *Westminster Gazette,* 20 March 1920   3. *Daily Mail,* Music Critic, 20 August 1919   4. *Western Daily Press.* 23 August 1919   5. *Western Daily Press,* 29 December 1919   6. Mother's letter (AB1) 7 April 1921   7. (E11)   8. (E7)   9. Ivor Brown: *The Saturday Review* 1 March 1924   10. (E7)   11. (E11)   12. Letters (E8)   13. (M1)   14. (D8)   15. (AL30)   16. *An Actor in His Time* by John Gielgud, p.64   17. Letters (C19)   18. Letters (D10)   19. Lettera (AL16)   20. *The Observer* 28 December 1924   21. Letters (B6)   22. *The Times.*   23. *Daily Graphic*   24. *Daily Sketch* 25. Letters (AK5)   26. Letters (AK11)   27. Letters (AK10)   28. Letters (AK4)   29. Letters (AK9) 30. Letters (AK8)   31. Letters (AK12)   32. 'The Oxen' by Thomas Hardy

Christmas Eve, and twelve of the clock.
"Now they are on their knees,"
An elder said as we sat in a flock
By the embers in hearthside ease.

We pictured the meek mild creatures where
They dwelt in their strawy pen,
Nor did it occur to us there
To doubt they were kneeling then.

So fair a fancy few would weave
In these years! Yet, I feel,
If someone said on Christmas Eve,
"Come; see the oxen kneel

"In the lonely barton by yonder coomb
Our childhood used to know,"
I should go with him in the gloom,
Hoping it might be so.

Chapter Three:

1. (S27), (AK10), (S28)   2. (J6)   3. (AH14)   4. (AH15)   5. Cecil's sonnet

A SONNET

For Gwen; before the First Night
of "The Immortal Hour" 30.1.1926

When the wise gods sum up our gutted hours,
Take scales to weigh our will against our deed
Baring the root of motive, hidden seed,
Whence actions spring - perfect or cankered flowers:
Then shall they praise, preserve and chase in brass
White hours of worship seeking beauty's shrine -
Immortal hours, whose living is divine -
And these shall stand, though Time itself should pass.

So, when to-night, the world quite laid aside,
Thy genius invests a magic part;
This is the height of life: be satisfied.
Thou can'st not, love, be happier than thou art.
The tale was woven and the music writ
For thy sweet beauty now to sweeten it.

Cecil

6. (AH3) 7. (AH4) 8. *Cape Times* Wednesday September 3 9. Marda's Journal p.4 10. This proved to be Marda Vanne's last will and testament. 11. Extracted from *Walter Sickert* by Richard Stone © 1988 Phaidon Press Ltd., p.67 12. (E17) 13. *Sunday Times* September 18, 1932 (Scrapbook 6) 14. (E17) 15. (E17 16. (E17) 17. (F1) 18. (AA45) 19. (E13) 20. (E13) 21. (B5) 22. (S18) 23. (F20) 24. (B26) 25. (F2) 26. (F2) 27. (F2) 28. (F3) 29. (F4) 30. (R35) 31. (Scrapbook 5) 32. (Scrapbook 7) 33. *Olivier: Confessions of an Actor* by Laurence Olivier, London 1982, p. 37 34. Marda's 1935/6 Diary p. 204 35. (L21) 36. Marda's 1935/6 Diary p. 383 37. Marda's 1935/6 Diary p. 387 38. (AE6) 39. (AE4) 40. (AE8) 42. (AE9) 43. (AE10) 44. (AE14) 45. (AE1) 46. (AE2) 47. *David Ffrangcon-Davies: His Life and Book (The Singing of the Future)* by Marjorie Ffrangcon-Davies, with an Introduction by Ernest Newman, London 1938 pp. 10/11 48. (AC1)

Chapter Four:

1. (AB6) 2. (AB7) 3. (E12) 4. (E12) 5. (E12) 6. (E12) 7. (M16) 8. (A1) 9. (A24) 10. (W33) 11. (AL14) 12. (J13) 13. (AL28) 14. (T19) 15. (T20) 16. (AM19) 17. (AM16) 18. (AD6) 19. (AD7) 20. (AD8) 21. (AD9) 22. (AD11) 23. (SB13) 24. (AD12) 25. (AD12) 26. (AD13) 27. (SB15) 28. (SB5), (BG) 29. Morley, Sheridan, *John Gielgud* London 2000, p.92 30. (AC3) 31. (AD29) 32. (AC2) 33. Morley, Sheridan, *John Gielgud* London 2000 p. 180 34. (AD17) 35. (AL8) 36. (S16) 37. (AJ9) 38. (AL33) 39. Guthrie, Tyrone, *A Life in the Theatre*, London 1960, p.19 40. (AL6) 41. (AV7) 42. South Africa, *Outspan* 30 July 1943 43. (AC38i) 44. (AC38i) 45. (AY81) 46. (SB15) *Theatre in South Africa* 14 August, 1941 47. (AD31) 48. (AC40) 49. (M22) 50. (AC18) 51. (AC17) 52. (AC18 53. (AD37) 54. (AD36) 55. (AD37) 56. (AC28) 57. (AC19) 58. (AF57) 59. (D4) 60 (C23) 61. (AM16)

Chapter Five:

1. (C7) see Appendix 2. (Q pp.9, 10) 3. (AR2) 4. (SB5 p.9) 5. (SB5 p.9) 6. (AV9) 7. (AV9) 8. (AV13) 9. (AV13) 10. (AV14) 11. (AV16) 12. (AV14) 13. (AV21) 14. (AV24) 15. (AV28) 16. (SB5 p. 22) 17. (SB5 p.22) 18. (D20) 19. (C7) 20. John Gielgud et al. *John Gielgud: An Actor and His Time* London 1979 p.23 21. (SB5 p. 31) 22. (AX35) 23. (SB5 p.33) 24. (SB5 p.33) 25. (SB5 p.33) 26. Jean Batters *Edith Evans* London 1977 p.134 27. (SB5 p.33) 28. (AV18) 29. (SB5 p.31) 30. (T6) 31. (G4) 32. Dodie Smith, *Look Back with Mixed Feelings* © Dodie Smith 1978, W.H.Allen Ltd. Pp. 210-11 33. As above p.268 34. Dodie Smith *Look Back with Astonish-ment*, London 1979 pp.43, 44...35. As above pp. 53, 54 36. (E13) 37. (G8) 38. (M5) 39. (AV16) 40. Dodie Smith, *Look Back with Gratitude* London 1985 p. 234 41. (AV17) 42. (SB5 p.91) 43. (SB5 p.71) 44. (R11) 45. (SB5 p.71) 46. (R13) 47. (S34) 48. (S39) 49. (AP35) 50. (AP41) 51. (AP36) 52. (AY21) 53. (AV31) 54. (AV12) 55. (U2) 56. (O3) 57. (O4) 58. (S2) 59. (S2) 60. (F8) 61. Many girls were christened Etain in the 1920s after the Etain of *The Immortal Hour*. Perhaps G. Ff-D. is acting here with such a one. 62. (SB5 p.38) 63. (C16) 64. (SB5 p.123) 65. (SB5 p.100) 66. (SB5 p.100)

Chapter Six:

1. 'A Juliet Remembered', a video, A Saffron Production, 1988...2. (1979 Diary, 11 October) 3. (C31) 4. (1979 Diary, 22 February) 5. (1979 Diary, 20 March) 6. (B24) 7. (B24) 8. Valerie Grove, *Dear Dodie*, London 1996, p.244 9. As above p. 293 10. Video, a Saffron Production for Anglia Television 1991 11. (AX 21-28) Filming in Tangiers 12. Nelson Mandela, *Long Walk to Freedom*, Abacus 1994, pp. 365-374 13. (AV24) 14. (SB5 p. 109) 15. (LA57) 16. (SB5 p.114) 17. (R10) 18. (SB p.120) 19. John Bunyan, *Pilgrim's Progress*, London 1918 p. 375 20. Bryan Forbes, *Ned's Girl*, London 1977 21. (SB5 p.125) 22. (B21) 23. (AL35) 24. (S36) 25. ((B15) 26. (B16) 27. (F9) 28. (F39) 29. (F30) 30. (AA23) 31. (AA38) 32. (AA17) 33. (AA33) 34. (BDii92) 35. (BDii90) 36. (AA6)

'Dear Miss Ffrangcon-Davies, I feel I must write to congratulate you and thank you for that lovely programme on TV. It was for me, and millions of others I am sure, an evening of pure enchantment indeed as Hugh Davenport pointed out in the Weekend Telegraph (I hope you read his article) it was sheer magic.

I have always loved your work ever since, as a student, I saw you as Elizabeth Moulton-Barrett. And then again in "Gaslight". I have a vivid memory of your hands in that play. When the gaslight flickered and you could hear the steps overhead, it was not only your voice and face but your whole body, especially your hands, that expressed your terror. I have never forgotten that.

Then there was, of course, "The Importance of Being Ernest". But my happiest memory, and certainly the most beautiful, is of your Anne of Bohemia in "Richard of Bordeaux" - not only because of your lovely performance but also because of a lovely thing you did.

I was a very young minister in my first appointment out of college, living in Sheffield. I had a committee meeting (I think) in London and stayed the night with friends - and I went to see "Richard of Bordeaux". I was so thrilled that I wrote both to you and John Gielgud asking for your autographs. I received a signed photo of JG which I still prize. But you went 'the extra mile'. You sent me a letter saying you had no photos but instead you sent me a copy of Theatre World as there were several pictures in it of the play. I thought then and I still do that it was a lovely thing to do. To take the trouble to send a charming letter and the magazine to an unknown fan was both generous and gracious.

So here I am writing to thank you for the letter you sent me fifty-five years ago. And I read it again this morning!

For me perhaps the most moving moments in the "Omnibus" programme were when you and Sir John sat talking together. I was remembering you both as Richard and Anne.

Yesterday I was telling my daughter about it all and I said "They were both so beautiful" and she said "And they still are!" And that is true.

I loved your closing words to Nigel Hawthorne but I also remember your closing words in a previous interview. You quoted from 'Back to Methuselah' – Lilith's last sentence "It is enough that there is a beyond".

Thank you for casting your spell on us for so long - and please come on TV again soon.'
37. (U2, 3, 4)

Epilogue:
1. St Paul's Letter to the Romans, Chapter 6 verse 9   2. (BE31)   3. (BE11)   4. (BE14)

INDEX

201